Managing Your Health

A guide for people living with HIV or AIDS

written and edited by
Brent Patterson and Francis Robichaud
revised and updated by
Craig McClure, Treatment Service Coordinator, CATIE, 1997

Produced by
The Community AIDS Treatment Information Exchange (CATIE)/
Réseau communautaire d'info-traitements sida
and
The Toronto People With AIDS Foundation (TPWAF)
1996

This handbook was funded by the AIDS Care, Treatment and Support Program under the National AIDS Contribution Program of the National AIDS Strategy, Health Canada. Revisions and reprinting, 1997, also funded by Health Canada and the AIDS Bureau, Ministry of Health, Ontario.

Many people contributed to the development of this handbook, as writer, editors, technical reviewers, and community advisors.

The national advisory committee was composed of Connie Connelly (Yukon), Brent Daum (Saskatchewan), Drew Ferrari (Alberta), John Graham (Ontario), Robert Guertin (Québec), Robert Hay (Northwest Territories), Jeff Lee (Saskatchewan), Kurt McGifford (Manitoba), George Mitchell (First Nations), Andrea Scott (PEI), James Shedden (Nova Scotia), Jeff Stevenson (New Brunswick), Sheila Wahsquonaikezhik (First Nations), Gordon Waselnuk (British Columbia), and Gerard Yetman (Newfoundland).

The editorial committee was composed of Chris Bearchell, Stewart Brown, Gerry Hunt, Eric Mykhalovskiy, and Darien Taylor. The French editorial committee was composed of André Dupont, Robert Guertin, and Roger Leclerc.

The medical advisory committee was composed of Dr. Robert Frederickson (Nova Scotia), Dr. Bernard LaPointe (Québec), and Dr. Andrew Patullo (British Columbia).

Copy editing was done by Irit Shimrat. David Vereschagin was responsible for the design and layout of the handbook. The illustrations were done by Alison Lang. Carmen Bourbonnais, André Côté, Christiane Devaud, and François Gagnon were responsible for the French translation. Stephen Chiu was the project assistant.

We would like to acknowledge the generous contributions of the following:

Mark Whitehead, co-author of the first edition of *Managing Your Health*.

Individuals who helped with the first edition:
Mary Louise Adams, Alex Berry, Santo Caira, André Chamberlain, Steve Chapman, Bernard Courte, Theresa Dobko, Dionne Falconer, Ron Foley, Wayne Hellard, Ayoka Junaid, Dianne Lodge, Ian Lumsden, Dr. Don MacAulay, Tim McCaskell, Eric Mykhalovskiy, Anthony Mohamed, Bill Naumovich, Glen Pelshea, Yvette Perreault, David Pickard, Charles Roy, Sean Waterson, Pat Williams

Deirdre Maclean for her assistance in the area of treatment information in the second edition.

Individuals who have helped with the second edition:

Darcy Albert, Maggie Atkinson, Kevin Barlow, Reeta Bhatia, Alan Boutilier, Pamela Bowes, Janet Dunbrack, Paul Groh, Sean Hosein, Dr. John Leutkehoelter, Craig McClure, Chester Myers, John Plater, Dr. Stan Reid, Judy Rogers, Marilynne Seguin, Bob Shearer, Peter Singer, Elisse Zack

We would also like to thank all of those individuals and organizations whose names may have been missed but who contributed their support and encouragement to this project.

Any errors that may remain are the responsibility of the Community AIDS Treatment Information Exchange (CATIE) and the Toronto People With AIDS Foundation.

ISBN 1-896135-13-7

◆ This handbook is dedicated to the memory of those we have lost, and to the strength and courage of those who continue to confront this syndrome.

Francis Robichaud
November 2, 1964–April 20, 1996

Contents

Introduction xv
How to use this book xv
A holistic approach to health xvi
Community-based health philosophy xvii
Advocacy xviii
Problems with health care in Canada xviii
A word about language xix
Reaching AIDS groups xix

1   **Life After Diagnosis** 1
Hooking up to AIDS groups 2
Stigma 3
Who to tell 4
    Family, partners, and friends 4
    Other people with HIV 5
    Your doctor 5
    Other people you deal with 6
    Sexual partners and people you share needles with 6

2   **Emotional and Spiritual Support** 9
HIV and your emotions 10
Prejudice and your emotions 10
Stress 11
Emotional effects of infections and medication 12
Thinking about death 12
Talking with other people living with HIV/AIDS 13
Counselling 14
Spirituality 15
Getting involved through activism and volunteering 15

v

3 **Your Immune System and HIV** 17
What are germs? 18
Your immune system 19
    Your lymphatic system 19
    The cells of your immune system 20
The stages of HIV infection 21
    Primary HIV infection 21
    Seroconversion 21
    Asymptomatic HIV infection 21
    Symptomatic HIV infection 22
    AIDS 22
Does HIV cause AIDS? 22

4 **Keeping Track of Your Health** 23
Tests for HIV infection 25
Blood tests 25
    Your blood 25
    Tests of immune system cells 27
    Viral load 28
    Other blood tests 28
Other tests 29
Types of tests for infections 31
Pulmonary function tests (PFTs) 32
Nervous system tests 32
Tests specific to women 33
Tests specific to men 34

5 **Health Care Professionals, Hospitals, and Home Care Services** 35
Doctors 35
    Finding a doctor 36
    Your first appointment with a new doctor 37
    What you can expect from your doctor 38
    What your doctor can expect from you 39
    Making the most of your appointments 40
Dentists 41
Gynecologists 41
Obstetricians 42
Community Health Representatives (CHRs) 42
Finding a complementary therapist or practitioner 42
Hospital HIV clinics 44
Centres locaux de services communautaires (CLSC) 45

vi

CONTENTS

Community health centres   45
Hospital stays   45
    Being admitted (checking in)   46
    Things to take with you   47
    Things your friends or family can bring or do   47
    Food   48
    Visitors   48
    Nurses   49
    Doctors   49
    Social workers   51
    Pastoral care workers   51
    Leaving the hospital   51
Home care programs   52
Care teams   54
Hospices   54
House calls   54
Other in-home help services   55

6 Health Options   57
Treatment isn't the whole story   58
Treatment issues   59
    Treatments during pregnancy   59
    Treatments for children   60
    Treatments for people with hemophilia   60
    Treatments for drug users   60
Anti-HIV treatments   61
    Reverse transcriptase inhibitors – nucleoside analogues   63
        Side effects of nucleoside analogues   64
        AZT   64
        ddI   65
        ddC   66
        d4T   67
        3TC   67
    Non-nucleoside reverse transcriptase inhibitors (NNRTIs)   68
    Protease inhibitors   68
        Saquinavir   69
        Ritonavir   69
        Indinavir   69
        Nelfinavir   70
    Drug interactions and antiretrovirals   70
    Final comments on antiretrovirals   70

Other anti-HIV treatments   71
    Compound Q   71
    Hypericin   71
    SPV-30   72
Immune modulators   72
    Interleukin-2   72
    Naltrexone   73
    DNCB   73
Complementary therapies   74
    Traditional Chinese medicine (TCM)   74
    Naturopathy   75
    Homeopathy   76
    Ayurvedic medicine   76
    Aromatherapy   76
    Oxygen therapy (superoxygenation
      or hyperoxygenation therapies)   77
    Massage and touch therapies   77
      Swedish massage   78
      Reflexology   78
      Therapeutic touch   78
      Reiki   79
      Rolfing   79
      Shiatsu   79
      Trager   79
    Chiropractic   80
    Exercise   80
    Yoga   81
    Tai Chi   81
    Meditation   81
    Sweat lodge   82
    Affirmations and visualization (guided imagery)   82
    Herbal medicine   83
    Other treatments   87
Nutritional approaches   88
    Diet   88
    Macronutrients   89
    Micronutrients   89
      Vitamins   89
      Minerals   91

    Supplementation 92

        Basic protocol (for every HIV-positive person) 92

        Additional protocol 93

        Other supplements 93

    Special diets 96

    Liquid food supplements 96

Water safety 97

Food safety 97

    Shopping for food 98

    Eating out 99

    Food poisoning 99

Other things to think about 100

    Pets and HIV 100

        Safe pet guidelines 100

    Travelling with HIV 101

    Suntanning 102

7 Opportunistic Infections and Related Conditions 103

What are opportunistic infections? 103

You won't get every infection 104

The germs that cause infections 104

Other conditions 105

Treatments 105

Bacterial infections 106

    Mycobacterium avium complex (MAC)/
      Mycobacterium avium intracellulare (MAI) 106

    Tuberculosis (TB) 108

    Pelvic inflammatory disease (PID) 111

    Bacterial pneumonia 112

    Other bacterial infections 113

Fungal infections 113

    Candidiasis (thrush or yeast infections) 113

    Cryptococcosis 115

    Histoplasmosis 117

    Pneumocystis carinii pneumonia (PCP) 118

Protozoal infections 120

    Toxoplasmosis 120

    Microsporidiosis 122

    Cryptosporidiosis and isosporiasis 123

Viral infections 125

    Cytomegalovirus (CMV) 125

        The Amsler grid 129

Herpes simplex virus   130

Herpes zoster virus (shingles)   131

Progressive multifocal leukoencephalopathy (PML)   132

Other viral infections   134

Hepatitis   134

Influenza   135

Hairy leukoplakia   135

Other AIDS/HIV-related conditions   136

Kaposi's sarcoma (KS)   136

Cervical dysplasia and cancer   139

Lymphoma   141

Peripheral neuropathy   143

AIDS dementia complex (ADC)   144

Skin problems   146

Seborrheic dermatitis   146

Psoriasis   147

Folliculitis   147

Molluscum contagiosum   148

Other skin problems   148

Sexually transmitted diseases (STDs)   148

Chlamydia   149

Gonorrhea   149

Syphilis   149

Genital herpes   150

Genital warts   150

Scabies   151

Safer sex   151

Using condoms   152

Oral sex   154

Sex toys   154

Using street drugs   155

Piercing and tattoos   156

Constitutional symptoms   156

Fever   157

Night sweats   157

Fatigue   158

Pain   158

Diarrhea   159

Weight loss   161

Wasting   164

8   Getting Treatments   165
   Approved and unapproved treatments   165
   How to get approved treatments   166
         The Drug Formulary and other government drug plans   166
         Private insurance coverage   168
         Off-label use of drugs   169
         Paying for treatments yourself   169
         HIV clinics   169
   How to get unapproved or experimental treatments   170
         The Emergency Drug Release Program (EDRP)   170
         Friends and buyers' clubs   171
         Compassionate access   171

9   Clinical Trials   173
   What is a clinical trial?   173
   Complementary therapies and clinical trials   174
   The phases of a clinical trial   174
         Phase 1: Is the treatment safe?   174
         Phase 2: Does it work?   175
         Phase 3: How well does it work?   175
         Combined phases   176
         Phase 4: Post-marketing trials   176
   Controlled trials   176
   Placebos   177
   Why join a trial?   178
   Who can join a clinical trial   178
   How to join a trial   179
   Informed consent   180
   Cost   181
   The clinical trial   181
         How the treatment is taken   181
         How much of the treatment to take   181
         When to take each dose   182
         How often you have to come to the site   182
         Trial schedules   182
         Trial rules   182
         Taking other medication   183
   Seeing your own doctor   183
   What happens if you get sick   183
   The principal investigator   184
   How your rights are protected   184
   Leaving the trial   185

Problems you could run into   186
How to decide   186
How to find a clinical trial   186

10   Practical Matters   189
Work   189
Money   191
  How to get financial help   191
    Appealing a decision   192
  Unemployment Insurance (UI) benefits   193
    Eligibility   193
    How to apply   194
  Social assistance/welfare   195
    Eligibility   195
    How to apply   196
    Start-up benefits   196
  Disability benefits   197
    Eligibility   197
    How to apply   198
  Canada Pension Plan disability pension and the
    Québec Pension Plan (le Régime de rentes du Québec)   199
    Eligibility   200
    How to apply   200
  Income tax credits and exemptions   201
    Medical expenses   202
    Property tax deferment   202
  The Federal Extraordinary Assistance Plan (EAP) and the
    Multi-Provincial/Territorial Assistance Program
    (MPTAP)   203
    Eligibility   203
  Non-Insured Health Benefits Program (NIHB)   204
  Credit/debt counselling   204
  Private insurance   205
  Group insurance   205
  Disability insurance   207
  Life insurance   208
  Living benefits   208
    Viatical companies   209
Housing   209
  Shared housing   210
  Housing co-operatives   210
  Subsidized housing   211

Supportive housing   212
Hospices and nursing homes   212
Hostels and community shelters   213
The YMCA/YWCA housing registry   213
Moving in with family   213
Aboriginal communities   214
Food   214
Meal programs   214
Food banks   214
Clothing   215
Transportation   215

11   **Legal Issues**   217
Your rights   217
Human rights legislation   217
Other ways to fight discrimination   220
Lawyers   221
Legal costs   221
Legal aid   221
Clinics   222
Planning ahead   222
Medical power of attorney and living wills   223
A registry for living wills   225
Suicide, assisted suicide, and euthanasia   226
Enduring power of attorney   226
Committeeship   227
Wills   228
How to write a will   228
Your executor   230
Bank accounts   231
Survivor benefits (CPP/QPP)   231
Memorials and funerals   232
Pre-paying   234

12   **Checklist for Managing Your Health**   235
Things to think about   235
Monitoring your health   236

xiv

CONTENTS

Phone Numbers of AIDS Resources   241
National agencies   241
Regional agencies   243
British Columbia   243
Alberta   246
Saskatchewan   248
Manitoba   250
Ontario   252
Québec   258
New Brunswick   262
Prince Edward Island   263
Newfoundland & Labrador   264
Nova Scotia   265
Yukon   266
Northwest Territories   267

Index   265

Introduction

WELCOME TO the revised and updated second edition of *Managing Your Health: A Guide for People Living with HIV or AIDS. Managing Your Health* is a joint project of the Community AIDS Treatment Information Exchange (CATIE) and the Toronto People with AIDS Foundation (TPWAF). This edition came about because of the overwhelmingly positive feedback to the first edition and the many requests received from people across the country for copies of the book. This edition has been revised and updated by CATIE due to the rapid emergence of new HIV/AIDS treatment options in 1996.

Managing Your Health is intended for people living with HIV/AIDS and their care givers. (HIV stands for Human Immunodeficiency Virus. AIDS stands for Acquired Immune Deficiency Syndrome.)

How to use this book

Managing Your Health tries to show you how to take action in order to be as healthy as you can. Currently there is no cure for AIDS, but there are things you can do which may help delay the progression of HIV disease and help you stay healthy longer. This book is not meant to tell you everything you'll ever need to know. It is a guide to some of the issues you may find yourself struggling with. There are lots of suggestions about where to start. It's set up in sections so that you can find what you need quickly. You don't have to read it all at once. Read it in whatever order you please. Start with the questions you need answered now. If you want, you can skip chapters or sections and go back to them when you're ready. Use the information that's relevant to you; don't feel bad about what you can't or don't want to do.

Information about HIV and AIDS changes so quickly that it's hard to keep track. People are still figuring out how to use medications and complementary therapies effectively. Check with your doctor or call your nearest AIDS group (see Page 243) for up-to-date information. You or your doctor can also call CATIE's HIV/AIDS Treatment Information Network (The Network) toll free at 1-800-263-1638.

We want to hear your comments about this guide. Send comments to:

The Community AIDS Treatment Information Exchange (CATIE)
420-517 College Street
Toronto, Ontario M6G 4A2 Canada
Phone: (416) 944-1916
(toll free in Canada) 1-800-263-1638
Fax: (416) 928-2185
E-mail: myh@catie.ca

or

The Toronto People With AIDS Foundation (TPWAF)
399 Church St., 2nd Floor
Toronto, Ontario M5B 2J6 Canada
Phone: (416) 516-1400
Fax: (416) 506-1404

xvi

INTRODUCTION
How to use this book
A holistic approach to
health

A holistic approach to health

Managing Your Health puts forward a holistic approach to health, which takes into consideration your physical, emotional, mental, spiritual, sexual, and social well-being. A holistic approach emphasizes the need to look at all the things that affect your health.

Community-based health philosophy

A community-based health philosophy is shaped by the health care needs identified by the members of a community. It is these needs and the people who identify them that determine how and which services will be developed. In this sense, such a philosophy is built from the bottom up. Historically, the leaders of community-based AIDS efforts have been gay men, lesbians, and people living with HIV/AIDS. This is due to the initial neglect of AIDS by governments, the medical profession, and social services. They saw AIDS as an illness affecting marginalized groups – people who were not considered part of the "general public" (whose health matters).

Lesbian and gay activists, and especially people with HIV/AIDS, organized politically to put pressure on the government to take action. They developed a community-based health promotion model that includes treatment, care, support, advocacy, education, and prevention. This model was strongly influenced by the experiences of feminists responding to women's health issues. People living with HIV/AIDS, gay men, lesbians, and people of colour raised the issue of HIV/AIDS within their communities. One of the challenges was to figure out how to address HIV/AIDS in a culturally appropriate way. Aboriginal people, people from different cultures, drug users (people who use alcohol, street drugs, glue, prescription drugs, etc.), prostitutes, people with hemophilia, straight women and men, ex-prisoners, and many others have since successfully organized community-based responses to the AIDS epidemic, both within their own communities and in coalitions (networks of different groups).

A community-based health philosophy focuses on empowerment and advocacy. It involves you, the service-user, working with others to make informed decisions and develop strategies for the best possible health and health care. It also recognizes that people need resources in order to do this, and it encourages people to work towards better and more equal access to these resources. A community-based approach, which emphasizes working with others, is particularly important in responding to government cutbacks to health care and other social services, which limit resources.

xviii

INTRODUCTION
Advocacy
*Problems with health
care in Canada*

Advocacy

Advocacy involves identifying and trying to reduce barriers to health care that may exist in institutions, government policies, or social systems. Advocacy can be done on an individual basis or systemically. In individual advocacy, an attempt is made to solve the problems of one person; for example, finding housing for someone. In systemic advocacy, an attempt is made to change the policies or behaviour of institutions or societies to improve the situation of many people; for example, finding government funds for housing projects. Advocacy can take many forms, including meetings with policy makers; research; using the media; demonstrations; legal challenges; and being persistent in getting answers from social assistance workers and health care givers.

Problems with health care in Canada

Canadians take pride in having universal health care, meaning that health care is supposed to be available to everyone, free of cost. But, in reality, there are differences in how easily people from different backgrounds can get health care, and in the kind of care they get. Sexism, racism, and homophobia (fear of homosexuals) in the medical system affect how health services are created and who gets them.

People also face different problems getting health care depending on where they live. Services vary from region to region and are often unequal. Those who live in rural and remote areas may have problems getting knowledgeable medical care, appropriate blood tests, etc., and may feel isolated.

Not having enough money can also be a problem. Currently many treatments are not covered by government health plans. This is particularly true of complementary therapies (see Page 74). Sometimes "user fees" – fees that you pay yourself – are charged for treatments or services. Due to government cutbacks and changing philosophies about the provision of health care, health care is increasingly becoming the responsibility of the person who is sick.

Drug companies often fail to provide experimental treatments to people not participating in clinical trials. (Providing these services for free is sometimes called "compassionate access" – see Page 171.)

These are just some of the ways in which getting health care in Canada can be a problem.

A word about language

Most information about HIV and AIDS is full of technical words that can be hard to understand. This book is meant to help you make informed decisions about preventing and treating disease by giving you information in plain language. But some of the concepts associated with HIV and AIDS are complicated. Many large, complex words have been replaced with easier ones. Definitions are given when technical words are used. Common or slang terms are given in brackets ( ) after many of the scientific words to help make the information clear. Talking with someone about the information in this book can also be helpful.

Reaching AIDS groups

This book is not going to answer all of your questions. There are many things we can only mention. However, many other resources exist which you can refer to for more specific information. You can get help, or more information, by contacting an AIDS group. Aboriginal people may want to contact the nearest Friendship Centre. If you live in an Aboriginal community, talk to your community health representative or nurse. At the back of the book, on Page 241, is a list of some telephone numbers you can call.

Managing Your Health est disponible en français sous le titre *Vous et votre santé*.

Life After Diagnosis

WHEN YOU'VE BEEN TOLD you have HIV or AIDS, it's natural to have questions like, "What will happen to my health?" "Can I or should I continue to have sex?" and "Should I tell my family?" It may seem that there are too many questions and no place to start.

People who have HIV or AIDS face many challenges. Having a weakened immune system is hard on your body. It can be emotionally overwhelming, and can leave you discouraged and despairing.

You are not alone. There are things you can do to stay healthy longer. The more we learn about HIV and AIDS, the longer people are living. There are ways to prevent infections and delay the progression of HIV disease. And if you do get sick, there are many new treatments that can help.

Figuring out how you're going to look after your health can help you avoid health problems. Your approach should be flexible so it can respond to changes in your life.

To take care of yourself physically, you can exercise, eat properly, take antiretroviral drugs, take treatments to prevent infections, take vitamins, and get plenty of rest. Mental and emotional health are just as important. It helps to talk about HIV to the people who are important in your life. Other people who have HIV may be able to understand your feelings and offer advice. You may want to check out a support group. Some community-based AIDS groups can provide counsellors and help you find other forms of emotional support. Consider becoming more involved in your community. For some people, spiritual and religious beliefs are helpful; you may find guidance from an Aboriginal elder or other religious leader, or through prayer, traditional Aboriginal healing, or meditation.

Different things will work for different people; find out what works for you. Your nearest AIDS group (see Page 243), other people living with HIV/AIDS, complementary therapists, and health care professionals can all give you advice. Make the changes that you feel comfortable with, and don't try to do everything at once.

Hooking up to AIDS groups

Some AIDS groups provide many kinds of services, information, and referrals that can be useful to you. They may offer people you can talk to (this sometimes includes peer support groups and counsellors), information on treatments, education about HIV infection, help with financial problems, legal services, political advocacy, needle exchanges, care teams or buddies, transportation, and many other things. And they can direct you to physicians, complementary therapists, counsellors, lawyers, social workers, clinics, hospitals, and detox centres. Larger cities have more groups and more resources. In some areas people have established AIDS groups to address their specific needs. For example, there are groups of gay men, women, Aboriginal 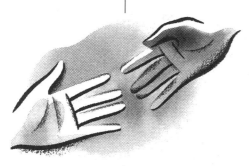 people, people from different cultures, deaf people, prostitutes, people with hemophilia, drug users, and prisoners. Services are available in several languages and are offered in ways that are sensitive to different cultural groups. If you have access to a computer you may be able to communicate with AIDS groups through the Internet. Contact your nearest AIDS group (see Page 243) to see what's available in your area.

Stigma

As someone living with HIV/AIDS, you may experience prejudice, or stigma (when someone tries to make you feel bad or ashamed). Too many people still don't understand how the virus is spread, and a social stigma is attached to many of the communities that have been most affected by AIDS. AIDS has been wrongly associated with the lifestyles of so-called "high-risk groups," rather than with risky activities. Add to this the misconceptions that HIV is easily spread and that testing HIV positive means you're on the verge of death, and it makes some people feel that those living with HIV/AIDS are dangerous.

Whether you're gay or not, you may have to deal with homophobia – fear and hatred of lesbians and gay men. If you are lesbian, gay, or bisexual, or if you don't label yourself in any of these ways but have sex with members of the same sex, homophobia can hurt you in a very personal way.

If you are straight, you may find it difficult to use the services of AIDS groups which mostly serve the gay community. And you may resent people being prejudiced against you because they think you are something that you aren't, especially if you dislike or fear homosexuality yourself.

The stigma associated with HIV/AIDS is much broader than homophobia. Gender, class, cultural beliefs, language, education, ability, etc., all affect how easily people can use services. If you are not connected to people who are affected by HIV or AIDS, you may find it difficult to get information and support.

It is the responsibility of different levels of government and of AIDS groups to overcome these barriers, but there are things you can do. For instance, you may want to help educate people about HIV and AIDS, or get involved in an AIDS group or activist group to help make changes. You'll have to figure out for yourself how to respond to prejudice. Remember, you don't have to educate everyone you meet about HIV and AIDS.

Stigma affects who you decide to tell about your HIV status.

Who to tell

Telling someone you're HIV positive is a very personal decision. Who to tell, when and how to tell them, and why you want to tell them are all important questions. One reason to tell someone you're HIV positive is to have someone to talk with about what you're going through.

4

LIFE AFTER
DIAGNOSIS
Who to tell
• *Family, partners, and
friends*

Family, partners, and friends

The people who are already close to you can give you support. To help you decide who to tell, you could ask yourself the following questions. Who do you feel ought to know? Who accepts and doesn't judge you? Who loves and values you? Who respects your privacy? Who is practical and sensible and reliable? Who has responded well to requests for help in the past? Who's a good listener? You may decide to tell different people for different reasons.

You may be afraid of how loved ones will react to your having HIV. Depending on your situation, there may be certain people who are hard to tell – maybe your parents, or your children, your partner, or your close friends. You may have to tell people things about yourself that they didn't know. If you're gay, or bisexual, and people don't know, talking to them about HIV can be difficult. This can also be true if you have been having sex outside a relationship, or if you use drugs, and people don't know. But many spouses, partners, friends, and relatives will be able to recognize the courage and trust it takes to talk about being HIV positive. Many people with HIV find that taking a chance and talking with people they trust results in deeper, closer relationships. You have to balance the risk of rejection with the possibility of support. A counsellor at your nearest AIDS group or needle exchange program (see Page 243) can help you decide whether, or when, to tell someone. A counsellor can also help you deal with your feelings about how people react when you do tell them.

You don't have to tell anybody until you're ready. And you don't have to tell everyone all at once. You'll probably find that you feel comfortable with different people at different times. Trust those feelings and do what feels right.

Other people with HIV

Talking with other people who have had the same kinds of experiences as you can give you support and practical tips about how to deal with issues. These people can help you develop a strategy for managing your health by sharing what has worked for them.

You may eventually decide that you want to be public about your HIV status. Speaking in public forums, attending conferences, and participating in AIDS activism can be interesting and rewarding. On the other hand, you may decide to tell only a couple of people who are close to you. This can be a very different issue depending on whether you live in a big city, small town, or rural or remote area. The important thing is that you choose who to tell and how to tell them, and that the people close to you respect your decision.

Your doctor

If you don't feel comfortable telling the doctor you go to now, it may be a good idea to find a new one. This can be hard if you don't live in a city, because there are fewer doctors to choose from. You may find yourself educating your doctor about AIDS. Your nearest AIDS group (see Page 243) can make referrals to knowledgable doctors and can recommend material for your doctor to read. You or your doctor can also contact the Community AIDS Treatment Information Exchange's HIV/AIDS Treatment Information Network (see Page 242) for treatment information. Finding a doctor who knows how to treat HIV/AIDS is important. Doctors who are not specialists but who know a lot about HIV/AIDS are sometimes called HIV primary care physicians. You can read more about finding a doctor in Chapter 5.

5

LIFE AFTER DIAGNOSIS
Who to tell
- *Other people with HIV*
- *Your doctor*

Other people you deal with

You have the right to privacy, and it's up to you to decide whether you're going to give personal information to someone. Unfortunately, some people still discriminate against those who have HIV. Use your judgement with people you don't know very well. If you don't want people you tell to tell anyone else, make that clear.

In most cases, your employer and the people you work with do not need to know. Landlords and neighbours do not need to know. Unfavourable reactions could affect your housing situation or cause other problems that you don't need.

Sexual partners and people you share needles with

Discussing your HIV status with someone you're having sex with is a very different issue from telling someone in order to receive support. It can be hard to decide whether and when to tell that person. Do you tell someone as soon as you meet him or her, or do you wait until you're going to have sex? Does it make a difference whether this is a one-night stand or an ongoing relationship? What if prostitution is how you make your living?

Some people say you should tell anyone you're having sex or shooting drugs with. Other people say you don't have to if you're practising safer sex and using needles safely (see Pages 151 and 155). This is something you'll have to think about. Talking about it with other people who are HIV positive may help you make up your mind.

You might consider contacting people who you have had unsafe sex with, or anyone you've shared needles unsafely with, so that they can decide whether they want to be tested or not. Unless you were tested anonymously, if you've just recently tested HIV positive you may be contacted by your local public health office and asked to give the names of recent sexual partners or people you've shared needles with. A counsellor at your nearest AIDS group (see Page 243) can help you figure out who needs to know and may be able to give you suggestions about how to deal with the public health office.

6

LIFE AFTER
DIAGNOSIS
Who to tell
• *Other people you deal with*
• *Sexual partners and people you share needles with*

There have been a couple of legal cases where people who knew they were HIV positive have been taken to court for infecting another person through unsafe sex. The law in this area keeps changing.

Sometimes people are afraid to talk about their HIV status or safer sex because of how other people may react. This fear can make a lot of sense, especially if you're worried about rejection or violence. No one should ever push you into sex that you don't want. If you need advice on how to get your partner(s) to have safer sex, or if you have fears about your relationship or safety, talk to someone at your nearest AIDS group.

There are sections on sexually transmitted diseases and safer sex in Chapter 7. You can also get information on safer sex from your nearest AIDS group or public health office. You (or you and your partner[s]) may also want to talk about sex with a counsellor. Counsellors are available at most AIDS groups.

Remember, deciding who you're going to tell is up to you.

7

LIFE AFTER DIAGNOSIS
Who to tell
• *Sexual partners and people you share needles with*

2

Emotional and Spiritual Support

9

TAKING CARE OF YOUR HEALTH when you have HIV isn't just a matter of finding a good doctor, getting the latest treatment, and taking care of your body. You also need to take care of yourself emotionally, mentally, spiritually, sexually, and socially.

People are usually shocked to find out that they're HIV positive. "I can't believe this is happening to me!" is a common reaction. Some days you may have more feelings than you can deal with. You may feel angry, depressed, afraid, or sad. And you may find that these feelings change from one minute to the next. This is completely normal.

Talking about your feelings can be really helpful, although it's not always easy. You may feel overwhelmed by your emotions and unable to express them. It's important to deal with your emotions in a way you're comfortable with. Different people – and people from different cultures – deal with emotions in different ways.

Some people find it helpful to write about their feelings. Others talk and cry with friends, relatives, or community elders, or join support groups or try different forms of therapy. Some find it helpful to keep busy and not think about themselves too much. Organized religion, traditional Aboriginal spirituality, meditation, and other ways of exploring spirituality can help.

Finding out about HIV and AIDS, and getting involved politically, can also be helpful.

10

**EMOTIONAL
AND SPIRITUAL
SUPPORT**
*HIV and your
emotions*
*Prejudice and your
emotions*

Use as many different supports as you need.

Many people living with HIV/AIDS find renewed purpose and deeper values as they come to terms with the effects of HIV on their lives. You may feel strength and a sense of accomplishment in your ability to take care of yourself. This can depend on many things, including your personal circumstances and history, what kind of support you get from family and friends, what kinds of services you get, and how much HIV is affecting your daily life.

HIV and your emotions

There is no "correct" way to respond emotionally to living with HIV and AIDS. And it's not simply a matter of dealing with your emotions and then having things go back to normal. Dealing with your emotions is always an ongoing process of adjusting and readjusting.

You may want to resist changes in your life and hold onto the way things were before you knew you were HIV positive. You may find yourself feeling angry and frustrated. Anger can take many forms. You may feel anger as well as sadness when friends or loved ones with HIV get sick or die. Anger can be a positive force, and it often drives people to become involved with AIDS activism.

For some people, discovering that they're HIV positive can actually bring relief from uncertainty. Or you may have been bothered by health problems without understanding why you had them. Finally knowing can bring some relief and allow you to take action.

Prejudice and your emotions

Because of the stigma attached to HIV/AIDS (see Page 3) many people feel guilty or ashamed after learning that they're HIV positive. Experiencing AIDSphobia (fear of people with HIV/AIDS), homophobia (fear and hatred of lesbians and gay men), or any kind of prejudice is hurtful. Some people worry about what others will think when they find out. Worries about HIV can bring up uncomfortable feelings about your sexuality or drug use. You may worry about infecting others, or think that AIDS is a punishment. The reality is that no one is at fault for being HIV positive.

You may need to develop ways to protect yourself emotionally from other people's prejudice, whether that means not telling people about your HIV status, or joining together with others to work for change.

Sometimes language is used to pressure you to deal with your emotions in ways other people think are right. Often the word "denial" is used in a way that is judgemental and assumes that there is a "correct" way to respond to HIV/AIDS. The word "anger" also gets misused. For example, you may complain about receiving poor health care and be told that you are "carrying around a lot of anger." This is insulting and a way to avoid addressing your concerns.

Stress

How you deal with stress makes a difference in how you cope with your feelings about being HIV positive. Too much stress can affect your health.

As a person living with HIV/AIDS, you may find that there is pressure on you to be "well adjusted." This pressure often comes from people who care about you but have their own ideas about how you "should" be behaving. It can create more stress for you. Try to help the people who care about you understand that how you live your life is your own business.

You may wish to explore different ways of reducing stress in your life. Exercise can be helpful; so can yoga, massage, and other forms of meditation and relaxation (see Chapter 6). Some AIDS groups offer free massages or stress management programs. Activities you enjoy, such as reading, going for walks, seeing movies, etc., can help you reduce stress and make you feel better. Some people use spiritual exploration as a way of finding inner peace and decreasing stress. You can also talk to someone at an AIDS group (see Page 243) or a nearby hospital, or check with your doctor, for more ideas about dealing with stress. There are resource books and tapes on stress reduction.

Stress can also be reduced by dealing with problems in your life. Some people feel better after leaving an abusive partner, getting a job, leaving a job, finding a better place to live, or making other changes. Financial and legal issues that may cause stress are dealt with in Chapters 10 and 11.

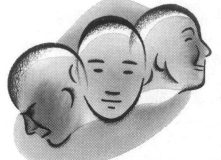

Emotional effects of infections and medication

12

EMOTIONAL
AND SPIRITUAL
SUPPORT
*Emotional effects of
infections and
medication
Thinking about death*

Changes in your physical condition or reactions to medication can cause shifts in your emotions. These feelings will often disappear when the infection is cleared up or the drug or treatment is finished. Ask your doctor about side effects related to drugs and treatments, and tell him or her about changes in your emotional state. Be careful about getting treatments for mood changes. Some doctors are quick to prescribe medication without giving thought to the long-term effects of drug dependency and overmedication. This is especially true for women. If you have questions about your medication, ask your doctor, and get a second opinion if you are uncertain. Complementary therapies can provide an alternative for dealing with some mood changes (see Page 74).

Drug reactions or interactions, and infections of the central nervous system, can cause depression or confusion, which seem like psychological problems.

You may have to cope with the emotional effects of specific illnesses. Chapter 7 deals with many of these in detail. In addition to these illnesses, you may experience physical changes such as weight loss or skin problems. You may worry about not looking as attractive as you once did. This can be damaging to your self-esteem. Talking with other people living with HIV/AIDS who have had similar experiences can be helpful.

Thinking about death

Being HIV-positive means having to face life and death issues. Thinking about death is difficult in our society, which doesn't deal with this subject openly. You may think about death more than usual when you first find out that you're HIV positive, when tests show a drop in your T4 or T8 cell count (see Pages 27 and 28), or a rise in your viral load (see Page 28), or when a friend gets sick or dies. The prospect of pain and suffering is disturbing. Thinking about death brings up feelings about the possibility of losing loved ones, or about things that you may not get to do. It's important to remember that having HIV doesn't mean you're going to die right away. But thinking about death is important, and may help you focus on what's important in your life.

Some people who have HIV think about suicide. This is not unusual. If you have such thoughts, don't panic or keep them to yourself. Talk to someone who will really listen, and who you know and trust. You may want to see a counsellor or psychiatrist if these feelings continue for more than a couple of days. It is important to be aware that psychiatrists are obliged to prevent you from harming yourself, so there is some risk that you may receive unwanted psychiatric treatment. Most areas have crisis lines that you can call (these are anonymous) – check the front of the phone book or call your nearest AIDS group (see Page 243).

13

EMOTIONAL
AND SPIRITUAL
SUPPORT
Thinking about death
Talking with other
  people living with
  HIV/AIDS

Talking with other people living with HIV/AIDS

Other people living with HIV/AIDS can be helpful. They can sometimes help you figure out how to solve problems by thinking about them in new ways. And they can give you support by helping you feel less lonely and more confident. Even hearing your problems described by someone who has been through the same thing can be reassuring. These and other new relationships may lead to friendship and a sense of community with people who are supportive and nurturing. Your nearest AIDS group (see Page 243) can help you connect with other people who are living with HIV/AIDS. AIDS groups can help you find (or start) a support group or meet with someone one-on-one. Some offer peer counselling by HIV-positive staff or volunteers. If there is no AIDS group close by you, use the list of national numbers on Page 241 to find a counsellor or other support. There are also some support groups on the Internet.

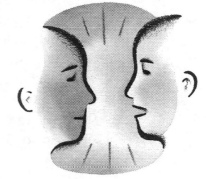

Counselling

When you can't quite figure out how to deal with a situation, when you feel overwhelmed, or if you want a regular time to deal with emotional troubles, you might want to go to a counsellor or therapist. There are different kinds, including psychologists, psychiatrists, social workers, peer counsellors, and religious and spiritual counsellors.

Psychiatrists are medical doctors with specialized training. They often deal with emotional problems as diseases which can be treated by prescribing drugs. Some also use psychotherapy. Their fees are covered by provincial or territorial health insurance (except in Québec) and they usually need a referral from your doctor.

Psychologists are not medical doctors and therefore can't prescribe medication. Their fees are not usually covered by health insurance, although some private insurance plans may pay part of them.

"Therapist" and "counsellor" are general terms that refer to someone who practises any one of many kinds of counselling. Anyone can say he or she is a therapist or counsellor, without having special training or a licence. Talk to a few counsellors over the phone before you make an appointment. Ask about what training they have had. This will give you a sense of what to expect and may help you decide what you want in a counsellor. Good counsellors will encourage this kind of research. Don't hesitate to ask about fees before your first appointment. Many counsellors charge on a "sliding scale" basis: if you can't afford their usual fee, they will charge you less. You have to negotiate this.

Counsellors usually use the first appointment as a "getting to know you" session. This allows both of you to see whether you can get along with each other before you decide to go on. Counselling can only help if you feel comfortable with the person you're talking to.

Many AIDS groups have counsellors or peer counsellors (people who are HIV positive who you can speak to) on staff or as volunteers. Counsellors who work for AIDS groups don't charge for their services. You can also ask other people who have HIV, your friends, or your doctor for suggestions.

Spirituality

Spirituality, whether in the form of organized religion, shared beliefs of a specific culture, or individual personal beliefs, is an important source of support for many people who have HIV/AIDS. Some find renewed purpose in their lives as they come to terms with HIV. You may find support and strength in exploring the spiritual traditions of your own culture.

Meditation (see Page 81) has helped many people who have HIV or AIDS find peace and acceptance and get in touch with their spirituality.

Priests, rabbis, ministers, nuns, imams, Aboriginal elders, and other spiritual leaders may be able to give you emotional support. They offer religious and spiritual advice, as well as company and comfort. But be aware that some organized religions don't accept homosexuality, sex outside of marriage, drug use, condom use, or the right to abortion. You can check out HIV support groups (see Page 243) to find people who share your religious or spiritual beliefs. Or you may want to try attending a church, synagogue, temple, or sweat lodge that has a supportive membership.

Exploring spirituality has helped some people deal with HIV and AIDS. If you're thinking about checking out programs or workshops, do some investigating. You can spend a great deal of money going to workshop after workshop. If you look around, you may find something that works for you at very little cost. Talk with other people who have HIV or AIDS and find out what's worked for them.

Getting involved through activism and volunteering

Taking an active part in your own health care can make you feel better. Making your own informed decisions, rather than leaving all the decisions to your doctor, is an important part of this. Although information on treatment may seem overwhelming, you can learn the basics. Staying informed is a good way to have more control over your health care. Being involved with an AIDS group and its activities helps

**EMOTIONAL
AND SPIRITUAL
SUPPORT**
*Getting involved
through activism
and volunteering*

you keep up with new information. And volunteer work can be very rewarding. You may want to try public speaking, peer counselling, or working for a food bank. If there isn't already a support group in your area that meets your needs, you may want to think about starting one. An AIDS group may be able to give you a hand, and other people would benefit from your efforts. Contact your nearest AIDS group (see Page 243) to find out how you can get involved.

Activism has been an important force in improving government policy and getting services for people who have HIV or AIDS.

Your Immune System and HIV

WHAT ARE GERMS? How does your immune system protect you against germs? What happens when your immune system is damaged? What usually happens to the immune systems of people with HIV? The answers to these questions can help you understand how HIV is thought to affect your body and how your immune system works. This information can help you better understand what's happening to you and how to interpret terms used by your doctor. In order to understand how HIV is believed to work, it helps to know something about germs and about how your immune system keeps you healthy.

The information in this chapter is complex. Don't worry if you can't take it in all at once. You may want to go over it with a friend, your doctor, or staff at your nearest AIDS group (see Page 243). You can also contact the Community AIDS Treatment Information Exchange's HIV/AIDS Treatment Information Network toll free at 1-800-263-1638.

What are germs?

A human body is made up of billions and billions of cells, but germs have only one cell. There are four different types of germs, or "microbes": bacteria, fungi, protozoa, and viruses.

Bacteria (the plural of bacterium), fungi (the plural of fungus), and protozoa (the plural of protozoan) are all single-celled creatures but each type behaves in different ways. Like all living things, these organisms breathe, eat, shit, and reproduce. Not all germs cause disease; in fact, some of them help keep us healthy.

Viruses are very different from the other three kinds of germs. Viruses do not breathe, eat, or shit, and they can't reproduce on their own. Viruses are simple structures that straddle the line between living and non-living matter. A virus is made up of genetic material called DNA (deoxyribonucleic acid) or RNA (ribonucleic acid), wrapped in a coat of protein. In order to reproduce, a virus must enter a living cell and take over some of that cell's parts. Only then can the virus make copies of itself.

HIV is a type of virus called a retrovirus. It is made up of two strands of the genetic material called RNA wrapped in a protein coat. This protein coat has spikes of something called gp120 all over it. These gp120 spikes work like keys. All of our body's cells have receptors on them. These receptors act like locks to let some things in and keep others out. HIV, with its gp120 spike, or key, is able to enter cells that have what's called a CD4 receptor, or lock.

There are several stages in the reproductive cycle of HIV. At each stage, chemical messengers called enzymes help the virus make copies of itself. As HIV enters a T4 (CD4+) cell, the virus sheds its protein coat. Then its genetic material, called RNA, must be changed to match the cell's genetic material, which is called DNA. An enzyme called reverse transcriptase allows the viral RNA to become viral DNA. In the next stage another enzyme, called integrase, helps the new viral DNA join, or integrate with, the cell's DNA. Once the viral DNA is joined with the cell's DNA, the cell begins to reproduce the virus, making hundreds of copies of HIV. Another enzyme, called protease (or proteinase), helps put together the parts of the virus. When the new viruses are ready, they burst out of the cell and into your blood or lymph (see Page 19).

Your immune system

Your immune system is a network of chemicals, cells, tissues, and organs found throughout your body. These work together to protect you from germs. Your immune system can tell the difference between what belongs in your body and what doesn't belong. When something that doesn't belong gets into your body, your immune system tries to destroy it in order to keep you healthy.

Your body has many ways of protecting itself. The first is your skin, the largest organ of your body. Your skin acts as a shield, and sweat glands in it get rid of waste. The small hairs and fluids in your body openings also protect you. Nostrils have hair and mucus (snot) to keep out germs carried in the air. The saliva (spit) in your mouth contains enzymes that can destroy germs. Your eyes are protected by eyelashes, eyelids, and tears. Your vagina (cunt), urethra (the tube you pee through), anus (asshole), and bowels (guts) are lined with mucous membranes, which protect them.

19

YOUR IMMUNE SYSTEM AND HIV
Your immune system
- *Your lymphatic system*

Your lymphatic system

Your lymphatic system is like a twin to your circulatory system. Your circulatory system is made up of your heart and the blood vessels called arteries, capillaries, and veins. Instead of blood, your lymphatic vessels carry a fluid called lymph. This clear fluid helps carry germs away from your body's cells. The germs are filtered and often destroyed through tissue called lymph nodes. There are 500 to 1,000 lymph nodes scattered through your body. Clusters of lymph nodes are found in your armpits, neck, abdomen (belly), and groin (crotch). Sometimes when you have an infection you will notice "swollen glands," which may be sore. These are your lymph nodes responding to the unwanted germs.

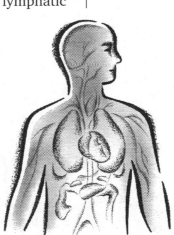

The cells of your immune system

The cells of your immune system are called white blood cells, or leukocytes. They are created in your bone marrow. Marrow is the material that fills the hollow parts inside many of your bones. Your immune system cells move throughout your body in both your bloodstream and your lymphatic system. There are several kinds of immune system cells. The white blood cells that are the most important in HIV infection are called macrophages and lymphocytes.

Macrophages (sometimes called monocytes) respond to things that don't belong in your body, like germs, by surrounding and eating them. Macrophages can also bring germs or pieces of germs to lymph nodes to "show" to lymphocytes.

Lymphocytes are cells that live in lymph nodes. Lymphocytes can travel through your body in either your bloodstream or your lymph fluid, but at any one time about 98 per cent of all the lymphocytes in your body are found in your lymph nodes.

There are two ways your immune system can respond when faced with an infection.

T lymphocytes (T cells) are the cells involved in the Th1 response. This type of response is also called cell-mediated immunity, because your T cells coordinate or mediate the response. T cells all look alike under a microscope but they can be divided into different groups according to what they do.

Some T cells are called T4 lymphocytes (T4 cells, or CD4+ cells). T4 cells release chemicals called cytokines, which "instruct" other cells to begin your immune system's response to anything that doesn't belong. These are the cells most commonly infected by HIV.

Other T cells are called T8 lymphocytes (T8 cells, or CD8+ cells). T4 cells "instruct" T8 cells to perform their role in your immune system's response to infection. Some T8 cells can destroy cells that are infected by germs. Once an infection is under control, other T8 cells cause the immune system to return to normal.

B lymphocytes (B cells) are mostly involved in the Th2 response. This type of response is also called humoral immunity, or the antibody immune response. B cells produce proteins called antibodies. Antibodies "stick" to germs and kill them before they get a chance to infect cells.

The Th1 response is useful when fighting off many of the infections seen in AIDS. After you become infected with HIV, your immune system's ability to make a Th1 response generally weakens over time.

20

YOUR IMMUNE
SYSTEM AND HIV
Your immune system
• *The cells of your
immune system*

The stages of HIV infection

Each person's experience of health and illness is different and everyone experiences HIV infection differently. It's important to remember that the stages of HIV infection will be different from one person to another. Some people have been HIV positive for many years and haven't developed an opportunistic infection. On Page 237, you'll find a checklist of things you may want to monitor with your doctor and care givers, in order to prevent or treat infections.

Primary HIV infection

This refers to the time when you're first infected with HIV. During this stage, which is also called acute infection, the virus multiplies rapidly. About two to four weeks after infection, you may feel ill, with flu-like symptoms such as fatigue, fever, sore throat, swollen lymph nodes (see Page 19), headache, loss of appetite, or skin rash. This may last for as long as a few weeks. Your T4 cell count (see Page 27) may drop during this period, and the amount of virus in your blood may be very high. You might test negative for HIV antibodies at this stage (see Page 25), but you can still pass HIV on to someone else.

Seroconversion

The word "seroconversion" refers to your body responding to HIV by making antibodies. After you seroconvert, a blood test for the HIV antibody will come back positive. This stage usually happens one to three months after infection.

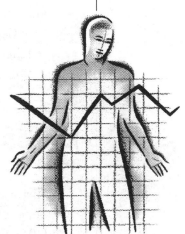

Asymptomatic HIV infection

"Asymptomatic" means without symptoms. In this stage, which may last years, you may feel perfectly well. However, you may have swollen lymph nodes (see Page 19) in two or more different areas (your

21

YOUR IMMUNE SYSTEM AND HIV
The stages of HIV infection
- *Primary HIV infection*
- *Seroconversion*
- *Asymptomatic HIV infection*

neck and armpits, for example). This is called "persistent generalized lymphadenopathy," and may last for months, or even years. Even if you have no physical signs of infection, your T4 cells (see Page 20) decrease in number.

22

YOUR IMMUNE
SYSTEM AND HIV
*The stages of HIV
    infection*
• *Asymptomatic HIV
    infection*
• *Symptomatic HIV
    infection*
• *AIDS*
Does HIV cause AIDS?

Symptomatic HIV infection

As your immune system is weakened by the virus, you may develop "constitutional," or whole-body, symptoms of HIV infection. These can include swollen lymph nodes (see Page 19), night sweats, fever, diarrhea, weight loss, and tiredness (see Pages 157 to 164). You may develop infections like thrush, persistent vaginal yeast infections, or oral hairy leukoplakia (see Pages 113 and 135).

AIDS

AIDS stands for Acquired Immunodeficiency Syndrome. "Acquired" refers to the fact that the condition is not hereditary – you acquire (get) it at some point in your life. "Immunodeficiency" is a weakness in your immune system. "Syndrome" is a combination of symptoms and/or diseases. AIDS is not a disease. Rather, it is a syndrome associated with HIV infection, decreased numbers of T4 cells (see Page 20), and one or more of the opportunistic infections listed by the Laboratory Centre for Disease Control (LCDC) in Ottawa, which can be reached at (613) 957-1777. Most of these infections are discussed in detail in Chapter 7.

Does HIV cause AIDS?

Historically there has been some debate about the relationship between HIV and AIDS. Most people, but not everyone, believe that HIV causes AIDS. Some people say HIV can't cause AIDS by itself, but can do so in combination with other things, called co-factors (such as different germs).

Keeping Track of Your Health

MONITORING YOUR HEALTH with a doctor or other health professional is usually done in three different ways. First, your doctor will take your history – how you feel overall, whether you have any symptoms, when the symptoms started, and how much they affect your life. This information is important; it will help your doctor figure out what, if anything, is going wrong, and what's going right.

The second step involves a physical examination. Your doctor will look for changes from your normal condition. Your "vital signs" – that is, your pulse, blood pressure, respiration (breathing) rate, and temperature – are taken and recorded. Your doctor may feel the lymph nodes (see Page 19) in your neck, armpits, and groin, and touch your abdomen (belly) in order to feel the edges of your liver and spleen. You may also be given a short neurological (nervous system) exam that will check your reflexes and sense of balance.

The third step is a series of lab tests. These may be tests done regularly to look for changes from your normal test results, or they may be done to discover the cause of a problem or symptom you might have.

The information received from your history, your physical examination, and the results of your lab tests can help you and your doctor make treatment decisions.

Some people pay a lot of attention to their regular lab tests. They get photocopies of their results and keep diaries. Others find it easier to have their doctors monitor these tests and then discuss the results with them. If you're interested in monitoring your tests, ask your doctor to discuss them with you and explain them in a way that you can understand. But try not to get too caught up in the meaning of the different numbers. What's important is that you understand what is happening and what you can do about it.

As you learn to read test results, you may want to keep in mind the following points:

◆ All test results are compared to the "normal range" – test results for most people who are healthy (with no active infections) fall between two values. There are always people whose results are naturally above or below the normal range. It's important to find out what's "normal" for you. Always compare your results over time; look for trends.

◆ The normal ranges are for the general population, and may be different for people with HIV.

◆ Test results can be affected by a lot of different things, including how you're feeling on any particular day, and the time of day you have the tests done. Here are some suggestions:
    ◆ Always test at the same time of day.
    ◆ Use the same lab every time. Ranges can vary from one lab to another.
    ◆ A woman's menstrual cycle may affect test results. Try to have tests done at the same time in your cycle.

◆ Labs can be wrong. Consider repeating tests before you make a treatment decision.

Most tests described in this chapter are paid for by provincial or territorial health plans. However, these tests are not equally available in different parts of the country. Some may require special handling and immediate testing at a specific laboratory, so doctors can't just send materials to the nearest city. Others, such as MRI scans (see Page 31), require very expensive equipment that may not be available in smaller hospitals. If you live in a smaller community, you can talk with your doctor about what options may be available.

Tests for HIV infection

These tests use a small sample of blood taken from a vein in your arm to find out if you've been infected with HIV. The tests look for antibodies (see Page 20) to HIV, not for HIV itself. HIV antibodies are made by B cells (see Page 20) as your body tries to get rid of HIV. Labs use two tests to look for these antibodies. The ELISA test is done first, as a general screening test. (ELISA stands for "enzyme-linked immunosorbent assay.") If the ELISA test is positive, a second test, called the Western Blot, is done to confirm the results. When both tests are positive, it means that the antibody to HIV has been found. Again, these tests don't look for the virus itself, but for evidence in your blood that your immune system has reacted to the presence of HIV.

Viral load tests show how much virus is in your blood. They can show whether you're infected, even if your immune system hasn't made antibodies to HIV. There are currently three different tests for measuring viral load. You should try to always use the same type of test if possible, as the results may not be comparable. At the time of writing, not all provincial health plans cover viral load testing.

KEEPING TRACK OF YOUR HEALTH
Tests for HIV infection
Blood tests
• *Your blood*

Blood tests

Your blood

Your blood contains different kinds of cells in a clear fluid called plasma. Blood carries nutrients (from your digestive system) and hormones (from your glands) to cells throughout your body. It also carries waste to your excretory system (the system that gets rid of what your body doesn't need). And blood can carry germs all through your body when you get an infection.

Testing your blood to see how many of each kind of cell you have can show whether there are any problems. Some drugs you may be taking can affect these tests. Your doctor may suggest you stop using a certain drug to see if it is the cause. Your blood cells are produced in your bone marrow (see Page 20). Several drug treatments used for HIV infection can affect bone marrow, which in turn can affect the levels of many of these cells.

◆ **Complete blood count (CBC)**: This is made up of several different tests. These are the most common blood tests, and they're done quite often. Your CBC can give you and your doctor a general sense of your overall health. Any count that is outside your normal range can suggest an infection or damage to your body, which tells your doctor to go on to do more specific tests. Your CBC studies three different kinds of cells: white blood cells, red blood cells, and platelets.

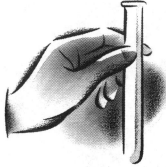

   ◆ **White blood cell (WBC) count**: White blood cells (also called leukocytes – see Page 20) are your immune system cells. This test measures the total number of white blood cells found in a sample of your blood. A low white blood cell count is called leukopenia. AZT (see Page 64), ganciclovir (see Page 127), and other medications can cause a drop in the number of your white blood cells. If you take these drugs, your doctor will probably monitor your WBC count every month.

      ◆ **Differential**: This test breaks down the WBC into different types of white blood cells and tells you what percentage of them are lymphocytes, macrophages (see Page 20), or other kinds of cells. Increases or decreases in the numbers of these cells can show different types of problems. You can discuss these issues with your doctor.

   ◆ **Red blood cell (or RBC) count**: Red blood cells give blood its red colour, which comes from iron. They carry oxygen from your lungs to all the other cells in your body. They also carry carbon dioxide from your tissues to your lungs, where it's breathed out. This count tells you how many red blood cells there are in a certain amount of blood.

   ◆ **Hemoglobin (Hgb)**: Red blood cells contain hemoglobin, which binds to oxygen in your lungs and carries it to tissues all through your body, where it's released. Even if you have enough red blood cells, you may not have enough hemoglobin.

      If you don't have enough red blood cells or enough hemoglobin, your body can't get enough oxygen. This results in a condition called anemia, which can leave you feeling really tired and breathless and looking pale.

   ◆ **Hematocrit**: Your blood is made up of plasma and red blood cells, white blood cells, and platelets (see below). The hematocrit measures the percentage of your blood that is made up of all these cells except the plasma.

◆ **Platelet count**: Platelets (also called thrombocytes) are tiny, colourless blood cells that help your blood clot. When the number of platelets in your blood is low, you can bruise easily, and can bleed for a long time when cut or injured. A platelet count below normal range is called thrombocytopenia, which can cause you to bleed for a long time when injured.

Tests of immune system cells

◆ **Absolute T4 cell count**: Also called the "absolute CD4+ count." This number is calculated from the results of three different blood tests. The absolute T4 count is the most common surrogate marker (a lab measurement that can show indirectly the effect of a treatment on a disease) used for people with HIV.

T4 cells are the white blood cells (see Page 20) most likely to decrease in people with HIV. These cells play an important role in controlling infections. T4 cells die about 24 to 36 hours after being infected with HIV. Your body is able to replace these cells and keep HIV in check for years. However, at some point your immune system will start to lose ground. Figuring out the number of T4 cells in a sample of blood can give you an idea of how your immune system is doing. Knowing your T4 count can help you decide when to take action and what to do.

The normal range of T4 counts can vary from one lab to another, depending on which procedures are used. For example, some labs may use 450-1150 cells per cubic millimetre as the normal range for adults; others may use 550-1250. Any single count of T4 cells is not a sure sign of how your immune system is doing. Two T4 cell counts done on samples of blood drawn from the same person twelve hours apart can be very different from each other. If one T4 cell count is way out of line with the pattern shown in the last several tests, it may be a good idea to get another test done. Your T4 cell count shows only one part of how your immune system is functioning. Always consider it as part of a bigger picture. Look for trends over time, rather than focusing on a specific result.

◆ **T4 (or CD4+) percentage**: This measures the percentage of T4 cells compared to the total number of lymphocytes (see Page 20) in your blood. T4 cells usually make up between 31 and 49 per cent (about one-third to one-half) of the total number of your

27

KEEPING TRACK OF
YOUR HEALTH
Blood tests
• *Your blood*
  • *Tests of immune
    system cells*

28

KEEPING TRACK OF
YOUR HEALTH
Blood tests
• *Your blood*
  • *Tests of immune*
    system cells
  • *Viral load*
  • *Other blood tests*

lymphocytes. As the number of your T4 cells drops, it makes up less and less of the total number of lymphocytes. This test is used together with your absolute T4 cell count to get a more complete picture of your immune system.

◆ **Absolute T8 count**: Also called the "absolute CD8+ count." This number is calculated from the results of three different blood tests. The absolute T8 count is another sign of whether people have HIV. People with HIV often have T8 counts above the normal range.

   As with T4 counts, the normal range of T8 counts can vary from lab to lab, depending on which procedures are used.

◆ **T8 (or CD8+) percentage**: This measures the percentage of T8 cells compared to the total number of lymphocytes (see Page 20) in your blood.

◆ **p24 antigen test**: The p24 antigen is one of the proteins that HIV makes. When HIV multiplies inside a cell, p24 antigen is released into your bloodstream. This test measures how much p24 antigen you have in your blood. High levels of p24 antigen suggest that HIV is multiplying rapidly. Many people with HIV/AIDS never test positive for p24 antigen, so this test is not very useful on its own.

Viral load

Viral load is the amount of HIV present in the blood. It is measured in number of copies per millilitre of blood. The tests currently available can measure viral load as low as 500 copies/ml and as high as one million copies/ml. A high viral load can indicate a greater risk for the progression of HIV disease. The risk of transmission of HIV from a woman to her fetus also increases if the viral load is higher.

Other blood tests

Your blood can also be tested for:

◆ **Amylase** (see Page 94), an enzyme produced by your pancreas. Amylase levels may be increased by pancreatitis (inflammation of the pancreas – see Page 65) or by certain types of drugs that affect your pancreas. If you use ddI, ddC, or pentamidine (see Pages 65, 66, and 119), your doctor will probably monitor amylase levels every month.

◆ **Creatinine phosphokinase** (CPK), an enzyme usually found in muscles. When your muscle tissue is damaged or destroyed, the CPK enzyme leaks out into your blood. This test can show muscle damage due to wasting (see Page 164) or drug side effects.

◆ **Erythrocyte sedimentation rate** (ESR, Sed Rate), a test that measures how long it takes red blood cells (erythrocytes) from a sample of your blood to settle at the bottom of a test tube. A high ESR can indicate inflammation (swelling or other signs of infection). This test can't identify a specific infection. However, you can monitor this test in the long term and, if there are any major changes, you should be looking for a possible infection.

◆ **Blood gases**: Testing of blood gases is done only in a hospital, when you're having extreme difficulty breathing. A sample of blood is removed from an artery in your wrist or groin (crotch), and the levels of oxygen, carbon dioxide, and bicarbonate are measured. The results of this test can help doctors measure how much oxygen to give you. Not enough oxygen can damage internal organs, and too much can destroy your lungs.

◆ **Electrolytes**: If you look at your blood test request form, you will probably see that your doctor regularly orders tests of sodium, potassium, and calcium. These salts are called electrolytes and they must be balanced properly. If you have bad diarrhea or vomiting, you can lose electrolytes because you're not keeping enough food or water in your body. If your electrolytes get too low, you may feel weak, dizzy, or confused, and you can get very ill.

Other tests

◆ **Liver integrity tests** (formerly known as "liver function tests"): Your liver is part of your digestive system, which includes your esophagus (the tube that connects your mouth and stomach), your stomach, and your small and large intestines (guts). Blood or urine (pee) tests that measure how well your liver is working are called liver integrity tests. These tests can show if there is any

KEEPING TRACK OF YOUR HEALTH
Blood tests
• *Your blood*
  • *Other blood tests*
Other tests

damage to, or stress on, your liver. Since your liver releases many different chemicals into your bloodstream, a separate blood test is done for each.

If you look at your blood test request form you will probably see that your doctor regularly orders tests of these liver enzymes:

◆ aspartate aminotransferase (AST, also known as SGOT)
◆ alanine aminotransferase (ALT, also known as SGPT)
◆ lactate dehydrogenase (LDH)
◆ gamma-glutomyltransferase (GGT)

If the levels of these four enzymes are higher than your normal range, there may be damage to the cells of your liver. This may be caused by excessive use of alcohol, by prescription or street drugs, or by infections like hepatitis B (see Page 134).

Your blood test form may also include a test of a fifth liver enzyme, alkaline phosphatase (Alk Phos). If the level of this enzyme is above your normal range then there might be damage to the parts of your liver called bile ducts. In some people, higher-than-normal levels of alkaline phosphatase may be seen before symptoms of MAC infection (see Page 106) develop.

You may have liver integrity tests done if you're having a hard time digesting food, if your skin is becoming yellow (this is called jaundice), or if your doctor thinks you may have one of the hepatitis viruses (see Page 134), which infect and can damage your liver. Several drugs you may be taking can also damage your liver, so your doctor may do these tests regularly.

◆ **Renal (kidney) function tests**: Your kidneys (along with your bladder) are part of the system that removes waste from your body. They also help recycle nutrients. Any test that measures how well your kidneys are working is called a renal function test. Blood urea nitrogen (BUN) and creatinine tests are done using a blood sample. Other renal function tests measure how much fluid your kidneys release as waste, by collecting and measuring how much you urinate (pee) in 24 hours. Urine can be analyzed to measure which chemicals or salts your kidneys are releasing. Too much or too little of these chemicals can be a sign of kidney damage. Several drugs can damage your kidneys, so your doctor may do these tests regularly.

Types of tests for infections

Some tests look for germs that may be causing problems, or may cause problems in the future. These include tests for the germs that cause such AIDS-related infections as toxoplasmosis (see Page 120), CMV (see Page 125), and MAC (see Page 106), as well as tests for several other infections (including TB [tuberculosis – see Page 108] and STDs [sexually transmitted diseases – see Page 148]) common in people with HIV. Examples of some tests are:

- **Stain**: Blood, stool (shit), mucus, urine (pee), sputum (saliva coughed up from your lungs), phlegm, spinal fluid, and tissue samples can be stained and examined under a microscope. If there are germs in the sample, the stain can make them easier to identify.
- **Culture**: Samples of body fluids or tissues can be tested by culturing them. Samples are observed to discover which germs grow in them. Some germs, like those that cause MAC (see Page 106), are very slow growing, so it may take several weeks before a germ can be identified.
- **Scope**: This is a very thin flexible tube with a light source and magnifying lens at one end. A variety of scopes are used to allow doctors to visually examine the inner parts of your body. A test done in this way is called an endoscopy. A gastro-scope is inserted through your mouth into your stomach; a colonoscope is inserted though your anus (asshole) or colon (large intestine [gut]); a bronchoscope is inserted through your nose into your windpipe and lungs; a colposcope is inserted into your vagina to examine your cervix. Scopes can allow doctors to see lesions (abnormalities) on internal tissues and to take samples (biopsies).
- **Biopsy**: A small sample of skin, muscle, lymph node (see Page 19), or even organ is removed from your body. The tissue sample is then examined under the microscope. The shape, number, and type of cells that make up the sample are studied and compared to the normal range. Biopsy samples may also be stained or cultured.
- **Imaging tests**: These tests include X-rays, computerized tomography (CT or CAT scans), and magnetic resonance imaging (MRI) scans.

KEEPING TRACK OF
YOUR HEALTH
*Types of tests for
infections*
*Pulmonary function
tests (PFTs)*
Nervous system tests

All create images of the inside of your body. A radiologist (a doctor who specializes in the study and interpretation of these tests) will examine the images in order to make a diagnosis. Each type of infection or tumour or broken bone will show a different pattern on the image. For example, the pattern of PCP (see Page 118) looks very different from the pattern of tuberculosis (see Page 108) on a chest X-ray.

Pulmonary function tests (PFTs)

"Pulmonary" means "of the lungs." This series of tests can give your doctor an idea of how well your lungs are working. These tests may be done if you're having trouble breathing, if you feel a tightness in your chest, or if you get tired easily when walking or climbing stairs. If you have symptoms of a lung infection, like PCP (see Page 118), your doctor may order these tests, as well as blood tests and an X-ray of your lungs. The tests are simple: first, you will be asked to breathe out though a tube in your mouth, as hard and as fast as you can. The tube is connected to a machine which measures the flow of air, the rate of the flow, and the volume of air. Second, you will be asked to breathe in through the tube, as deeply as you can. The results of these tests can help your doctor figure out the cause of your shortness of breath.

Nervous system tests

Your brain and nervous system control all of your body functions. An infection or lesion (abnormality) in your brain or spinal cord may cause you to feel weak, unfocused, or disoriented. You may also have severe headaches; trouble speaking or seeing; loss of memory, concentration, or other mental abilities; weakness; loss of sensation (feeling); or lack of coordination. Your doctor can do tests to see how your nervous system is damaged or weakened. Some examples are:

◆ **Tests of your reflexes**: Reflexes are automatic responses. The most familiar reflex test is the "knee reflex." A rubber mallet is used to tap the tendon just below your kneecap while you're sitting down. This causes your lower leg to kick out, by reflex. There are many other reflexes which can be tested

◆ **Tests of your sensitivity to touch**: Pricking your skin lightly with a pin, passing a cotton ball over your skin, and touching a finger or toe joint with a vibrating tuning fork are some of the ways your doctor may test your sensory system.

◆ **Tests of your sense of balance**: You may be asked to walk by placing your heels in front of your toes in a straight line, then asked to walk on your toes and then your heels.

Tests specific to women

Regular gynecological examinations (tests of your reproductive system) can help diagnose infections. Early diagnosis of a problem usually means it can be treated with fewer drugs or minor surgery.

There are two parts to a regular gynecological examination, and a rectal examination (an examination of the inside of your ass) may be done as well.

◆ **External visual examination**: Your doctor examines the outside of your vulva (cunt) for lesions (such as herpes – see Page 130), genital warts (see Page 150), or any other evidence of infection.

◆ **Internal examination**: While wearing latex gloves, your doctor will insert two fingers into your vagina and gently press the other hand on your abdomen (belly). If there is any swelling of your uterus (womb) or ovaries, this may feel uncomfortable or even painful. Discomfort or pain can indicate an infection. Next, your doctor may insert a plastic speculum into your vagina. The speculum keeps your vagina open and allows your doctor to do a Pap smear. A tiny brush and a wooden spatula are brushed gently over your cervix (the entrance to your uterus). Fluid and cells cling to the brush and spatula. The sample is sent to the lab for testing.

◆ **Internal rectal examination**: Although these exams are more commonly done for men, women may request them as well. Infections that usually appear inside your vagina can "travel" to your rectum (the inside of your ass). This is especially true of genital warts. The doctor will insert one gloved finger into your rectum.

33

KEEPING TRACK OF YOUR HEALTH
Nervous system tests
Tests specific to women

Tests specific to men

Regular physical examinations of your genitals, anus (asshole), and rectum (the inside of your ass) can help diagnose infections. Early diagnosis of a problem usually means it can be treated with fewer drugs or minor surgery.

◆ **External visual examination**: Your doctor examines the outside of your penis and scrotum (balls) for lesions (such as herpes – see Page 130), genital warts (see Page 150), or any other evidence of infection.

◆ **Internal rectal examination**: Your doctor will insert one gloved finger into your rectum to feel your prostate gland. Swelling of this gland can indicate cancer. Infections that usually appear on your penis or scrotum can "travel" to your anus or rectum, especially genital warts and herpes lesions. The doctor may also do a rectal Pap smear (see Page 33).

Health Care Professionals, Hospitals, and Home Care Services

Doctors

Your doctor should help you bring together the different parts of your health care to make sure all your medical needs are met. If you've been seeing the same doctor for years and have a good relationship with him or her, you may not need to change doctors when you learn you are HIV positive. But if he or she has very little experience with HIV/AIDS or seems prejudiced, you may decide to find someone who is more accepting or knows more. This may not be easy, especially if you live in a rural area and have a limited number of doctors to choose from.

HEALTH CARE
PROFESSIONALS,
HOSPITALS, AND
HOME CARE
SERVICES
Doctors

• *Finding a doctor*

Finding a doctor

Your relationship with your doctor is important. You need to feel comfortable with him or her. A doctor who has experience in working with people living with HIV/AIDS is sometimes referred to as an HIV primary care physician. In some big cities, primary care physicians have formed networks in order to share information. Your nearest AIDS group (see Page 243) can refer you to a such a doctor if there is one available in your area. One way to find a doctor who knows something about HIV is to talk with other people who are HIV positive. Ask them who they go to and whether they're happy with the care they're getting. Get three or four names and shop around; talk with doctors to see whether they have the qualities that are important to you.

Ask yourself what type of doctor you want. Do you want one who tells you what to do (which may make you feel secure), or one who will work with you in weighing the pros and cons of a treatment? Do you want a doctor who will help you explore alternative treatments? Do you want a female doctor? Do you want a gay doctor? Do you want a doctor who can speak with you in your first language? Who has experience working with interpreters? Who is sensitive to your cultural and spiritual beliefs? Do you want someone close to home? Someone who has experience with drug users?

Answering these questions can help you decide which doctor is right for you. But you may not have any choice, especially if you live in a rural or remote area. You may have to help educate your doctor if he or she is new to HIV/AIDS. The checklist in Chapter 12 can be helpful in discussing your health with your doctor. You can also suggest that he or she get in touch with one of the HIV mentoring programs offered in several provinces. These programs allow doctors who are new to HIV/AIDS to work with more experienced doctors in order to increase their understanding. The Canadian HIV/AIDS Mentorship Program (CHAMP) (see Page 241) and the Canadian HIV/AIDS Physicians (CHAP) (see Page 242) can both provide more information on these programs. You and your doctor can also get information about specific HIV-related infections and treatments from the Community AIDS Treatment Information Exchange's HIV/AIDS Treatment Information Network (see Page 242).

Your first appointment with a new doctor

There are some things you can do to prepare for your first appointment:

- **Make an appointment to talk with the doctor.** Make sure you will have enough time to get to know the doctor and give the doctor a sense of your medical history and current state of health.
- **Make notes about the questions that you want to ask during your visit.** If you're nervous, or worried that there may be too much information to remember, you can make a list, or take a friend along to help you keep track.

After the appointment, ask yourself:

- Was I given enough time?
- Did the doctor give me a chance to ask questions?
- Did he or she answer them in a way I could understand?
- Was he or she knowledgeable about HIV/AIDS? Was he or she willing to learn?
- Did he or she listen to what I had to say about my specific conditions or situation?
- Is he or she knowledgeable about the conditions specific to people in my situation (drug users, women)?
- Is he or she willing to try different approaches to treatment?
- Is he or she willing to work with me as a partner in my health care?
- Did he or she seem to be prejudiced against me in any way?
- Did I feel comfortable with this doctor? Was he or she friendly?

One visit doesn't commit you to a relationship. If you have some worries, you may want to shop around some more.

Once you have chosen a doctor, arrange to have your last one pass on your medical records. This will give your doctor a better idea of your history. Sometimes it costs money to have documents transferred. There is no standard fee; your doctor determines the cost based on the amount of paperwork and photocopying. However, you can expect to pay around $25 for a simple chart transfer.

You will also need to make an appointment for a complete physical exam. Complete exams usually take about 45 minutes. This will give your doctor a picture of the state of your health right now. This is called a baseline. It will be used to compare with how you're doing later.

HEALTH CARE
PROFESSIONALS,
HOSPITALS, AND
HOME CARE
SERVICES
Doctors

- *Your first appointment with a new doctor*
- *What you can expect from your doctor*

What you can expect from your doctor

- **You have the right to be treated with dignity and respect.** Your concerns should be taken seriously, whether they're HIV-related or not.
- **You have the right to hope.** Your doctor should be encouraging and should keep your well-being in mind.
- **You have the right to ask questions.** Your doctor should be willing to answer any questions you might have in a manner which is understandable to you. He or she should not respond defensively when you ask challenging questions.
- **You have the right to honesty.** Your doctor should be willing to explain what your symptoms mean, what the lab tests say, and whether treatments are working. If your doctor can't treat something, he or she should be willing to say so, and perhaps refer you to a specialist.
- **You have the right to get a second opinion.**
- **You have the right to confidentiality.** Your doctor should keep your medical information completely confidential (private). Whether or not your doctor is required by law to report your HIV status to the ministry or department of health varies from place to place; so does whether those laws are enforced. This means that, depending on where you live, even though you may have tested anonymously (in a way that is supposed to protect your privacy), your doctor could report your HIV status. Ask your doctor how he or she will ensure confidentiality. If you're not satisfied with the answer, think about finding another doctor.

In general, your doctor must get your permission before he or she gives out any information to your partner, family, insurance company, or employer. But if your doctor thinks you're putting a sexual partner at risk and you refuse to tell that partner, he or she may inform the partner or report the situation to public health authorities, after telling you of his or her intention.

- **You have the right to up-to-date, balanced information.** Your doctor should be willing to tell you about both the good and bad effects of treatments. It's difficult even for excellent doctors to stay on top of everything. Your doctor should be open to new information.

- **You have the right to accept or refuse any treatment.** Your doctor should respect your wishes, although he or she doesn't have to give you a treatment that he or she feels may be harmful or worthless. Your doctor should respect your right to see other health professionals, including complementary or alternative practitioners (see Page 42). In some circumstances, refusing a treatment can affect whether or not you can get private insurance.

- **You have the right to your doctor's full attention.** A regular appointment lasts between fifteen and 30 minutes. Book more time if you need it for specific tests, etc. Your doctor should take all your concerns seriously. He or she should actually do a check-up before prescribing treatment. (It's not enough just to hear you describe your symptoms.) Your doctor should complete all forms for lab tests, prescriptions, and referrals to other agencies (such as welfare, housing, or disability insurance).

- **You have the right to get important news from your doctor in person.** Nobody should ever get their HIV results or the results of immune tests, viral load tests, or other serious tests, over the phone. Nurses, receptionists, and lab technicians don't usually discuss this information with you. However, some community-based health clinics have nurses or counsellors who are trained to do this.

What your doctor can expect from you

Your doctor is a human being like you and deserves to be treated with the same dignity and respect that you deserve. Be honest – don't keep information from him or her about new or complementary treatments you may be trying, any treatment that you stop, or anything you do that might affect your treatment plan. Your doctor can look into possible drug interactions (ways that different drugs you're taking can affect you in combination with each other) and sudden

HEALTH CARE PROFESSIONALS, HOSPITALS, AND HOME CARE SERVICES
Doctors
- *What you can expect from your doctor*
- *What your doctor can expect from you*

improvements in or deterioration of your health. If you don't feel you can be honest with your doctor, consider changing doctors, if possible.

Try to understand that your doctor may have bad days occasionally. And there is a limit to what your doctor can do for you.

Making the most of your appointments

Here are a few things you can do to get the most out of doctors' appointments:

40

**HEALTH CARE
PROFESSIONALS,
HOSPITALS, AND
HOME CARE
SERVICES**
Doctors
- *What your doctor can
  expect from you*
- *Making the most of
  your appointments*

- ◆ **Prepare for appointments. Write down key questions ahead of time. Decide what you want to talk about.** Think about what decisions need to be made first. If possible, bring along written materials about any new treatment you want to ask about. Make a list of any symptoms, or changes in your health since your last visit, which you want checked. You may want to keep a medical diary.

- ◆ **Make sure you understand what your doctor is testing or treating you for.** How accurate are the tests? What are the side effects of each drug or treatment? If the treatment doesn't work, what are the alternatives?

- ◆ **Keep a written list of all the medications you're taking.** This includes drugs, vitamins, minerals, and herbal remedies. Some medications can interact (react with each other) in bad ways. You can help your doctor watch out for this by bringing along a list every time you see him or her.

- ◆ **Keep a list of all the instructions your doctor gives you.** If your doctor wants you to go for blood tests or X-rays, write that down. Find out whether there's anything you need to do to prepare for a test. If your doctor suggests that you stop taking a medication for a period of time, make a note of it.

- ◆ **Make sure you understand your doctor's instructions.** At the end of the appointment, go over what your doctor wants you to do: Make another appointment? Get some lab tests done? Call a specialist for an appointment? Change your diet? Decrease the amount of a particular medication you're taking?

- ◆ **Learn about HIV and your immune system.** Reading the latest issue of *TreatmentUpdate/Traitementsida* (a publication of the Community AIDS Treatment Information Exchange –

see Page 242) or other treatment publications and newsletters can help you stay on top of things. The more informed you are, the better able you'll be to make decisions about your health care. Don't diagnose yourself; different infections can cause similar symptoms, so always talk to your doctor.

◆ **Keep appointments and get tests done even if you don't feel sick.** Regular appointments and tests will give you a clearer picture of your health and a better chance of getting illnesses or infections treated early on.

Dentists

Taking care of your mouth is important, because being HIV positive can increase the risk of cavities and of inflammation (redness, swelling, or irritation) of your gums and damage to the bones that support your teeth. Certain problems related to HIV/AIDS, such as thrush (see Page 113), can also appear in your mouth. For these reasons it is useful to let your dentist know you're HIV positive, if you feel comfortable telling him or her. Some dentists may not accept you as a client due to your HIV status. If possible, see a dentist who has experience with HIV/AIDS. Other people living with HIV/AIDS, or your nearest AIDS group (see Page 243), may be able to recommend a dentist. Have a check-up every six months, if you can.

Gynecologists

If you have gynecological (related to women's reproductive organs) problems that your doctor can't treat, it's important to try to find a gynecologist (a doctor who specializes in this area) who knows about HIV/AIDS, because several of the gynecological symptoms related to HIV/AIDS may not be as quickly diagnosed and treated by a doctor or gynecologist unfamiliar with HIV/AIDS. For more discussion of symptoms specific to women, see Page 33.

HEALTH CARE
PROFESSIONALS,
HOSPITALS, AND
HOME CARE
SERVICES
Doctors
• *Making the most of
  your appointments*
Dentists
Gynecologists

Obstetricians

Obstetricians (doctors who specialize in the care of pregnant women) who have experience with HIV/AIDS can best help you deal with your pregnancy and delivery, and with the care of your new baby. They should be aware of the symptoms of HIV/AIDS in women. Also, they can give you information about pregnancy and your health. Some doctors may advise you against pregnancy due to your health or to the risk of passing on HIV to your child. You may want to discuss these issues with someone you trust. Your nearest AIDS group (see Page 243) may be able to put you in touch with other HIV-positive women who have given birth. The decision of whether or not to have a child is yours. For more information on pregnancy and HIV/AIDS, see Page 59.

Community Health Representatives (CHRs)

CHRs are health care workers located in Aboriginal communities. They are employed by your Band or regional health board. The role of the CHR will vary depending on the availability of other health care workers and how close the community is to a hospital. Generally, CHRs provide health information, counselling, and first aid. They also make referrals and appointments, dispense some prescription drugs, provide advocacy, and advise on government policy. Not all CHRs will know much about, or be comfortable with, HIV/AIDS.

Finding a complementary therapist or practitioner

Complementary therapists or practitioners (see Page 74) are people trained to use forms of treatment that are different from conventional medical care (see Page 57). Only a few complementary therapists see large numbers of people living with HIV/AIDS. Outside of big cities, it may be difficult to find such a therapist. You may already have some

42

HEALTH CARE
PROFESSIONALS,
HOSPITALS, AND
HOME CARE
SERVICES
Obstetricians
Community Health
  Representatives
  (CHRs)
Finding a
  complementary
  therapist or
  practitioner

idea of how a particular complementary therapy works, but it's useful to consult with the therapist about his or her philosophy and practice. As with doctors, shop around.

The following questions may help you choose a therapist:

◆ What is the treatment being offered, and how can it benefit you?
◆ What is the therapist's experience in treating people living with HIV/AIDS?
◆ What experience and training does he or she have in diagnosing HIV/AIDS-related illnesses?
◆ What qualifications does he or she have?
◆ How can the treatment be combined with conventional medicine?
◆ How much does he or she charge? Does he or she charge on a "sliding scale" (offer a reduced rate if you can't afford his or her regular fees)? Are other costs involved? (Some private insurance policies cover a percentage of the costs of some complementary therapies.)
◆ Is he or she prepared to visit you at home or in the hospital if necessary?

Any claim that a treatment can cure AIDS or an AIDS-related infection completely, or change your HIV status from positive to negative, should make you cautious. If you're not sure about a particular therapy or therapist, try to contact someone who has had that therapy or been treated by that therapist. You can also call the Community AIDS Treatment Information Exchange's HIV/AIDS Treatment Information Network toll free at 1-800-263-1638. Or talk to someone at the professional association of those who practise the therapy. Many of the questions and issues raised on Page 36 also apply to finding a complementary therapist or practitioner.

43

HEALTH CARE PROFESSIONALS, HOSPITALS, AND HOME CARE SERVICES
Finding a complementary therapist or practitioner

Hospital HIV clinics

If you live in a big city, your doctor may refer you to a clinic or centre at a nearby hospital with a special focus on HIV/AIDS. These clinics primarily provide medical care during the day to people living at home ("outpatients").

HIV clinics don't take the place of your own doctor, who should keep looking after you and help coordinate your contacts with the rest of the medical system. HIV clinics are often attached to "teaching" hospitals. These hospitals train medical students (interns) and resident doctors who may be involved in your care, so you may not be seeing the same doctor all the time.

HIV clinics can give information and follow-up care to people who have HIV. Their services may include counselling and support as well as keeping track of your health. Often they have people who specialize in medicine, psychology, social work, psychiatry, nutrition, or nursing. You may not need all of these services, but you can ask for a referral when you do need one of them.

HIV clinics are usually run by a specialist in infectious diseases or immunology (the study of the immune system). Because they are connected to hospitals, HIV clinics can help you get other hospital services. For example, if you need a blood transfusion or IV medication (IV means intravenous, or injected directly into a vein), this can often be done at the clinic or elsewhere in the hospital. You don't have to stay overnight in the hospital to get most kinds of medical care.

Doctors who work in HIV clinics are often involved in studies of new drugs to treat HIV or the infections that people living with HIV can get. Chapter 9 talks about how clinical trials (drug studies) are done. If you want to join one of these studies, you may be able to sign up through an HIV clinic. Some primary care physicians (see Page 36) are also involved in clinical trials.

HIV clinics don't provide emergency services. They usually have limited hours. And they can be very busy, so you may have to wait a while to get an appointment.

44

HEALTH CARE
PROFESSIONALS,
HOSPITALS, AND
HOME CARE
SERVICES
Hospital HIV clinics

Centres locaux de services communautaires (CLSC)

CLSCs are unique to Québec. They are government agencies that offer health and social services locally. They provide an easy way to get into the often complicated system of health and social services. Each centre offers different services and some have developed services specifically for people living with HIV/AIDS. Contact your nearest AIDS group (see Page 243) or CLSC to find out what services are offered and how to use them. As hospital budgets are cut back, more services are being provided through CSLCs.

Community health centres

Smaller communities may have community health centres and clinics instead of hospitals. In larger cities, these centres have been set up to meet the needs of specific groups of people, such as recent immigrants, women, Aboriginal people, people from different cultures, street youth, and drug users. They offer a wide range of services, which vary depending on the region and the people being served. Some communities have nothing but a community health centre, which provides health care for everyone.

If you don't have health insurance you may be able to get free health care from a community health centre. Contact your nearest AIDS group (see Page 243) if you don't have health insurance and require health services.

Hospital stays

You may feel anxious about staying in a hospital. But there are things you can do that will help you prepare for a hospital stay and cope while you're there.

If you live in a small community and are concerned about confidentiality, you may want to look into the possibility of going to a hospital somewhere else. But remember that this would mean being farther away from your partner, family, and friends.

45

HEALTH CARE PROFESSIONALS, HOSPITALS, AND HOME CARE SERVICES
Centres locaux des services communautaires (CLSC)
Community health centres
Hospital stays

HEALTH CARE
PROFESSIONALS,
HOSPITALS, AND
HOME CARE
SERVICES
Hospital stays

• *Being admitted
  (checking in)*

Having your partner, family, and friends close by is important not only for emotional support but for practical help as well. Due to government cutbacks, more and more of the responsibility for care is being placed on the individual and his or her care givers. Communities affected by HIV/AIDS need to challenge the government and health care professionals to provide better health care.

Many of the suggestions in this section and chapter may feel too overwhelming for you to address on your own, especially if you're sick. Whenever possible, try to get others to assist you.

Being admitted (checking in)

Admission procedures can be complex and can take a while to complete. Take a friend with you for support. To make admission go smoothly, bring your health card, hospital card, insurance policy number, and the name and telephone number of your welfare worker, if you have one.

You can be admitted either through the hospital's emergency department or at the admissions desk. If you come through the emergency department, be aware that at times it will be very busy and that priority is given to people needing immediate medical attention. You may have to wait for several hours. If your doctor refers you to the hospital, report to the admissions desk during regular office hours.

The hospital puts patients in different kinds of rooms on the basis of availability of beds and medical need. You may be moved as beds become available or priorities change. If you wish to stay in a private room it will be expensive, unless you have medical insurance that covers private rooms. Be sure to check your insurance policy before you're admitted to the hospital. You're more likely to be put in a semi-private (two-bed) room. Regular wards usually have four beds to a room.

The palliative care unit provides beds for those who are dying and no longer want medical treatment. (Palliative care means being looked after when you're dying.) For more information on palliative care in general, you can refer to the AIDS Committee of Toronto (see Page 253) and le projet Accès publication, *Living with Dying – Dying at Home,* or Casey House Hospice (see Page 256) and Mount Sinai Hospital's publication, *Palliative Care.*

Things to take with you

◆ Bring all the drugs, therapies, and vitamins that you're taking, and a list of all of them. And if you have allergies to drugs or foods, write them down. Hospitals will probably take away any medication you bring with you and give it to you when you need it. If you want to keep any medication with you, make sure the nurses know you have it, so you don't end up getting too much of it.

◆ Bring along a nightgown or robe, a couple of pairs of pyjamas, some clean socks, underwear, slippers, and a couple of changes of your own comfortable clothes (preferably loose-fitting). Hospital gowns are impersonal, and they don't close completely, so they can be drafty; your own clothes will feel much more comfortable.

◆ If you're going to be in for a few days or more, bring along some personal things – pictures, books, a favourite stuffed animal, or a portable tape player and some of your favourite music or books on tape. These can help you feel more at home.

◆ Bring you own hairbrush, razor, toothbrush, toothpaste, soap, deodorant, and shampoo.

◆ If you have a living will (see Page 223), you may want to register it at the hospital when you get there. Check with your local hospital about their policy on this.

47

HEALTH CARE PROFESSIONALS, HOSPITALS, AND HOME CARE SERVICES
Hospital stays
- *Things to take with you*
- *Things your friends or family can bring or do*

Things your friends or family can bring or do

◆ Bring plants and cut flowers to brighten your room.

◆ Bring books, magazines, puzzles, games, pens, and paper, so you have things to read and do.

◆ Look after your plants and pets at home, pay the bills, take out the garbage, or do whatever else needs to be taken care of while you're away.

A trusted friend or relative can pay your rent and deal with banks, insurance companies, and your employer. You can have someone act for you when you can't act for yourself, by giving them power of attorney (see Page 226). If you're too ill to take care of paying your bills on time and no one else can do it for you, have someone tell your creditors that you're in the hospital.

Food

Hospital food is often bland and boring. If you'd like your friends to bring extra food, let them know what kinds you want. If you're especially hungry, you can order two portions of food from the hospital menu. You can usually request vegetarian or Kosher foods, although some hospitals aren't very flexible. You can ask to see the hospital dietitian, who can help you decide what foods to order from the regular menu. He or she can sometimes get you special foods, especially if there are things you can't eat. Be sure to fill in your daily menu choices; if you don't, you will get "standard fare." Sometimes you are told not to eat or drink during a particular period of time because of a test or treatment you're taking. It's important to follow these instructions.

Visitors

Be clear with visitors about what you want. You may prefer to eat alone, for example. If you don't want a lot of people around, say so. You have a right to set limits on how many people visit you in a day. Try asking people to call first. You may want to get someone to make signs that can be posted on your door, such as, "I'm feeling tired. Please come back another day." You may want to ask people who have colds or other contagious infections not to visit until they are better.

Hospitals can sometimes feel very lonely. So make sure to let your friends and family know if you'd like lots of visitors. Tell them how long you'd like them to stay, and how you'd like to spend your time together – talking, watching television, sitting quietly, or whatever you're in the mood for. Hospitals have set visiting hours, but most are flexible. Some may limit how often children can come in, or only let in children above a certain age.

48

HEALTH CARE PROFESSIONALS, HOSPITALS, AND HOME CARE SERVICES
Hospital stays
- *Things your friends or family can bring or do*
- *Food*
- *Visitors*

If you belong to a religious or spiritual community, you may want to ask another member to visit you. You may also request that certain ceremonies be performed in the hospital.

People from your nearest AIDS group (see Page 243) are often happy to visit you in the hospital if you want them to.

Nurses

Nurses know how hospitals work, how to get what you need, and how to make a complaint. Many nurses are excellent, and most are good at their jobs, even if they don't take time to chat or check in on you as often as you'd like. You need to learn when a nurse isn't doing his or her job properly – in which case you can complain – and when he or she is just busy or overworked. Funding cutbacks have reduced the number of nurses and other staff, which has reduced the quality of care in many hospitals.

Each bed has a buzzer for calling the nurse. Use it when you're feeling ill, if a treatment is bothering you, if you need some pain medication, or if you need other kinds of help. You can also ring to ask the nurse to contact a doctor or counsellor. If you can wait, it's good to make a list of your needs and let the nurse know next time he or she is in the room.

Nurses have to be careful with blood, as well as urine (pee) and feces (shit). They may wear gloves, and possibly hospital gowns, if they're taking a blood sample, or changing sheets or clothing stained with blood.

Doctors

You may not see your own doctor while you're in the hospital. If you're in a "teaching hospital," the doctor in charge of your care will probably be the one who checked you in – usually a specialist of some kind. Specialists often admit patients, then have their residents do most of the regular medical work (depending on the hospital and the specialist). Residents are students who have finished medical school and are now studying a specialty. You may end up getting most of your medical care from a resident. Each resident reports back to a

50

**HEALTH CARE
PROFESSIONALS,
HOSPITALS, AND
HOME CARE
SERVICES**
Hospital stays

• *Doctors*

specialist on staff at the hospital, so residents aren't acting alone. They can ask the specialist about any problems and concerns you have.

Staff physicians often lead "hospital rounds." Rounds are used to teach student doctors; the physician takes groups of residents around to see patients and talk about their cases. If your doctor isn't leading the rounds and the group is made up of students you don't know, you can decide whether or not to let them examine you or ask you any questions. You can always refuse to be examined during rounds. Discuss it with the doctor in charge of your care.

You have the right to ask a doctor about any new medication: what it is, what it's for, and what side effects it may cause. If the new medication is being given by a resident and you're not sure you want to take it, you can ask to speak to your specialist first. The same goes for medical tests.

You also have the right to refuse any medication. You should be asked to give your informed consent to get any treatment or procedure. That means you must fully understand what the treatment or procedure is, how it's going to be given, its benefits, and any possible risks or side effects.

If your first language isn't English (or French if you live in Québec or a francophone community), it may not be enough to have a friend or family member translate for you. It's better to use a professional translator, in order to make sure the medical information is accurate. Some hospitals may be able to provide translators, although often these are not professional – ask a hospital social worker for help.

If you're deaf, a hospital social worker can arrange for a professional interpreter, who will make sure you get accurate information. You may have to pay for this. The nearest office of the Canadian Hearing Society may also be able to assist you. If you're hearing impaired, make sure that doctors, nurses, and other staff know that you have difficulty hearing and how they can make communication easier.

You have the same rights and responsibilities when dealing with hospital doctors as you do with your own doctor (see Page 39). You can stop any part of your medical care at any time if you feel you're not getting better. Most hospital specialists are good at their jobs, but if you find yourself disagreeing strongly with the doctor in charge of your care, you can make a complaint to the chief of medicine.

Social workers

Some hospitals will send a social worker to visit you. Others will wait for you to ask. If you don't want to talk, that's your choice, and it should be respected. Social workers can be very helpful with problems you may have while in the hospital, and can also help you get ready to go home. For example, a social worker can arrange for home care (see Page 52), or help you contact the welfare office. If you've been getting support and counselling from someone before going into the hospital, you can still see that person now, or a social worker can arrange for other counselling. Social workers can also act as advocates; if you are dissatisfied with any part of your care, the social worker can make sure your concerns are dealt with.

Pastoral care workers

Pastoral care workers are religious counsellors who are either paid staff or volunteers at the hospital. They can provide religious and spiritual support to you, your family, and your friends. The pastoral care worker can put you in touch with a church, synagogue, mosque, or temple, and arrange for visits from members of your religious community. Religious services are usually available at the hospital (although these are most often Christian). You can also ask your own spiritual or religious counsellor to visit you in the hospital. Tell hospital staff if you do or don't want to be visited by a pastoral care worker or a representative of your religious beliefs.

Leaving the hospital

Leaving hospital is called being "discharged," and the arrangements for sending you home are called "discharge planning." You may get a visit from a nurse or social worker whose job it is to make sure you'll have everything you need at home. Fill prescriptions at the hospital pharmacy before you leave, so you won't have to go out as soon as you get home.

If you live alone, you may want someone to stay with you when you first get home. Part of your discharge planning should be making sure you have regular nursing visits at home if you need them. The

51

HEALTH CARE
PROFESSIONALS,
HOSPITALS, AND
HOME CARE
SERVICES
Hospital stays
• *Social workers*
• *Pastoral care workers*
• *Leaving the hospital*

HEALTH CARE
PROFESSIONALS,
HOSPITALS, AND
HOME CARE
SERVICES
Hospital stays
• *Leaving the hospital*
Home care programs

hospital social worker or your doctor can arrange for a home care program to look after these things (see below). The hospital can't send you home if you need home care and they haven't arranged for it, or if you need 24-hour care and there's no one at your home to help.

Hospital funding is being cut back. Sometimes hospitals send people home too soon. And they like to empty their beds before weekends or holidays. If you don't think you're ready to go home, talk to your doctor.

Home care programs

Home care programs differ from region to region, but generally they provide nursing and other professional services to make sure you can keep living independently at home. Home care may not be available in rural areas. In most provinces and territories, it is paid for by the ministry or department of health. To get home care, you must be covered under the provincial or territorial health insurance plan. You must have a stable place to stay, where the nurse can visit you on a regular basis. Once your doctor has referred you to a home care program, a worker will talk with you (either by phone or in person) to find out what you need and to tell you about the services offered.

The assessment process can be long and complicated. It often involves communicating with hospital clinics, doctors' offices, insurance companies, and the district home care coordinator. This can be hard when you're sick. Get a friend or your nearest AIDS group (see Page 243) to assist you with the process if possible.

From the time of registration, it can take several weeks for an assessment to be completed. However, you can begin the registration process before you actually need care. By pre-registering, you ensure that you will have quicker access to services when you need them.

Home care programs can arrange nursing care, homemaking, physiotherapy, occupational therapy, speech therapy, nutrition, laboratory tests, transportation, counselling, and palliative care (see Page 46).

Nursing care can range from just one visit a week to four visits a day, seven days a week. However, many people find that not enough hours of care are provided. Someone may have to coordinate additional support for you.

Nurses can help with medication, changing your IV equipment (IV means intravenous, or injected directly into a vein), advice on medication and nutrition, and health counselling. Homemakers can help with tasks such as bathing, going to the toilet, changing diapers, house cleaning, laundry, and washing dishes. The home care program can arrange for a social worker to visit. Hospital equipment (such as a hospital bed, a bedpan, canes, wheelchairs, and walkers) and medical supplies (such as a thermometer, antiseptic or rubbing alcohol, bandages, latex gloves, and diapers) can also be provided for free or at a discount. Your nearest AIDS group or disability organization may be able to get you equipment on loan. All your medication is paid for, just as it is when you're in the hospital. Many laboratory tests can be done in your home.

You lose your privacy when there are nurses and home care workers in your home. This can be difficult for you and for your partner or family. Also, new staff and volunteers have to get to know your home and your needs.

If you don't qualify for home care, you can call a nursing agency, but you'll have to pay for the service yourself, unless you have private insurance, which may cover some of the costs.

If you're leaving the hospital, your doctor will fill out a referral form if he or she feels you need home care. If you're at home, you can call the nearest home care program directly and give them the name and number of your doctor. You can ask a doctor or social worker for information about home care. Your nearest AIDS group can also refer you to a home care agency.

In Québec, home care is available through CLSC (see Page 45). Services may vary from one CLSC to another, but generally they provide physical assistance and homemaking.

For a more detailed description of long-term care services in Canada, see Health Canada's publication, *Description of Long-Term Care Services in Provinces and Territories of Canada*, available from the Publications Unit of Health Canada (see Page 242).

53

HEALTH CARE
PROFESSIONALS,
HOSPITALS, AND
HOME CARE
SERVICES
Home care programs

Care teams

Care teams are groups of people (for example, partner, friends, family, and sometimes volunteers from an AIDS group) who come to your home to keep you company, assist you with homemaking, and help you run your errands. As a team, they provide care for you when you're too sick to take care of yourself. Care teams work together with you, and may also be supported by home care workers (see above). Members of a care team will often prepare food, help you eat, give you your medication, help you bathe or go to the toilet, and change your diapers and dressings. Because of cutbacks to health care, more and more people are being cared for by partners, friends, family, and volunteers. If possible, have someone plan for this in advance; it's a lot of work. For information on how to set up a care team, refer to the AIDS Committee of Toronto (see Page 253) and le projet Accès publication, *Living with Dying – Dying at Home*.

Hospices

Hospices are places where people who are very sick can receive 24-hour care and palliative care (see Page 46). It is nurses, with the help of volunteers, who do all the care giving. Unfortunately, due to the cost of running hospices, space is limited and there are often waiting lists. And there are no hospices in rural areas.

House calls

Sometimes you may want to see your doctor about something that's not an emergency, but you can't get to his or her office. If your doctor won't make house calls, community health centres in some cities have doctors and nurses who will. But they usually only send someone to your house if you're already one of their clients.

54

HEALTH CARE
PROFESSIONALS,
HOSPITALS, AND
HOME CARE
SERVICES
Care teams
Hospices
House calls

Other in-home help services

Some agencies provide meal programs (see Page 214) which will deliver meals to your home. In many cities, drug stores will deliver prescription drugs for free. Some AIDS groups provide transportation services, such as taking you to the doctor or pick-up and delivery of prescriptions. Some community groups and agencies have volunteers who can help you at home and with your shopping. A few AIDS groups will help with pet care.

55

HEALTH CARE
PROFESSIONALS,
HOSPITALS, AND
HOME CARE
SERVICES
*Other in-home
help services*

6

Health Options

AS YOU LEARN ABOUT TREATMENTS, you'll find that there are different ways of grouping them together. In this sense, HIV is no different from the common cold. When you want to treat a cold, you have various options. You can use natural remedies like honey and lemon, a pharmaceutical drug like Dristan, or both. You can decide to treat the symptoms – like blocked sinuses – or to strengthen your immune system by getting plenty of rest, or to do both. There are different ways to get well. It's the same with HIV.

Health is a balanced state of physical, emotional, mental, spiritual, social, and sexual well-being. Some people call this way of looking at health "holistic." A holistic health approach treats you as a whole person and uses various methods of keeping you healthy. Making informed decisions about treatment options is an important part of taking charge of your health. Many of these treatments may not apply to your situation, or you may not want to do any or all of the things suggested. Use what makes sense for you.

In this book, the term "conventional medicine" is used to refer to mainstream, modern, Western medicine (also called allopathic medicine). Conventional treatments have been studied by scientists in laboratories and by medical doctors in clinical settings. The drugs used are tested first in test tubes (*in vitro*), then in animals, and finally in people (*in vivo*). If studies show that a drug seems to work, the

Health Protection Branch (HPB) of Health Canada may approve it for sale. You can get approved treatments from a doctor or hospital or pharmacy. These can be drugs, procedures (such as radiation therapy – see Page 137 – or surgery), or medical devices.

Alternative therapies are treatments used instead of conventional ones. Some people with HIV choose not to use conventional medicine at all, and use only alternative therapies. Complementary therapies are treatments that are not part of conventional medicine, but can be used together with conventional treatments. In other words, the two approaches to treatment complement each other. Many people living with HIV choose to use both conventional and complementary therapies. Some examples of complementary therapies are herbs, plant extracts, and techniques like massage, acupuncture, yoga, and meditation (all of which are discussed in this chapter).

Most complementary therapies use methods that have not been studied by scientists and approved by the HPB. Some complementary therapies, such as traditional Chinese medicine (see Page 74), have been studied extensively, but are rarely used by conventional medical doctors.

Taking care of your health can involve both conventional and complementary therapies. Often, conventional treatments like drugs can be used in combination with complementary treatments like acupuncture (see Page 74) in the hope that they'll work well with one another.

The authors make no claims for any of the therapies or treatments mentioned in this book.

Treatment isn't the whole story

While you're reading about treatments, keep in mind that these are only one part of your health care. Also, treatment information changes quickly, and new treatments become available. The information in this book is current as of the time of writing. Contact your nearest AIDS group (see Page 243) or the Community AIDS Treatment Information Exchange's HIV/AIDS Treatment Information Network (see Page 242) to get updated information.

When your doctor (or any health professional) prescribes a treatment for you, it's important to follow his or her prescribed dosage schedule as closely as possible. Make sure you understand how much of the treatment you're supposed to take, and when. Ask if there are any side effects, and whether it can interact (react badly) with other treatments you're taking. Tell your doctor about any other medication (such as over-the-counter drugs) and any type of complementary therapy (such as herbs or supplements) you're using. Street drugs can also interact with medications. It's best to discuss this with your doctor.

Treatment issues

Treatments during pregnancy

If you are asymptomatic (see Page 21), it seems that being pregnant will not cause you to develop AIDS faster. There's no proof that pregnancy will cause you to develop symptoms. If you already have symptoms or have AIDS, pregnancy may cause health problems and lead to AIDS-related illnesses. While you are pregnant, your T4 cell count (see Page 27) will drop. After your baby is delivered, your count may slowly rise again.

Drugs may have an effect on how your fetus develops, especially during the first trimester (the first fourteen weeks) of pregnancy. Your doctor may advise you to avoid all drugs during this period. If you are pregnant and have a T4 count of less than 200, your doctor will suggest treatments to prevent PCP (see Page 118). The College of Family Physicians of Canada advises that TMP/SMX, dapsone, and aerosolized pentamidine (see Page 119) seem to be safe to use during pregnancy. Acyclovir (see Page 131) may be used safely late in pregnancy (after your baby's organs have formed completely). AZT (see Page 64) can reduce the chance of passing on HIV to your baby. Other antiretrovirals are also being studied to help prevent transmission. Talk with your doctor about the most up-to-date information regarding what's best for you and your baby. It seems to be safe to use after the first trimester. For more information on treatment during pregnancy, see Modules 1 and 2 of Health Canada's *A Comprehensive Guide for the Care of Persons with HIV Disease*, developed by the College of Family Physicians of Canada. These are available through the National AIDS Clearinghouse (see Page 242).

HEALTH OPTIONS
Treatment isn't the whole story
Treatment issues
- *Treatments during pregnancy*

HEALTH OPTIONS
Treatment issues
- *Treatments for children*
- *Treatments for people with hemophilia*
- *Treatments for drug users*

Treatments for children

The treatments that are now available can both improve the quality of life of many children with HIV and increase their life span. Most of the same treatments used for adults are also used for children. Not all antiretrovirals which have been approved for adults have been studied in HIV-positive children. Since normal T cell counts (see Page 27) in children are different from those found in adults, different guidelines are used to decide when prophylaxis (preventive treatment) is necessary. Contact your local AIDS group (see Page 243) to see if any pediatric (children's) AIDS clinics are available in your area. For more information on treatment for children who are HIV-positive, see *Module 2: Infants, Children & Youth* of Health Canada's *A Comprehensive Guide for the Care of Persons with HIV Disease* (see Page 59).

Treatments for people with hemophilia

Drug treatments used for HIV/AIDS may interact with drugs used to treat hemophilia. Some drugs may affect clotting time, and should not be used. Talk to your doctor or nearest hemophilia group to see if any drugs you are taking can harm your health. In particular, you should avoid Aspirin (ASA). Many people with hemophilia, and some people who have had transfusions, may be infected with hepatitis C (see Page 134) and should therefore consider the effect of any therapy on liver function. A hematologist and a hepatology specialist should be consulted.

Treatments for drug users

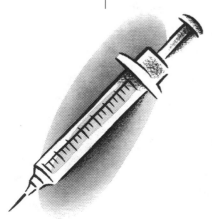

Not a lot is known about the effects of street drugs on HIV/AIDS or how those drugs will affect different treatments. A small amount of alcohol (one or two drinks a day) doesn't seem to increase damage to your immune system or cause you to get AIDS faster. However, drinking lots, or often, over a long period of time puts stress on your liver and other internal organs, which makes them less able to help your body use any medications you're taking. Alcohol and drugs can make it harder for your body to absorb important vitamins and minerals, which can contribute to health problems. Drug use increases the risk of getting bacterial infections such as bacterial pneumonia (see Page 112), sepsis (a blood infection), and endocarditis (an inflammation of the heart). Always clean your skin with an alcohol swab before shooting up. Tuberculosis (see Page 108) and hepatitis B (see Page 134) are also major concerns for drug users. Also, it can be difficult to tell the difference between problems related to drug use and symptoms of some infections associated with AIDS. This may prevent the early diagnoses of some infections.

Several important drug interactions (drugs reacting badly with each other) happen with methadone (a narcotic used to help people get off heroin). Rifampin (see Page 110), rifabutin (Mycobutin – see Page 107), and phenytoin (used for the treatment of seizures in patients with central nervous system infections) cause the elimination of methadone, which leads rapidly to withdrawal symptoms. This can be prevented by increasing your daily methadone doses. Drug inter–actions between street drugs and antiretroviral combinations are still not fully understood. If you are taking combination antiretroviral (anti-HIV) therapy (see below) you should try to decrease the amount of whatever street drug(s) you are using and monitor the effect the drug(s) has on you compared to when you were not taking antiretro-viral drugs. For more information on drug interactions call the Community AIDS Treatment Information Exchange's HIV/AIDS Treat-ment Information Network (see Page 242).

Because of the effects of some drugs and of alcohol on your body, you may want to think about the pros and cons of cutting down, switching drugs, or quitting. A worker at a detox centre or your near-est AIDS group (see Page 243) may be able to help you choose which drugs are the most harmful and how to reduce or use them safely. Decisions about drug use are your own business. Set goals that you're comfortable with.

Anti-HIV treatments

Because HIV is a type of virus called a "retrovirus," drug treatments taken to fight HIV are properly called "antiretrovirals," but people usually use the simpler word "antivirals." Antivirals interfere with the life cycle of HIV by slowing down or stopping the process by which the virus makes copies of itself. When there are fewer viruses available to

HEALTH OPTIONS
Treatment issues
• *Treatments for drug users*
Anti-HIV treatments

infect T4 cells (see Page 20), the number of those cells may increase. When you take antiviral drugs, your doctor will test your T4 count every three to six months, as well as your viral load.

T4 cell counts and viral load are surrogate markers of HIV infection. Surrogate markers are lab measurements that can show indirectly the effect of a treatment on a disease. So if your T4 count increases and your viral load decreases after you start taking antivirals, this shows that the treatment is working against HIV. If your T4 count decreases and/or your viral load increases, or the treatment doesn't work for you, you may decide to try another drug or combination of drugs.

HIV can mutate (change) so that a drug no longer has an effect. This is called resistance. Taking two or more anti-HIV drugs at once (combination therapy) makes it harder for HIV to change in ways that allow it to resist any one drug. Combination therapy has a longer-lasting benefit than monotherapy (taking one drug only).

In 1995, the results of two long-term studies of antiviral drugs confirmed what many people had come to believe: combination therapy provided greater survival benefit (fewer people died in the arm of the trial studying the combination than in the arm receiving the monotherapy), slowed disease progression (the process of getting sicker), and produced greater improvement in surrogate markers than did monotherapy.

The greatest benefit from combination therapy is achieved if you take the drugs as they are prescribed. This is called "compliance." Many people may have difficulty complying, since it may involve remembering to take your pills a number of times per day. Some drugs must be taken on an empty stomach, others with a meal. It is very important to think about how you will comply before you begin taking a particular combination of drugs.

Choosing which drugs to combine can be difficult. Some drugs should not be used in combination because they produce the same side effects. For example, both ddI and ddC (see Pages 65 and 66) can cause peripheral neuropathy (see Page 143). Using them together can increase the chances of developing this problem. Certain other drugs should not be used in combination because HIV can mutate to resist the effects of both drugs. This is called "cross-resistance."

The "right" combination for you will depend on what drugs you have taken before, which side effects you may experience, how able you are to comply with the dosing requirements, and other infections or health problems you may have.

Although combination therapy may be the best approach for most people, it may not always be an option. Not everyone can tolerate the side effects of two or more antiviral drugs. You may have health problems which make taking two or more drugs a serious risk. Or you may not have access to all (or any) of the combinations because your provincial or territorial health insurance doesn't pay for these treatments and you may not be able to afford them.

The following types of antiviral drugs are, or soon will be, available in Canada: reverse transcriptase inhibitors, including nucleoside analogues and non-nucleoside reverse transcriptase inhibitors (NNRTIs), and protease (or proteinase) inhibitors. For up-to-date information on antivirals, contact the Community AIDS Treatment Information Exchange's HIV/AIDS Treatment Information Network (see Page 242).

Note: Doses of drugs are given in numbers of "mg"s. This stands for "milligrams."

Reverse transcriptase inhibitors – nucleoside analogues

There are several stages in the reproductive cycle of HIV. At each stage, chemical messengers called enzymes help the virus make copies of itself. Some drugs can inhibit (slow down or stop) the actions of these enzymes. It is hoped that when the enzymes can't do their work, the virus won't be able to reproduce as quickly.

Reverse transcriptase (RT) is one of the enzymes that HIV needs to make copies of itself. RT inhibitors work early in HIV's life cycle, just after it has infected a cell.

Nucleoside analogues are a class of drugs that include AZT, ddI, ddC, d4T, and 3TC. HIV needs to change its genetic material (RNA) to match the genetic material of your cells (DNA). Nucleoside analogue drugs work by interfering with this "conversion" process. Genetic material, whether it's RNA or DNA, is made up of nucleosides. An analogue is one chemical compound that is very similar to another. Nucleoside analogues are compounds that are almost the same as the basic components of genetic material. As the viral RNA is being turned into DNA, nucleoside analogues bind to the DNA and block the conversion process.

HEALTH OPTIONS
Anti-HIV treatments
- *Reverse transcriptase inhibitors – nucleoside analogues*
  - *Side effects of nucleoside analogues*
  - *AZT*

Side effects of nucleoside analogues

The side effects most commonly reported by people who use these drugs include nausea and vomiting, headaches, diarrhea, chills, and fever. Not everyone will experience these side effects. Many people are able to "dose through" side effects by continuing to take the drugs and letting their bodies get used to them. Others choose to take lower doses and gradually add more until they are able to take the full recommended dose. Some people can't tolerate the side effects and have to change drugs, use very low doses, or not take these drugs at all. See below for the side effects caused by specific drugs.

AZT

AZT (also called azidothymidine, zidovudine, ZDV, or Retrovir) is the best-known antiviral (see Page 61) drug. It was originally developed in the 1960s as an anti-cancer drug, but didn't work. In 1985 researchers found that it stopped HIV from multiplying in the test tube, so they began testing it on people who had HIV. AZT is approved for use by people whose T4 cell count (see Page 27) is below 500, although this restriction is under review. It is available in pills, or as a syrup for children. The usual dose is 300 to 600 mg per day. AZT is able to get into the brain, which means it may have an effect on HIV in the central nervous system. For this reason AZT may help treat AIDS dementia complex (ADC – see Page 144), at doses of 1,000 to 1,200 mg per day. Some people have also used it to try to prevent other problems with memory, concentration, and difficulty in thinking clearly, or to make such problems less severe.

Side effects

AZT may damage bone marrow (see Page 20). Your bone marrow is where new blood cells in your body come from. This damage may cause the number of your red blood cells and white blood cells (see Pages 26 and 20) to drop. A serious drop in the number of your red blood cells is called anemia (see Page 26), and a drop in the number of white blood cells known as neutrophils is called neutropenia. Neutropenia makes it harder for your body to fight infections.

People who develop these symptoms are usually advised to take lower doses of AZT, or stop taking it completely, until their bone marrow can recover enough to start making more red and white blood cells.

AZT can also cause muscle wasting (see Page 164). After taking it for more than six months, some people start to develop weakness and aches in their muscles, especially in their buttocks (butt), upper arms, and thighs. This muscle damage is referred to as AZT myopathy.

After taking AZT for more than six months, some people get blue, brown, or black lines or streaks down their fingernails and toenails. This doesn't look nice, but does no harm. Some people of colour have reported that their skin gets darker, and people with curly hair sometimes report that their hair uncurls.

Drug interactions

AZT may interact (react badly) with other drugs you're taking. It can interfere with the work these other drugs are supposed to do. And other drugs can cause some of the same side effects as AZT. For example, ganciclovir (see Page 127) can cause neutropenia (see Page 64). If you take AZT and ganciclovir, this problem may get worse. Your doctor may recommend taking less AZT, or going off AZT, while you're on these other medications.

ddI

ddI (also called didanosine, dideoxyinosine, or Videx) is another approved nucleoside analogue. It is available in chewable tablets or as a powder you mix with water. An ingredient is added to help reduce the acid in your stomach for easier digestion of the ddI.

Side effects

ddI's most serious side effect is pancreatitis – a swelling or inflammation of your pancreas. Only a small number of people who take ddI develop this disorder, which can kill you if it is severe. If you are taking ddI and you experience nausea, vomiting, and gut pain, which are symptoms of pancreatitis, tell your doctor. To reduce the chances of this happening, your doctor can test the amylase (see Page 28) and triglyceride levels in your blood every month or so. If you develop pancreatitis, you should never use ddI again. ddI can also cause peripheral neuropathy (see Page 143).

65

HEALTH OPTIONS
Anti-HIV treatments
- *Reverse transcriptase inhibitors – nucleoside analogues*
  - *AZT*
  - *ddI*

HEALTH OPTIONS
Anti-HIV treatments
- *Reverse transcriptase inhibitors –*
  nucleoside analogues
  - *ddI*
  - *ddC*

Drug interactions

If you take ddI with certain drugs, the risk of developing pancreatitis increases. These drugs include sulfonamides, cimetidine (Tagamet), and ranitidine (Zantac). ddI can decrease levels of oral ganciclovir (see Page 127) by as much as 20 per cent, and may reduce the effectiveness of the drug. ddI may interact with pentamidine (see Page 119), a treatment and preventive treatment given for PCP (see Page 118). Drinking alcohol when you're on ddI can also increase the risk of pancreatitis. Any drug that must be absorbed with food should be taken separately (at least two hours earlier). Examples of drugs that shouldn't be taken at the same time as ddI are ketoconazole (Nizoral – see Page 114) and dapsone (see Page 119). Check with your doctor or pharmacist to see if any other treatment you are taking would be affected by ddI.

ddC

ddC (also called dideoxycytidine, zalcitabine, or Hivid) is another approved nucleoside analogue.

Side effects

ddC can cause peripheral neuropathy (see Page 143). Rarely, it may cause pancreatitis (see Page 65). If you're taking ddC, it's very important to call your doctor right away if you get any of the symptoms of pancreatitis, such as nausea, vomiting, or gut pain. ddC can cause ulcers (sores) in your mouth or esophagus (the tube that connects your mouth and stomach).

Drug interactions

Other drugs that cause peripheral neuropathy and pancreatitis should be used with caution or avoided when you're taking ddC. These include ddI (see Page 65), disulfiram, ethionamide, ganciclovir (see Page 127), isoniazid (INH), phenytoin (see Page 61), vincristine, hydrazaline, and metronidazole. Ask your doctor or pharmacist if any other treatments you're taking might cause problems in combination with ddC.

d4T

d4T (also called stavudine, or Zerit) is another approved nucleoside analogue.

Side effects

In general, d4T appears to produce fewer side effects than the other nucleoside analogues (see Page 63). Peripheral neuropathy (see Page 143) is the most serious side effect. Like AZT, d4T can cause neutropenia (see Page 64). An increase in liver enzymes (which is not good for you) has also been reported.

Drug interactions

Other drugs that cause peripheral neuropathy should be used with caution or avoided when you're taking d4T. These include ddI, ddC, foscarnet, amphotericin, and dapsone (see Pages 65, 66, 128, 116, and 119). Using both ganciclovir (see Page 127) and d4T may increase the risk of developing pancreatitis (see Page 65).

3TC

3TC (also called lamivudine, or Epivir) is another approved nucleoside analogue. Researchers have reported a "synergistic relationship" between AZT and 3TC, as well as d4T and 3TC, which means they work better as a team than either drug works by itself.

Side effects

Since 3TC is a new drug, there is little information available about its long-term side effects. The most common side effects reported by people using the 3TC and AZT combination are headaches, fatigue, fever and/or chills, nausea, diarrhea, and neutropenia (see Page 64). 3TC and AZT are approved for use in children. Pancreatitis (see Page 65) is the most serious side effect seen in children.

HEALTH OPTIONS
Anti-HIV treatments
- *Reverse transcriptase inhibitors – nucleoside analogues*
  - *d4T*
  - *3TC*

Non-nucleoside reverse transcriptase inhibitors (NNRTIs)

Like nucleoside analogues, this class of drugs works against reverse transcriptase (see Page 63). But NNRTIs have a different chemical structure. At the time of the writing of this book, these drugs are not approved for sale in Canada. Two of them, nevirapine (Viramune) and delavirdine (Rescriptor) are currently available through compassionate access programs (see Page 171). Ask your doctor for more information about these programs. HIV becomes resistant to all the NNRTIs very quickly. For this reason they must be used in combination with at least two other antiretroviral drugs.

Delavirdine is made by Pharmacia & Upjohn. Headaches and skin rash are the most commonly reported side effects.

Nevirapine is made by Boehringer Ingelheim. The most commonly reported side effect is skin rash.

Loveride is a third NNRTI, made by Janssen. The most commonly reported side effects of loveride are skin rash and itching.

Protease inhibitors

Protease (or proteinase – see Page 18) is an enzyme HIV needs at a later stage in its reproductive cycle than when it uses reverse transcriptase (see Page 63). Protease inhibitors are a new class of anti-HIV drugs which work by inhibiting (slowing down or stopping) the action of protease. When this enzyme can't do its work, HIV makes defective copies of itself, which can't infect other cells. Like reverse transcriptase inhibitors, protease inhibitors may reduce the amount of HIV  that can be measured in your blood. They may also increase T4 cell counts (see Page 27). Protease inhibitors will probably work best when combined with one or two reverse transcriptase inhibitors.

Protease inhibitors are new drugs. Their side effects and benefits over the long term are not clear. It also isn't clear which combinations work best with these drugs.

Saquinavir

Saquinavir (also called Invirase) is the first protease inhibitor approved for sale in Canada. Approval was based only on changes in surrogate markers (see Page 62). The best results from the studies were seen in people who used saquinavir with both AZT and ddC (see Pages 64 and 66). But the combinations of saquinavir with AZT, and saquinavir with ddC, produced similar results. Saquinavir was approved at a dose of 600 mg, taken three times a day.

Side effects
The most commonly reported side effects are diarrhea, abdominal discomfort (feeling bloated), and nausea.

Ritonavir

Ritonavir (also called Norvir) is approved for sale in Canada. The standard dosage of ritonavir is 600 mg twice daily with food.

Side effects
Nausea, vomiting, diarrhea, fatigue, and numbness or tingling of the mouth are the most commonly reported side effects. Some people can "dose through" these side effects, which means that after a period of time taking the drug the side effects go away. Pancreatitis (see Page 65) may be another side effect.

Drug interactions
People who take ritonavir may have to cut their dosages of some drugs, or stop using them entirely. These drugs include codeine, keto-conazole (Nizoral – see Page 114), Monostat-4, Hismanal, Seldane, Tagamet, Paxil, Valium, Xanax, and Halcion.

Indinavir

Indinavir (also called Crixivan) is approved for sale in Canada. The standard dosage of indinavir is 800 mg every eight hours on an empty stomach.

HEALTH OPTIONS
Anti-HIV treatments
- *Protease inhibitors*
  - *Saquinavir*
  - *Ritonavir*
  - *Indinavir*

Side effects

The most serious side effect is kidney stones. To reduce the risk of developing them, people taking indinavir should try to drink at least a litre and a half of water every day.

Nelfinavir

Nelfinavir (also called Viracept) will likely be approved for sale in Canada in 1997. The standard dosage of nelfinavir is 750 mg three times daily with food.

Side effects

Mild to moderate diarrhea is the most commonly reported side effect.

Drug interactions and antiretrovirals

All of the antiretrovirals have interactions with some other drugs. You may need to modify the dosage of these drugs or stop taking them entirely while taking antiretrovirals. Ritonavir, in particular, has a long list of drug interactions with some of the medications used commonly in HIV disease. You can get detailed information about specific drug interactions from CATIE's HIV/AIDS Treatment Information Network at 1-800-263-1638 or by email: info@catie.ca.

Final comments on antiretrovirals

Combination therapy with antiretroviral drugs may help you delay the progression of HIV disease by slowing down the replication (reproduction) of HIV. This can prevent damage to your immune system. Combination therapy is not a cure for HIV/AIDS. However, there are new drugs and new formulations of existing drugs being developed that will make it easier for people to comply. For people who can tolerate the drugs and comply with the dosing requirements, combination therapy offers the possibility of living with HIV as a chronic, manageable disease.

HEALTH OPTIONS
Anti-HIV treatments
- *Protease inhibitors*
  - *Indinavir*
  - *Nelfinavir*
- *Drug interactions and antiretrovirals*
- *Final comments on antiretrovirals*

Other anti-HIV treatments

Compound Q

Compound Q (also known as GLQ233) comes from the Chinese cucumber (*Trichosanthes kirilowii*), and has been shown to kill HIV in the test tube. It is usually given intravenously (IV, or injected directly into a vein). It has been studied since 1988 for its effect on the immune system and against HIV. Studies done in test tubes suggest that it may stop HIV from multiplying inside T4 cells (see Page 20). What makes Compound Q different from other anti-HIV drugs, however, is that it may also kill HIV-infected macrophages (see Page 20). Early trials in humans showed increases in T4 cells and lower levels of p24 antigen (see Page 28). But several recent trials have shown no significant changes in these signs.

Compound Q is still being studied for safety and usefulness. Researchers have found that it can be dangerous. Some people using it have developed headaches, muscle aches, and flu-like symptoms. One person who took it died from an allergic reaction. Because of the risks and side effects associated with this treatment, it should only be taken under the care of a health professional who has experience working with it.

HEALTH OPTIONS
Anti-HIV treatments
• *Other anti-HIV treatments*
  • *Compound Q*
  • *Hypericin*

Hypericin

Hypericin and pseudohypericin are extracts of the herb St. John's wort (*Hypericum triquetrifolium*). In test tube studies both compounds have shown anti-HIV activity. Other reports suggest that hypericin may work against several other disease-causing viruses, including CMV (see Page 125) and herpes simplex (see Page 130). This is called "broad spectrum activity." It has also been tested as an antidepressant in Europe.

A synthetic form of hypericin was given intravenously (IV, or injected directly into a vein) to a small group of people with HIV. However, the study was stopped early due to photosensitivity (a tingling or burning sensation in the skin when exposed to light), which is one of the side effects of this treatment. A pill form of synthetic hypericin is currently being studied.

St. John's wort is available as an extract at health food stores. An increase in liver enzymes (which is not good for you) has been reported in some people who use this herb.

SPV-30

SPV-30 is a herbal compound derived from the boxwood tree, made by a French company called Arkopharma. Studies have shown SPV-30 to act as an antiretroviral and small reductions in viral load were measured.

HEALTH OPTIONS
Anti-HIV treatments
- *Other anti-HIV treatments*
  - *SPV-30*
- *Immune modulators*
  - *Interleukin-2*

Immune modulators

Immune system modulators, or immune boosters, strengthen your immune system. Several drugs may do this. Some immune boosters are meant to increase your T4 cell count (see Page 27). Others work on other parts of your immune system (see cell-mediated and humoral immunity – Page 20).

Some researchers believe that the best treatment for a weakened immune system would be a combination of anti-HIV treatments and immune boosters, but research in this area is lacking. The following are a few examples of immune modulators:

Interleukin-2

Interleukin-2 is a cytokine, which is a naturally occurring chemical messenger in the body. In some studies it has been shown to increase T4 cells. It can also cause an increase in viral load, so antiretrovirals must be taken together with Interleukin-2. Interleukin-2 used to be called T-cell growth factor. It is approved for use in kidney cancer, and is sometimes used "off label" in HIV. Side effects include severe flu-like symptoms.

Interleukin-2 is one of many cytokines being studied to stimulate or suppress different parts of the immune system.

Naltrexone

Naltrexone is used in the USA (under the name Trexan) to help former heroin addicts stay drug-free. People with HIV sometimes have low levels of a hormone called beta endorphin, which has an important role in controlling your immune system. Naltrexone can cause your body to make more beta endorphin. Some doctors who prescribe it have seen their patients' T4 cell counts (see Page 27) stop going down. It has also helped some people stay well longer. Naltrexone is available in Canada through the Emergency Drug Release Program (see Page 170). The usual dose being given by doctors in the USA is 3 mg a day at bedtime, six nights a week. Since the tablets contain 50 mg, you or your pharmacist should mix two tablets in 100 ml (millilitres) of water and allow it to dissolve. Then use 3 ml in a glass of water (you can use a syringe – 3 cc [cubic centimetres] equals 3 ml).

DNCB

DNCB (Dinitrochlorobenzene) is a chemical compound used in photography. When applied to your skin, it brings on an immune reaction like a reaction to poison ivy, called delayed type hypersensitivity (DTH). The DTH response may stimulate the cell-mediated part of your immune system (see Page 20). Since this part may be weakened when you have HIV, DNCB has been used as an immune booster. One study of DNCB in people with HIV showed increases in T8 cell counts (see Page 28). In some people, the production of HIV in their blood either decreased or remained the same. But the doctors who did this study think that DNCB had no effect on the production of HIV. DNCB users report that skin infections (such as molluscum – see Page 148) may be controlled with long-term use (between three and eight months). DNCB must be used according to product instructions, otherwise it may cause severe burns to the skin.

73

HEALTH OPTIONS
Anti-HIV treatments
- *Immune modulators*
  - *Naltrexone*
  - *DNCB*

Complementary therapies

Aside from drug therapies, there are many other therapies that may help you repair immune damage or treat symptoms.

Be wary of claims that a therapy or treatment can cure AIDS or reverse HIV antibody status (from positive to negative). Try to inform yourself by talking with other HIV-positive people who have used the therapy or treatment you're interested in, or contact your nearest AIDS group (see Page 243) to see if they have information.

Get in touch with qualified people who practise complementary therapies. Ask what kind of training they've had, how long they've been practising, and whether they have any experience treating people with HIV. Find out how their therapies will combine with the other things you're doing to take care of your health. Are there any side effects? How often do you get the therapy?

Complementary therapies usually aren't paid for by government or private insurance programs; you may have to pay for them yourself. So you'll need to find out how much they cost and decide if you can afford them and, if you can, whether they seem worth it.

Many complementary treatments aren't easy to find. You may have to go to a health food store or order the treatment from a buyers' club (see Page 171).

Traditional Chinese medicine (TCM)

This system sees illness as an imbalance in your body's energy flow. This energy, known as "qi," moves along invisible pathways in your body, called meridians. Meridians connect your body's organ systems to each other and to pressure points (specific points on your body). Acupuncture needles (thin stainless steel needles) may be stuck into your skin at these points to balance your meridians. (This is not supposed to hurt.) Moxibustion is a method used in acupuncture practice. It involves the application of ignited cones or sticks of mugwort (an herb) over the acupuncture points in order to stimulate your body with heat. Chinese herbal medicine is often used along with acupuncture to treat blockages of energy within your body. Usually many different herbs are used together. Often the combinations are tailor-made to suit your health needs.

TCM is being studied to see what it can do for people who have HIV. Some people using acupuncture and Chinese herbs have reported improvements in such symptoms as diarrhea, tiredness, night sweats (see Page 157), weight loss, swollen lymph glands (see Page 19), and peripheral neuropathy (see Page 143). And some have felt generally better and more energetic.

Although the idea of health being related to the flow of energy in the body is only just beginning to be accepted in North America and Europe, it is common to most Eastern approaches to health.

Naturopathy

The word "naturopathy" comes from the Greek words "*naturae*" and "*pathos*," and means "a natural way to relieve suffering." Naturopathic doctors (naturopaths) see disease as your body's attempt to get rid of toxins and restore balance. They use a holistic approach to healing that can include herbal medicine, nutrition, supplements, homeopathy, traditional Chinese medicine, chiropractic (spinal manipulation), massage, and counselling. (Most of these techniques are discussed in this chapter.)

Using natural substances and procedures, naturopaths try to help the natural healing powers of your body work as well as possible. By teaching you the basics of healthful living, they help you take an active part in staying healthy, which includes both preventing and healing disease.

Some naturopaths are also trained as medical doctors. Some may have a special interest in a particular area, such as homeopathy or Chinese medicine. If you're looking for a particular kind of therapy, you should ask about a naturopath's specialty.

Naturopaths use research from various areas, including botanical medicine, homeopathy, acupuncture, and nutrition. Naturopathic colleges do research. For example, the Canadian College of Naturopathic Medicine in Toronto is doing research on the treatment of HIV infection with Chinese herbs.

HEALTH OPTIONS
*Complementary
    therapies*
- *Traditional Chinese
   Medicine (TCM)*
- *Naturopathy*

Homeopathy

Homeopathy is a system of medicine that began in Europe 200 years ago. Unlike standard medicine, homeopathy is based on the principle of "like cures like." This means that the symptoms of a sick person are treated with small doses of a medicine that would cause the same symptoms if a full dose were given to a healthy person. Most homeopathic medicines are found in nature (animals, minerals, and plants) and are taken as tinctures (dissolved in alcohol) or in mini-tablets.

In Western medicine, ten different people who all have the same condition would be treated with the same medication. In homeopathy, however, those ten people may each be treated with different remedies, according to the needs of each of their bodies. Homeopathy is practised by a wide variety of health care workers, including not only homeopaths but also medical doctors and naturopaths (see above).

Ayurvedic medicine

Ayurvedic medicine is the oldest recorded medicine on earth, and comes from India. It is more than 5,000 years old, and has only recently started to be studied again. "Ayurveda" literally means "science of life." The central belief of ayurvedic medicine is that the mind/consciousness creates matter. This means that you can affect your health through what you think or believe. Ayurvedic medicine uses such natural healing methods as nutrition, herbs, exercise, massage, and meditation to bring your body to a healthy state.

Aromatherapy

Aromatherapy is a unique branch of herbal medicine that uses the medicinal properties found in the essential oils of various plants. The oils are extracted from flowers, leaves, branches or roots, through a process of either steam distillation or cold-pressing. Essential oils can be either applied directly to an infection, inhaled (breathed in), placed in bathwater, or burned as incense.

Oxygen therapy (superoxygenation or hyperoxygenation therapies)

Hydrogen peroxide can be used as a mouthwash to treat thrush (see Page 113), or topically (on your skin or in a bath) to treat skin infections. But it can be deadly if it's not watered down, so use food-grade hydrogen peroxide in a 3 per cent solution, and don't swallow any.

Ozone, which is a form of oxygen, has been shown to make HIV inactive (harmless) in the test tube. Ozone can be administered from a home air or water ozonator with a tube inserted rectally (up your bum) or vaginally (up your vagina), or it can be inhaled (breathed in). There is no evidence that HIV-positive people receive any benefit from this therapy.

Blood ozonation is done by removing blood from a vein, adding ozone, and returning the ozonated blood into the vein. It is controversial, and two studies conducted by medical researchers in Ottawa showed that ozone had no effect on either T4 cell counts (see Page 27) or any other signs of immune function.

There have been reports of deaths due to improper use of ozone therapies.

Hyperbaric medicine involves the breathing in of pure oxygen while the body is under increased pressure inside a sealed chamber. It is approved for a number of conditions and sometimes used "off label" by people with HIV, though there has been little research into this therapy in HIV disease.

Massage and touch therapies

Massage is an ancient healing art, which is very popular these days. Physically, massage can relax your body and improve the circulation of your blood and other body fluids. Massage and other touch therapies often affect you emotionally as well, relieving stress and giving you a sense of well-being. In many cases, just being touched can be a healing experience. It may help give you a sense of self-worth, as well as physical pleasure. And you can be massaged not only by professionals, but also by friends with loving hands. Some AIDS groups (see Page 243) provide massage therapy for free.

HEALTH OPTIONS
Complementary therapies
- *Oxygen therapy*
- *Massage and touch therapies*

HEALTH OPTIONS
*Complementary
    therapies*
- *Massage and touch
    therapies*
    - *Swedish massage*
    - *Reflexology*
    - *Therapeutic touch*

Swedish massage

This is the kind of massage most people know about. The massage therapist uses different techniques to massage your body in order to stimulate the circulation of your blood and loosen knotted muscles. The kneading, stroking, pressing, and stretching that make up Swedish massage can help your joints move better and give you relief from pain, stress, and tiredness. Swedish massage can also help your immune system work better by helping you relax.

Reflexology

Reflexology comes from ancient Egyptian and Aboriginal healing traditions. It's based on the idea that there are places on your head, hands, and feet that are connected to each gland and organ in your body. Through both gentle and deep pressure massage of these points, reflexologists stimulate your organs and glands.

Therapeutic touch

This is different from most other kinds of massage because, in spite of the name, the therapist does not actually touch you. Therapeutic touch is based on the belief that all living things share in a life-energy field. When you're healthy, this life energy flows freely through your body. When you get sick, the flow of energy is blocked. Therapeutic touch helps unblock the energy and bring your body back into balance. The person giving you the massage holds his or her hands about four inches from your body, and works the energy in a way that clears areas where it's blocked and spreads it to where it's needed. Many people feel energy moving throughout their bodies during a therapeutic touch massage. Many feel a warmth and heaviness in their hands and feet and feel their breathing deepening; these are signs of relaxation.

Reiki

The word "reiki" means "universal life energy." Like therapeutic touch, reiki is based on the belief that living things share life energy. When that life energy is blocked, it results in an imbalance that may appear as illness. Unblocking the energy helps you get back into balance. A person giving you a reiki massage uses his or her hands in different ways to help channel (guide) your energy and unblock your emotions.

Rolfing

Rolfing is a method of straightening your body by working on your fascia – the connective tissue that surrounds your muscles. A rolfing practitioner massages you hard in order to move your fascia and muscles into place. This balances your posture and allows your body to move more efficiently and freely. Rolfing often releases pent-up emotions.

Shiatsu

Shiatsu (acupressure) is a Japanese system of massage that aims to balance the energies in your body. It is believed that energies that are out of balance can cause disease and tiredness, and make your immune system work less well. The word "shiatsu" means "finger pressure." The therapist presses specific points on your body. Each point connects to a specific organ in your body through lines called meridians (see Page 74). Pressing a certain point stimulates the organ it's connected to. Shiatsu uses the same pressure points as acupuncture (see Page 74), but uses the pressure of fingers, palms, and elbows instead of needles. Both shiatsu and acupuncture work to calm the energy ("qi") that flows in a continuous cycle through your body.

Trager

Trager is a form of gentle and pleasurable massage that releases tension from body joints. The Trager practitioner uses various rhythmic, rocking, and stretching movements to do this.

HEALTH OPTIONS
Complementary
therapies
- *Massage and touch*
  therapies
  - *Reiki*
  - *Rolfing*
  - *Shiatsu*
  - *Trager*

Chiropractic

The word "chiropractic" means "done by hand." It is based on the theory that health and disease are life processes related to the function of your nervous system. Your nervous system can be irritated by physical, chemical, or psychological factors, which can cause disease. The chiropractor identifies what is causing the irritation in your nervous system and attempts to remove it. A chiropractor may physically straighten your body by manipulating (moving around) your spine. He or she may also use heat, light, and electric and water therapies, and may recommend exercises or diet programs.

Exercise

Moderate exercise done regularly can help you stay physically and emotionally healthy. Besides making your muscles, skeleton, and circulation stronger, a reasonable amount of exercise is thought to make your immune system work better. It can also help you relax, improve your digestion and your ability to get rid of body wastes, and make it easier for your body to take in and use oxygen. Exercise is extremely useful in relieving stress and depression and reducing anxiety.

There are many types of exercise and, as with everything else, you need to decide what works for you. You may want to talk to your doctor before beginning any new exercise program. Include plenty of time for slow stretching. If you get tired, take a break. And if you have any problems that won't go away, talk to your doctor.

You may want to try taking an aerobics class or doing other aerobic exercise, such as going for brisk walks, swimming, cycling, or dancing. Aerobic exercise moves lots of oxygen through your body and strengthens your heart.

It's usually suggested that people with HIV should focus on weight training, since this builds lean body mass (see Page 161). (Aerobic exercise may burn too many calories without promoting muscle mass.) Doing exercise that gets your heart and lungs going for at least 20 minutes causes your body to produce endorphins – chemicals that relieve pain and make you feel good.

Physical exercise can give you a chance to socialize and have fun. It's important to create an exercise program that you can enjoy. Many gyms have trained staff to help you decide on an exercise plan that works for you.

Yoga

The practice of yoga helps establish a balance between body and mind. In yoga, you use deep breathing, stretching, holding of positions, and meditation techniques. Some people claim that this increases body oxygen levels and decreases carbon dioxide levels. Yoga can give you better control of your voluntary and involuntary muscle systems, including your digestive system. (A voluntary muscle is one that you move on purpose. Involuntary muscles move on their own.) Instructors working with HIV-positive people report that yoga relieves swollen glands, improves stamina, and helps reduce chronic fatigue (constant tiredness).

Tai Chi

Tai Chi is a form of Chinese martial art involving a series of slow, rhythmic movements. This relaxing exercise tones your muscles and increases your energy, strength, and stamina. Tai Chi improves your posture, breathing, and circulation. It requires coordination between mind and body. It has been popular in China for many centuries as a way to get, and stay, healthy.

Meditation

Meditation is an exercise of the mind. It may help you relax and can give you a sense of calm, peace, joy, and efficiency in everyday life. Some people say it has given them a clearer view of reality. Most people meditate sitting up. You concentrate on a specific image, a mantra (a meaningless word that you repeat in your mind), or your breathing. One good time to meditate is early in the morning. A session may be as short as ten minutes, or as long as feels comfortable.

HEALTH OPTIONS
Complementary
    therapies
- *Exercise*
- *Yoga*
- *Tai Chi*
- *Meditation*

If meditation interests you, you should be able to find a program that suits you. Your nearest AIDS group (see Page 243) may be able to help you find one.

Sweat lodge

The sweat lodge is an Aboriginal ceremony of renewal and purification. It is used as a tool for freeing your body, mind, and spirit from negativity. A group of people is seated in a circle in a small, round, dark structure with a central pit. A ritual is carried out in which stones are heated and placed in the lodge. A small fire can also be made. Four herbs (tobacco, cedar, sage, and sweetgrass) are combined to make what is called a "smudge." When burnt, they produce smoke that is believed to carry prayers to the Creator. Spirits are summoned with songs to hear the prayers of those attending. As you pray for help and health, you let go of fear, anger, and hurt. Sweat lodges have been organized specifically for people with HIV.

Affirmations and visualization (guided imagery)

No one doubts that a positive attitude is a vital part of healing. An affirmation is a statement of something you want to happen. Some examples of positive affirmations are: "I am strong and healthy," "I love myself," "I am capable of making positive medical decisions," and "All hands that touch me are healing hands."

Visualization (guided imagery) is one way of developing positive thinking that has become popular with some HIV-positive people and people who have cancer or other life-threatening illnesses. A long-standing practice in many cultures, visualization is now well known in North America, partly because of the work of people like O. Carl Simonton, author of *Getting Well Again*, and Bernie Siegal, author of *Love, Medicine and Miracles*.

In visualization, you make pictures or images in your head of how you would like yourself to be, or ways in which you would like your health to improve. Anyone can do it; all you need to do is use your imagination and believe in your own inner strength. Visualization can

82

HEALTH OPTIONS
*Complementary
therapies*
• *Meditation*
• *Sweat lodge*
• *Affirmations and
visualization
(guided imagery)*

help you relax and give you a sense of participating in your own healing. It's also thought to make your immune system work better.

Many people use cassette tapes (like those made by Dr. Emmett Miller, Shakti Gawain, Louise Hay, and others) to guide their visualizations.

Herbal medicine

The first medicines anyone ever used were herbs. Many medicinal herbs, both Eastern and Western, are being used by people who have HIV. They are natural substances that come from things like flowers, weeds, and parts of trees. A single herb may be used to treat several different conditions. Herbs that are grown organically (without artificial fertilizers, herbicides, or pesticides) are usually considered best.

Herbal medicines are used by herbalists, doctors of Chinese medicine, naturopaths, homeopaths, aromatherapists, and ayurvedic doctors (see Pages 74 to 76). They can be purchased in several forms. Dried herbs can be mixed in water or juice, put in capsules, or used as infusions or decoctions. Infusions are prepared like tea but are steeped longer, so they become considerably stronger. Decoctions are made by gently simmering the dried herb in water for ten to 20 minutes. Tinctures are infusions made with alcohol. Some herbal products, such as aloe vera and tea tree oil (see below and Page 87), can be applied directly to your skin.

If you're thinking about taking herbal treatments, it's always best to consult a health care professional to find out which herb is best for you, and what dosage would be effective and safe. You may also want to refer to an herbal dictionary or book to help you make decisions about dosages (amounts) and safety. Remember that herbal treatments are not paid for by the government, so you have to pay for them yourself. You can get herbs from herbal, health food, or supplement stores, and sometimes from pharmacies and buyers' clubs (see Page 171).

Your immune system is composed of many different elements. Not all of these are damaged in HIV-positive people. Some "immune boosting" herbs may stimulate parts of your immune system that are already overactive, while suppressing (weakening) parts that are not. For example, some herbs may boost your antibody immune response, which would tend to suppress your cell-mediated response (see Page 20). It's been shown that your cell-mediated response is naturally

HEALTH OPTIONS
Complementary therapies
- *Affirmations and visualization (guided imagery)*
- *Herbal medicine*

suppressed when you have HIV, while your antibody response is over-active. Therefore, antibody-producing herbs may not be beneficial for you. Ask your naturopath or herbalist, or do your own reading, to find out how various herbs stimulate your immune system and whether they would be helpful for you.

There are many kinds of herbs used by people with HIV. Some of the more common ones are described here.

◆ **Aloe vera** has long been used to heal burns and cuts. Acemannan (brand name Carrisyn) is a concentrated powder form of the juice of the aloe vera plant. Test tube studies have shown that aloe vera works against bacteria, fungi, and viruses (see Page 18), and also as an anti-inflammatory. (The word "anti-inflammatory" refers to anything that reduces swelling and other signs of infection.) Most oral (taken by mouth) aloe vera products contain only small amounts of juice from the plant, so it's doubtful that these would slow down viruses or kill bacteria. However, aloe vera is known to aid in the healing of stomach problems, ulcers, and constipation and other colon (bowel) problems.

◆ **Apple cider vinegar** is used as an antifungal mouthwash against thrush. Swish and gargle with a small amount of vinegar, then spit it out. If you have sores in your mouth, the acidity of the vinegar may cause discomfort or pain. You may want to dilute it with water. Apple cider vinegar can also be used to aid digestion (if you have an upset stomach) and may help prevent germs from growing in your urinary tract (the tube you pee through) and bladder, and causing infections.

◆ **Bee propolis** is a resin from tree buds that is collected by bees. It contains vitamins, minerals, amino acids, enzymes, and other nutrients. It's been shown to fight bacterial infections and works in the test tube against four types of herpes viruses (see Page 130). You can chew it as a remedy for thrush (see Page 113), or apply it directly to cuts and sores as an antiseptic.

◆ **Bitter melon** is the fruit of a plant called *Momordica charantia*. A tea is usually made from the fruit, leaves, and stems of this plant, and is taken as an enema (fluid injected into your rectum [ass]). A few test tube studies have shown that components of bitter melon can slow down HIV. Bitter melon can also bring on an abortion. There have been no clinical trials of bitter melon.

◆ **Blue-green algae** is harvested from the surface of lakes and oceans. It contains amino acids, minerals, and many other nutrients. Some people use it as a general immune booster or to give them more energy. A study by the American National Cancer Institute showed that it works against HIV in the test tube. It's available in powder and capsule form.

◆ **Curcumin** is a substance found in the spice turmeric, which is used in Indian curries. Curcumin has been used to aid digestion and fight intestinal (gut) parasites (see Page 159). Test tube studies have shown that it can stop HIV from reproducing. But early results in tests on humans have shown no effect on T4 cell counts (see Page 27). Curcumin is available in many health food stores. Turmeric can be used in cooking, but it is thought to be impossible to eat quantities high enough in curcumin to affect HIV just by using this spice.

◆ **Echinacea** is also called purple coneflower. It's found all over North America and has long been used by Aboriginal peoples. Test tube studies have shown that echinacea can increase levels of the cytokine (see page 20) TNF-alpha. High levels of this cytokine can cause fevers and wasting (see Page 164) and can stimulate HIV reproduction. Echinacea is used to heal wounds; it may activate your antibody immune response (see Page 83) against viruses and bacteria. Some herbalists suggest that HIV-positive people not use this herb, or use it for only a couple of days when they feel a cold or flu coming on. Echinacea is available in a tincture (dissolved in alcohol) and in dried plant form (which is made into a tea or taken in capsules).

◆ **Essiac tea** contains burdock root, sheep sorrel, slippery elm bark, and turkey rhubarb root. This tea was developed by the Ojibway nation. There are no reports of either test-tube studies or clinical trials of Essiac tea. It has been used as an immune booster. Some people say that it has cured certain types of cancer, but there is no proof. People with HIV have reported improvements in well-being, but more information is necessary about the specific effects on HIV-positive people.

◆ **Garlic** has been found to have an effect against some bacteria and fungi (see Page 18). After you have recovered from an infection, garlic may be useful in keeping it from coming back. You can eat it raw or take it in odourless capsules. Raw garlic can sometimes cause diarrhea or nausea.

HEALTH OPTIONS
Complementary
therapies
• *Herbal medicine*

◆ **Grapefruit seed extract** is sold under the brand names Citricidal and Nutribiotic. It's a liquid that fights bacteria and fungi (see Page 18). It can be used as a mouthwash for thrush (see Page 113) and topically (on the affected area) for many types of skin and mouth infections. Some people use it to disinfect vegetables and fruits (as an alternative to using bleach – see Page 98). It's also available in tablet form.

◆ **Herbal combinations** are mixtures of different herbs, usually used for a special purpose. It's important to note that many of these products claim to be "immune boosting," but may just boost your antibody immune response, which might not be good for you (see Page 83).

◆ **Hyssop** (*Hyssopus officinalis*) is an herb that's been used as a treatment for coughs and respiratory (breathing) problems associated with colds and flu. It's being studied in people with HIV to see if it has any effect on infections. Reports suggest that it may be useful in the treatment of MAC (see Page 106), herpes (see Page 130), and KS (see Page 136), although this has not been proven. It is prepared as a tea for drinking. A compress (to treat herpes, cold sores, or wounds) can be made by soaking a cloth in the tea.

◆ **Licorice root** is a common ingredient of Chinese herbal remedies. It's known for its anti-inflammatory (see Page 84) and immune-boosting properties. It's also been used to improve liver function and treat liver disease. One of its active ingredients is glycyrrhizin, which has been found to work strongly in the test tube against HIV and the herpes simplex virus (see Page 130). Glycyrrhizin, under the brand name Glyceron, is approved for treating hepatitis B (see Page 134) in Japan.

◆ **Milk thistle** contains silymarin, which may help protect your liver from the toxic (poisonous) effects of certain drugs. It may also protect your liver from the effects of alcohol, and help you recover from hepatitis (see Page 134).

◆ **Pau d'arco**, also known as Taheebo, is made from the inner bark of a South American tree. It's thought to fight fungi (see Page 18) and is sometimes used to treat candidiasis (including thrush and yeast infections – see Page 113).

◆ **SPV-30** (see also Page 72) is an extract from the European boxwood tree. It's being studied as a possible treatment for HIV. Preliminary studies have shown increases in T4 cell and

T8 cell counts, and decreases in viral load (see Pages 27, 28, and 25).

◆ **Tea tree oil** (sometimes called te tre oil) comes from the Australian tree *Melaleuca alternifolia*. It is used as an antiseptic and to fight fungi (see Page 18). It's been used successfully as an alternative treatment for candidiasis (including thrush and yeast infections – see Page 113), as well as infections of the skin.

Other treatments

◆ **Shark cartilage** contains compounds that may reduce the growth of new blood vessels. KS (see Page 136) lesions are abnormal growths of blood vessels, so shark cartilage may slow down or stop the development of KS. However, in one study involving thirteen HIV-positive people, the researchers concluded that shark cartilage was not an effective treatment for KS. Shark cartilage has a foul taste and is therefore generally taken as an enema (fluid injected into your rectum [ass]).

◆ **Kombucha "mushroom"** (also known as Manchurian "mushroom") isn't a mushroom at all. It's composed of bacteria and yeast cultures, and is shaped like a large pancake. It's placed in a large glass bowl with a solution of water, tea, and sugar. The culture grows there for a week or so. During this time, the solution ferments to produce a "tonic," or tea. Users report improvements in their sense of well-being and general health, as well as increases in energy. There are some concerns for people with HIV – the tea may grow other yeasts or bacteria that could cause infections in your body. There is no scientific evidence of any benefit to be derived from this treatment. No information is available about how Kombucha interacts with other drugs used by HIV-positive people. The FDA (U.S. Food and Drug Administration) has issued a warning about Kombucha; the deaths of two HIV-negative women who were known to have used it regularly are being investigated.

Nutritional approaches

Eating well is one of the first steps in taking care of yourself. Eating nutritious food helps your immune system fight diseases and gives you energy. Malnutrition and malabsorption (see below) are major problems for HIV-positive people. Your body uses up vitamins and minerals faster than normal. It gets harder for your body to absorb what it needs from your food. Even your stomach has a hard time breaking down your food into a form your body can use. It's important to watch what you eat.

Diet

During a state of chronic (long-term) illness, your body requires more food than normal. Multiple nutritional deficiencies are shown to occur early in the course of HIV infection. Deficiencies of certain nutrients weaken your immune system, including T cell function (see Page 20) and count (see Page 27).

Several factors affect this:

 ◆ **Malnutrition** (not eating enough food, or your body not being able to use food)
 ◆ **Malabsorption** (your intestines [guts] being unable to absorb nutrients properly)
 ◆ **Increased need for nutrients** (since your body needs more to do the extra work required to fight infection)
 ◆ **Diarrhea** affects absorption by making your food go through your body too fast
 ◆ **Nausea, loss of appetite, and vomiting** can lower the amount of food available for digestion
 ◆ **Metabolic changes** (changes in the way your body uses the nutrients in your food)
 ◆ **Sores and ulcers in your mouth and/or esophagus** (the tube that connects your mouth and stomach) can make it hard to eat and swallow food

Although it's good to eat regular meals, it may be easier for you to eat smaller meals more often. It's really important to eat in a way that makes you comfortable, and to be comfortable when you eat.

Macronutrients

Getting a balance of basic nutrients like proteins, carbohydrates, and fats is important. These are called macronutrients, and make up the largest part of your food. Good sources of protein include meat, fish, eggs, milk, cereals, and vegetables. Being HIV positive means that your body may need more protein than it did before. Carbohydrates are found in starchy foods. The best kinds are high in fibre. These include grains and cereals. Sugar is also a carbohydrate – but remember that too much sugar may cause thrush (see Page 113) to develop more rapidly.

Micronutrients

Vitamins and minerals are found in your food and are called micronutrients.

Vitamins

It's generally suggested that people living with HIV/AIDS take higher doses of vitamins than is normally recommended. You should consult with your nearest AIDS group (see Page 243) or call the Community AIDS Treatment Information Exchange's HIV/AIDS Treatment Information Network toll free at 1-800-263-1638 about dose levels.

- ◆ **Beta-carotene** is used by your body to make Vitamin A, which is essential for vision, proper cell development, and the health of your skin and mucous membranes. Doses of more than 10,000 international units (IU) of Vitamin A can be dangerous. It's safer to take most of your dosage in the form of beta-carotene. Your body absorbs beta-carotene more efficiently if it's taken with fatty food.

    Beta-carotene can be found in carrots, sweet potatoes, strawberries, tomatoes, broccoli, sweet peppers, peas, beans, spinach, and pumpkins.

HEALTH OPTIONS
Nutritional approaches
- Macronutrients
- Micronutrients
  - Vitamins

◆ **The B vitamins** should be taken together in the form of a B-complex supplement. They play an important role in the function of your nervous system. B vitamins can be found in seeds, nuts, whole grains, wheat germ, liver, and kidney. The B vitamins are:
   ◆ **Vitamin B1 (thiamine)**
   ◆ **Vitamin B2 (riboflavin)**
   ◆ **Vitamin B3 (niacin)**
   ◆ **Vitamin B5 (pantothenic acid)**
   ◆ **Vitamin B6 (pyridoxine)**
   ◆ **Vitamin B12 (cyanocobalamin)**

◆ **Folic acid** is needed for energy production and the formation of red blood cells (see Page 26). Not having enough folic acid in your body seems to increase your likelihood of getting several types of cancer.

Folic acid may also reduce the likelihood of developing anal lesions (ulcers, tumours, or abscesses on your asshole) and cancers.

◆ **Vitamin C** is also known as ascorbic acid, and functions as an antioxidant. (Antioxidants are vitamins, minerals, or enzymes that help protect your body from the effects of "free radicals," which are atoms or groups of atoms that can cause damage to your cells.) It may also work against viruses, bacteria, and fungi (see Page 18). It's usually best to start with a low dose and slowly build up. Some people get diarrhea because of the high acidity of ascorbic acid, in which case "buffered" Vitamin C, or esther C, can be used.

High-dose Vitamin C therapy should be monitored by a health care provider experienced with this therapy.

Vitamin C is found in citrus fruit, cherries, and kiwi fruit.

◆ **Vitamin E** is an antioxidant (see Page 90) that helps protect cells from damage and is important for proper immune function. The suggested dose is 400-800 IU per day. For people with hemophilia, people taking anticoagulants (blood-thinning drugs), or people with Vitamin K deficiency, taking doses greater than 400 IU per day may result in abnormal bleeding. If you fall into any of these groups, it's best not to supplement with Vitamin E without the approval of your doctor.

Vitamin E is found in seeds, grains, and wheat germ.

Minerals

- **Zinc** helps promote the healing of wounds. Your body can't produce immune system cells, and particularly T4 cells (see Page 20), without it.

  Zinc is found in shellfish, tuna, salmon, and pumpkin seeds.

- **Copper** is essential for respiration (breathing) and for making antioxidants (see Page 90). It also has an anti-inflammatory effect (see Page 84). It works together with iron to ensure the proper functioning of hemoglobin (see Page 26). Zinc supplementation may reduce the amount of copper in your body so you might want to supplement with copper if you take zinc. But don't take them at the same time of day.

  The suggested dose is 2-4 milligrams (mg) per day.

  Copper is found in wheat germ and seafood.

- **Magnesium** is necessary for many body functions, including the production of energy, the building of bones, and the proper functioning of your heart, nerves, and muscles.

  Magnesium is found in oranges, peaches, pears, apples, bananas, grapefruit, and spring water.

- **Selenium** is an antioxidant (see Page 90) that helps glutathione (see Page 95) and Vitamin E (see above) work. Many researchers believe that it's one of the most important nutrients for preventing cancer and plays an important part in immune function.

  Selenium is found in nuts, grains, liver, and kidney.

- **Molybdenum** is a mineral that helps with many enzyme reactions. It's required by ddI (see Page 65) for the breakdown of the drug; therefore it's suggested as a supplement for people on ddI. The suggested dose is 50-150 micrograms (mcg), three times per day.

  Molybdenum is found in nuts, grains, liver, and kidney.

- **Iron** is critical for red blood cell formation and plays an important role in carrying oxygen to your cells. It can help prevent or eliminate anemia (see Page 26) caused by iron deficiency. The suggested dose is 10-15 mg per day.

  Iron is found in spinach and meat.

HEALTH OPTIONS
Nutritional approaches
- *Micronutrients*
  - *Minerals*

Supplementation

Any program of dietary supplements should be based on a good diet, with adequate amounts of good proteins, good fats, and good carbohydrates. However, deficiencies of some vitamins and minerals may occur early on in HIV infection. This may happen even before T4 cell counts (see Page 27) start to drop. Many experts on HIV and nutrition suggest supplementing your diet with extra nutrients. The recommended daily allowance (RDA) was developed for healthy people and is the minimum amount required to prevent a deficiency. For a person with HIV to get sufficient levels of many of these nutrients, supplementation may be required. Several studies have shown a relationship between nutrient deficiencies and getting sick.

Some doctors and nutritionists may not be aware that HIV-positive people require higher doses of vitamins. You may want to talk to more than one nutritionist.

Most vitamins, minerals, and supplements aren't covered by insurance plans, so you usually have to pay for them yourself.

The following suggestions are based on the protocol developed by Chester Myers, Ph.D. (an HIV and nutrition expert in Toronto).

Basic protocol (for every HIV-positive person)

◆ A daily multivitamin (choose one that contains 2,500 to 10,000 international units [IU] of Vitamin A; at least 25 milligrams [mg] each, preferably 50 mg, of Vitamins B2 and B6; and 1 mg of folic acid. It should also contain 50 micrograms [mcg] each of chromium, selenium, and molybdenum, and 10-15 mg of iron. Multivitamins that contain these are usually balanced with the other vitamins and minerals that you need)

◆ Vitamin C: 1,000 mg, taken in separate doses (500 mg, twice per day, or 250 mg, four times per day)

◆ Zinc: 30-50 mg per day

◆ N-acetyl cysteine (NAC – see Page 95): 500 mg, three or four times per day

◆ Vitamin B12 by a non-stomach route: sublingual (under the tongue), twice daily; nasal gel (in the nose), once daily; or injections, three times weekly

Additional protocol

- A daily multimineral (choose one that contains chromium, manganese, calcium, potassium, zinc, iron, selenium, and molybdenum)
- Extra minerals
  - Iron: 2-3 mg per day, especially for women
  - Magnesium: 200 mg per day
  - Selenium: 200 mcg per day
  - Copper: 3 mg every other day, to balance zinc
- B-complex (B-50 or B-75)
- Beta-carotene: 25,000 IU
- Vitamin E: 200-400 IU
- Increase Vitamin C to 4 grams per day (spread out in several doses)

Other supplements

- **Acidophilus and bifidus** are bacteria that naturally live in your intestines ("friendly" bacteria) and aid digestion. They may help control the growth of candida (see Page 113) and may help with diarrhea. Supplements containing acidophilus and bifidus can help balance the bacteria in your gut after you use antibiotics, which kill not only bad bacteria, but also good ones. Most formulas must be refrigerated. Many contain dairy products, so if you are lactose-intolerant (have difficulty digesting milk or milk products), use a non-dairy formula. The suggested supplementation is two capsules or teaspoons per day. Acidophilus can be found in yogurt with active (live) bacteria.
- **Bioflavonoids** work with Vitamin C to increase its disease-fighting ability. They're usually found in foods that are brightly coloured and have large amounts of Vitamin C (such as fruits and berries). They also help fight bacteria and viruses, and work as antioxidants (see Page 90). Several types of bioflavonoids are available. Quercetin, which can come from blue-green algae (see Page 85), has shown some effect in fighting HIV in the test-tube. It is also found in garlic, onions, grapes, and citrus fruits. Pycnogenol is a powerful antioxidant.

HEALTH OPTIONS
Nutritional approaches
- *Supplementation*
  - *Additional protocol*
  - *Other supplements*

◆ **Co-enzyme Q10** (ubiquinone) is an antioxidant (see Page 90) that may help maintain the strength of your heart. Your body produces ubiquinone naturally. It's important in supplying energy to cells and is critical for immune function. The suggested dose is 30-100 mg per day. Co-enzyme Q10 is found in red meat.

◆ **Digestive enzymes** help your body break down food in your stomach and intestines (guts). There are three types available: amylase, protease (or proteinase), and lipase. Amylase breaks down carbohydrates such as starch, protease helps you digest protein, and lipase aids in fat digestion. Many foods (including papaya and pineapple) are excellent sources of some of these enzymes. Enzymes are also sold in health food stores.

◆ **Essential fatty acids (EFAs)** help cells multiply and may help prevent some diseases. They can also play an important role in your immune system's response to illness. Flax seed, borage, and evening primrose oils are rich sources of EFAs. Salmon, mackerel, and sardines are good sources of fish oil, which is also high in EFAs. If you are taking fish oil as a supplement, follow product directions.

◆ **L-carnitine** is an amino acid that helps move fatty acids into and within cells. Your body produces l-carnitine naturally, and Vitamin C is important for its formation. Researchers have shown that this amino acid is low in many people in the advanced stages of AIDS. Supplementing with store-bought l-carnitine may improve immune function, increase energy, help reverse muscle wasting (see Page 164), normalize levels of fats in your blood, and protect against nerve damage such as peripheral neuropathy. The suggested dose is 250-1,000 mg per day. L-carnitine is found in red meat.

◆ **L-lysine** is an amino acid that may speed up recovery from herpes infections (see Page 130) and may keep them from coming back as often as they otherwise would.

◆ **Melatonin** is a hormone that is released by your pineal gland, a pea-sized structure at the centre of your brain. At night, melatonin is produced to help your body regulate your sleep-wake cycles. Melatonin serves two roles in your body – hormone regulation and antioxidant (see Page 90) protection. In its hormonal role, it regulates your body clock, enhances sleep, boosts your immune system, and may help protect you against cancer. You should discuss the use of melatonin with your doctor before starting. This is particularly true if you fall into one of the following groups:

- ◆ People taking steroid drugs such as cortisone and dexamethasone, since melatonin may work against the effect of these medications
- ◆ Pregnant women and women wanting to become pregnant, since melatonin has not been studied in pregnant women, and it is known that doses greater than 10 mg may prevent ovulation in some women
- ◆ People with severe allergies or autoimmune diseases (when parts of your immune system attack your own body), since melatonin stimulates your immune system and could exaggerate these responses
- ◆ People with immune system cancers such as lymphoma (see Page 141) and leukemia, since melatonin can further stimulate your immune cells
- ◆ Children, who have naturally high levels of melatonin; the effects of adding more are not known, except in the cases of some children suffering from certain mental and physical disabilities, who have benefited a great deal from melatonin

◆ **Monolaurin** (lauric acid) is a type of fat found in human milk that seems to work in the test tube against several viruses, including herpes simplex (see Page 130), CMV (see Page 125), and influenza (see Page 135). It can also be found in coconut oil, butter, and milk. It has a slight effect against HIV in the test tube.

◆ **N-acetyl cysteine (NAC)** is an amino acid usually prescribed for acetaminophen (Tylenol) overdose. It raises levels of glutathione in your cells. Glutathione levels tend to become low in people in the early stage of AIDS. Glutathione is an antioxidant (see Page 90) needed for boosting energy and immune function. It may also help restore the function of T cells (see Page 20) and reduce the wasting (see Page 164) seen in later stages of AIDS. In Canada, NAC is currently being studied to see if it will prevent hypersensitive reactions to TMP/SMX (see Page 119).

Special diets

Be careful of diets that advertise themselves as cures for HIV. If you want to check out special diets, get all the information you can about them – your nearest AIDS group (see Page 243) may be able to answer your questions. These diets often have many good points. But many are dangerous because the people who promote them don't really know about the problems that HIV-positive people can have. For example, the macrobiotic diet may have many good features, yet most versions of it are likely to cause deficiencies in zinc and Vitamin B12 (see Pages 91 and 90), and these may be hard to get enough of when you have HIV. The anti-candida diet(s) may include good advice about keeping sugar low, but may steer you away from other foods that can be good for you.

Liquid food supplements

When symptoms such as nausea, vomiting, mouth sores, or oral and esophageal candidiasis (see Page 114) affect your ability to eat, liquid food supplements can be used to either supplement your diet or replace meals. Liquid supplements can also be used if your body can no longer absorb or digest food. This can be done in three ways.

Liquid food supplements can be taken orally (by mouth); some brand names are Peptamen, Nutren, Vivonex, Isocal, Isosource, Ultra Clear, Ultra Maintain, MiluVita Plus, and Impact (Impact is sold only in the USA). You can also make your own blender drinks (see Page 161). Products such as Advera and Opti Healthgain have been specially developed for people with HIV. Provincial and territorial (or private) drug plans may cover the cost of some of these. Avoid protein drinks such as Boost and Ensure, which contain large amounts of sugar that will encourage the growth of thrush (see Page 113). They contain poor-quality fat and don't have dietary fibre.

Enteral nutrition is used when you can still digest food but have problems eating or swallowing. There are several ways this can be done. A tube (called a naso-gastric tube) can be put through your nose and down your esophagus to your stomach. Liquid food supplements are then poured through it. Another method, called PEG (percutaneous endoscopic gastrostomy) can be used in one of two ways. If your body can still digest food, a tube is inserted directly into your stomach through a cut in your abdomen (belly). The liquid food

96

HEALTH OPTIONS
*Nutritional
approaches*
• *Special diets*
• *Liquid food
supplements*

used (called semi-elemental) is similar to the oral formulas. If your body can no longer digest food properly, a similar tube can be inserted directly into your intestine (gut). The liquid food used (called elemental) is pre-digested and ready to be absorbed.

Total parenteral nutrition (TPN) is used when your body can't digest or absorb food any more. Liquid food is given intravenously (IV, or directly into a vein), and is ready for your body to use as is.

HEALTH OPTIONS
*Nutritional
   approaches*
• *Liquid food
   supplements*
Water safety
Food safety

Water safety

Tap water and well water may contain harmful bacteria and parasites (see Page 159). What would be harmless levels of *Cryptosporidum parvum* (which causes cryptosporidiosis, see Page 123), *microsporidium* (see Page 122), and mycobacteria (like the germs that cause MAC – see Page 106) for most people can cause infections in people with HIV (especially if their T4 cell count – see Page 27 – is below 100). Water from a tap should be boiled for at least five minutes and then cooled before drinking. It can also be distilled (evaporated and then condensed into water again), or passed through a filter, such as a reverse osmosis filter. Carbon filters, such as Brita filters, are not effective against bacteria and parasites. Only bottled water that's distilled or ozonated is completely free of germs.

Food safety

When your immune system is weak, it may be a good idea to watch not only what you eat, but also how you prepare your food. Some uncooked foods may put you in danger of bacterial or other infections. Avoid undercooked or raw meat or fish (although salt water fish is generally safe if prepared professionally). Meat should be well done (thoroughly cooked). Raw eggs and unpasteurized milk carry a risk of *Salmonella* infection (see Page 99). Avoid salad dressings (such as Caesar salad dressing) and eggnog if they are unpasteurized or contain raw eggs. Use pasteurized eggs (frozen or processed) rather than fresh eggs when making homemade ice cream, eggnog, and mayonnaise. When cooking eggs, make sure that the yolks and whites are firm, not runny.

Raw vegetables and fruit must be washed to remove germs. Cut off any mouldy parts. You can use grapefruit seed extract (see Page 86) or bleach in the water when you wash these foods if you want to be extra careful. About ten to 20 drops of grapefruit seed extract or one teaspoon (4 millilitres) of bleach per litre of water should kill organisms on the surface of the vegetables or fruit.

Before you handle any food, wash your hands with soap. Wash them again after you touch any raw meat or fish. Try to buy your meat fresh or thaw it quickly. Use one cutting board for meat and another one for fruit and vegetables. Plastic cutting boards are easier to keep clean than wooden ones. Wash your cutting boards with hot soapy water immediately after use. Keep shelves, counter tops, cutting boards, refrigerators, freezers, utensils, and dish towels clean.

Keep hot foods hot, cold foods cold. Properly cooking food can protect you from food poisoning. Heat kills bacteria. Most cookbooks give cooking times and temperatures for various foods. A minimum temperature of 60° Celsius (140° Fahrenheit) is necessary in order to kill bacteria. When reheating leftovers or heating partially cooked foods, heat to a temperature of at least 70° Celsius (160° Fahrenheit). Don't taste before cooking is finished.

If you are using a microwave oven, first heat the food at full power, then heat for another five minutes at a lower power – 20 or 30 per cent.

Shopping for food

It's important to read food labels when shopping. Avoid products that may contain bacteria that can cause food poisoning (see Page 99). Use milk and cheese products only if they have been pasteurized. Avoid unpasteurized honey. Products that contain any raw or undercooked meat or dairy products should be avoided, and so should products with a "best before" or "best used by" (expiry) date that has passed. Buy packaged peanut butter, rather than freshly ground peanut butter, which may grow mouldy.

It's a good idea to put packaged meat, poultry, or fish into a plastic bag before putting it in your shopping cart. This prevents drippings from touching other foods, which lowers the risk of bacteria from one food contaminating another. After shopping, get chilled and frozen foods into the refrigerator or freezer as soon as possible. Storing them in the car or even just carrying them around for a couple of hours can raise their temperature enough to allow bacteria to grow.

Eating out

Restaurants must follow guidelines established by the health department to ensure cleanliness and good hygiene. Always order meat medium to well done. Check how well cooked poultry or meat is by cutting into the centre of it. Fish should be flaky, not rubbery, when cut.

Order fried eggs well cooked, and avoid scrambled eggs that look runny. Caesar salad dressings and hollandaise sauce should also be avoided, if they contain raw eggs. If you're not sure about the ingredients in a particular dish, ask before ordering.

Raw seafood can pose a serious risk of food poisoning. Raw shellfish, like raw meat and poultry, may contain harmful bacteria. It's a bad idea to eat oysters on the half shell or raw clams. Lightly steamed seafood, like mussels and snails, may also contain harmful bacteria.

Food poisoning

You can't always tell by looking, tasting, or smelling if food has bacteria on it that can cause food poisoning. But such bacteria can cause serious infections in people with weakened immune systems. These infections can cause severe vomiting and diarrhea, and are often hard to treat. This can further weaken your immune system.

Most food poisoning is caused by food that's been badly handled or prepared. You can protect yourself by being careful about buying, preparing, and storing food. It's also useful to know about the following common, harmful bacterial infections and the foods you can get them from. Many kinds of bacteria can cause food poisoning, but three kinds are especially dangerous to people with HIV:

◆ **Salmonellosis** is the illness that can develop from eating foods containing *Salmonella* bacteria. It causes flu-like symptoms, and sometimes also nausea, vomiting, cramps, and diarrhea. Symptoms can develop six to 48 hours after eating infected food, and may last up to a week. The foods that most

HEALTH OPTIONS
Food safety
• *Shopping for food*
• *Eating out*
• *Food poisoning*

HEALTH OPTIONS
Food safety
• *Food poisoning*
**Other things to
    think about**
• *Pets and HIV*
    • *Safe pet guidelines*

often cause salmonellosis include raw or undercooked meat, poultry (chicken, turkey, etc.), and fish.

◆ **Campylobacteriosis**, or *Campylobacter* infection, can cause belly pain, diarrhea (which can be watery and/or contain blood), nausea, headache, muscle pain, and fever. Symptoms begin two to five days after eating bad food and generally last seven to ten days. These bacteria are found in raw or undercooked poultry, unpasteurized milk, and unchlorinated water.

◆ **Listeriosis**, the disease caused by *Listeria*, gives you flu-like symptoms: chills, fever, and headache, and sometimes also nausea and vomiting. These early symptoms can appear two to 30 days after eating the bad food, and can be followed by meningitis (see Page 115) or encephalitis (see Page 121). Foods that can contain *Listeria* are unpasteurized milk and cheeses and raw or undercooked meat, poultry, and fish.

Other things to think about

Pets and HIV

Your pets can be an important part of your life and can make you happy. But pets can also give you harmful parasites (see Page 159) or bacteria, so be careful about looking after them. Make sure your pet has had all its shots (vaccinations). If you have had your pet for a long time, and especially if it stays indoors, you have little to worry about.

Safe pet guidelines

◆ Wash your hands often, especially before eating or smoking.

◆ Keep your pet well groomed, and make sure that both your pet and its living and feeding areas are clean.

◆ Avoid contact with your pet's body fluids, such as feces (shit), urine (pee), saliva (spit), and vomit. Clean up messes with a disinfectant (1 tablespoon of bleach in 1 litre of water); then wash your hands. You should either wear gloves or have somebody else clean up.

◆ Your pet's nails should be clipped short so that you can avoid scratches. If you are bitten, wash the bite well.

Travelling with HIV

HEALTH OPTIONS
Other things to think about
• *Pets and HIV*
   • *Safe pet guidelines*
• *Travelling with HIV*

Canadians often forget that many parts of the world have more contagious diseases than are found in North America. Vaccination against many of these diseases is available. But be careful of "live" vaccines (made with live germs), since they can cause infection in people with weakened immune systems. Discuss your options with your doctor or nearest infectious disease clinic.

Food and water can contain germs and parasites (see Page 159) that can cause serious diarrhea or vomiting if you're not used to them. Unboiled water and raw vegetables and fruit can cause the worst problems. Try drinking hot drinks, bottled water, or bottled or canned soft drinks. Don't use ice, unless it's made from bottled water or water that's been boiled for five minutes. Brush your teeth with bottled water (not tap water). Avoid salads. Wash fruit well and then peel off any skins, rinds, or shells.

Don't be surprised if you feel fine while you're away but get sick as soon as you get home. Sometimes this happens because of changes in temperature or climate, or because of jet lag or exhaustion. You may feel weak or nauseous, or have diarrhea. See your doctor right away if you come back from a vacation feeling sick.

Drink lots of water (follow safe water guidelines – see Page 97) and other non-carbonated fluids on the plane.

Keep all your medicine with you on the plane, in case your luggage is lost or delayed. If you're carrying a lot of medicine, allow extra time to clear customs.

More than 50 countries put travel restrictions on people who have HIV. This means they have rules about whether you can travel there, or how long you can stay, if you are HIV positive. (Officials may be able to figure out that you're positive if, for example, you're carrying certain medications.) Most of these rules have to do with people who plan to stay for a long time – in order to study or work, for example. Many countries won't let HIV-positive people stay for good. The U.S. government doesn't let HIV-positive people into the country, even to visit, without a special permit. Canada allows HIV-positive visitors.

Every country has different rules, so check with the embassies or consulates of the countries you plan to visit to get up-to-date information about whether you need to get a visa.

It's usually recommended that you get extra health insurance every time you leave the country, since most provincial health plans don't cover out-of-country medical expenses. Some private insurance policies have a "pre-existing condition" clause. This means that any infections or problems that you already had before you left won't be covered. Some plans consider HIV infection a pre-existing condition. Others cover people with HIV as long as their health is stable and they don't have any active infections. Check with your insurance carrier for such restrictions. Regardless, it's a good idea to buy health insurance, since HIV and AIDS are not the only causes of hospitalization or illness. Accidents do happen, and any problems should be treated right away, rather than waiting till you get back.

Suntanning

You've probably heard about the hole in the ozone layer and the risk involved in getting too much sun. Your skin tans because of damage caused by the sun. Over time, this can lead to skin cancer. You can be exposed to ultraviolet light (the damaging rays of the sun) on both sunny and cloudy days. If you're going to be outside for long, use a lotion with a high level of sunblock.

Sunlight may cause HIV and herpes (see Page 130) viruses to multiply. And spending time in the sun can be a problem when you're taking certain drugs and treatments. Many drugs cause photosensitivity – your skin may react to sunlight by getting red, and you may have tingling and burning sensations. Staying in the sun too long can cause you to burn more easily or quickly.

However, lying in the sun can be a positive experience; soaking in its energy can help you relax. If you enjoy doing this, it's important to use a sunblock and only go out for short periods of time. Suntanning is also used as a treatment for several types of skin conditions. It may be beneficial for many minor skin complaints which are more common in people living with HIV/AIDS.

HEALTH OPTIONS
Other things to
*   think about*
• *Travelling with HIV*
• *Suntanning*

7

Opportunistic Infections and Related Conditions

What are opportunistic infections?

The human immunodeficiency virus (HIV) causes gradual damage to your immune system (see Chapter 3). When your immune system is damaged, you can get sick from germs that wouldn't normally cause diseases. These germs take advantage of the opportunity created by your weakened immune system to cause an infection. This is why they're called opportunistic infections. They're also sometimes called secondary infections, because they happen after, or second to, HIV, which is believed to be the primary (main) infection.

OPPORTUNISTIC INFECTIONS AND RELATED CONDITIONS
You won't get every infection
The germs that cause infections

You won't get every infection

A damaged immune system affects each person differently. One person may get certain symptoms or infections and another may get completely different ones. You won't get all of them. You may not get any. Men and women, children and adults, and people from different parts of the world get different kinds of infections. And you may still get ordinary colds and flus.

The first cases of AIDS were reported in the early 1980s. At that time, AIDS seemed to be a condition that killed people very quickly. Those people had probably been living with HIV for many years without showing any symptoms. And, when they did get sick, there were very few treatments available. Now it is known that most people can live with HIV for many years without showing any signs of illness. And when people with HIV do get sick, there are many new treatments that can help control and prevent infections. Although there's still no cure, it's important to remember that lots of progress has been made in managing HIV disease.

The germs that cause infections

Many of the germs that cause opportunistic infections are widespread and common in daily life. For example, approximately half the adult population of Canada has been infected with CMV. When people with healthy immune systems are infected with CMV they may have no symptoms at all or they may have a short, flu-like illness. People with weakened immune systems, such as people who have received organ transplants or people with AIDS, can develop serious problems from CMV.

Some germs can cause problems in people with healthy immune systems. For example, the bacteria that cause food poisoning (see Page 99) can make anyone sick. But people who have HIV are much more likely than others to get sick from them.

There are four kinds of germs that can cause opportunistic infections: bacteria, fungi, protozoa, and viruses (see Page 18).

Bacterial infections that can cause disease in people who have HIV include Mycobacterium avium complex (MAC), tuberculosis

(TB), and bacterial pneumonias. Protozoa can cause toxoplasmosis, microsporidiosis, cryptosporidiosis, and isosporiasis. Fungi can cause Pneumocystis carinii pneumonia (PCP), thrush, cryptococcosis (which can cause meningitis and pneumonia), and histoplasmosis. Viruses that can cause problems for people with HIV include cytomegalovirus (CMV), herpes zoster (which causes shingles), and herpes simplex.

Other conditions

OPPORTUNISTIC
INFECTIONS
AND RELATED
CONDITIONS
The germs that cause infections
Other conditions
Treatments

People who have HIV disease can also develop other conditions that may or may not be caused by a germ. These include cancer of the cervix, Kaposi's sarcoma (KS), lymphoma (cancer of the lymph system), wasting, AIDS dementia complex (ADC), and skin problems.

This chapter discusses all these infections and conditions.

Treatments

Most drug treatments are used to control or get rid of an infection. Others deal with specific symptoms caused by an infection (for example, controlling pain). You may be taking anti-HIV drugs like AZT (see Page 64) or ddI (see Page 65), as well as drugs to prevent or fight otherinfections. At some point, you may find that you're taking a lot of different drugs. Many drugs can cause unwanted side effects. Sometimes these side effects can be just like the symptoms of an infection (for example, fever or chills). And drugs can interact (react with each other) in ways that may either hurt you or make the drugs work less well. Your doctor may have to adjust your medications from time to time.

New drugs are constantly being developed. Some of the drugs listed in this chapter are still being studied and may not be available yet. But remember, treatment information is changing all the time. Contact the Community AIDS Treatment Information Exchange's HIV/AIDS Treatment Information Network toll free at 1-800-263-1638 for up-to-date information.

Note: In the following discussions of drug treatments, doses are referred to in numbers of "mg." This stands for "milligrams."

Bacterial infections

Mycobacterium avium complex (MAC) / Mycobacterium avium intracellulare (MAI)

MAC stands for Mycobacterium avium complex, which is sometimes also called Mycobacterium avium intracellulare (MAI). It is caused by at least two different bacteria: *Mycobacterium avium* and *Mycobacterium intracellulare*. These bacteria can get inside certain cells in your body. Because they hide in your body's cells, they can be very hard to treat.

The bacteria that cause MAC are in the same family as those that cause tuberculosis (TB – see Page 108). MAC cannot be passed from one person to another. MAC bacteria can be found in soil and water. Probably most people have been exposed to MAC, but they don't get sick from it. Their immune systems are strong enough to fight it off. But when your immune system is damaged, MAC can cause infection.

Symptoms

MAC can be found in many parts of the bodies of people who have AIDS. This is called disseminated MAC infection. The most common symptoms of MAC infection are persistent fever and tiredness, accompanied by night sweats (see Page 157), loss of appetite, abdominal (belly) pain, and chronic diarrhea. It can also cause serious weight loss (see Page 161), swollen lymph glands (see Page 19), an enlarged spleen and liver, and anemia (see Page 26).

Diagnosis

When you visit your doctor, you will be asked if you have any problems or symptoms. If you report symptoms that sound typical of MAC infection, and if your T4 cell count (see Page 27) is below 100, your doctor may order some lab tests. There are two blood tests that can be done to check for MAC infection. The first test can show if your blood sample contains bacteria from the Mycobacteria family. But it can't tell the difference between MAC and other Mycobacteria, including the one that causes tuberculosis.

OPPORTUNISTIC
INFECTIONS
AND RELATED
CONDITIONS
Bacterial infections

- *Mycobacterium avium complex (MAC) / Mycobacterium avium intracellulare (MAI)*

The second test used is a blood culture. The lab will put a sample of your blood in a dish and watch to see if MAC will grow. It can take several weeks to get results. Because MAC can be a serious illness, doctors almost always recommend treatment as soon as they think you have it. Your doctor can always change the treatment if the results show that something else is causing your symptoms.

Prevention

The risk of developing MAC increases if your T4 cell count (see Page 27) is below 50. You may be able to reduce the risk of getting MAC by taking special care in preparing foods. Wash and peel all fruit and vegetables carefully. The Food and Drug Administration in the USA says to "boil it, peel it, cook it, or forget it." These precautions can help you avoid other germs as well. See the sections on water safety and food safety (Pages 97 and 97) for more information.

The drugs rifabutin (Mycobutin), azithromycin and clarithromycin cut the risk of getting MAC in half for people with T4 counts below 100. If you have fewer than 100 T4 cells, you may want to talk to your doctor about taking drugs to prevent MAC.

The most common side effects are nausea, abdominal (belly) pain, and skin rash. A rare but serious side effect of rifabutin is neutropenia (see Page 64). If you take rifabutin, your doctor will check your white blood cells regularly. The urine (pee), feces (shit), saliva (spit), sweat, tears, and skin of people who take rifabutin may be coloured orange or brown. Soft contact lenses may be permanently stained.

Treatment

Treatment for MAC infection is lifelong. Once the infection has been brought under control, it requires permanent treatment to keep the bacteria from making you sick again. Combinations of several different antibiotics are the usual treatment for MAC infection. For example, you may be given clarithromycin (Biaxin) or azithromycin (Zithromax), plus ethambutol, and rifabutin. Other antibiotics that may be used are ciprofloxacin, ethambutol, and amikacin. The choice of drugs depends on how well you tolerate them, which drugs are most effective for you, and how expensive they are. Clarithromycin and azithromycin are new drugs, and they are very expensive. Provin-

107

OPPORTUNISTIC INFECTIONS AND RELATED CONDITIONS
Bacterial infections
• *Mycobacterium avium complex (MAC) / Mycobacterium avium intracellulare (MAI)*

cial or territorial drug programs and many private drug insurance programs may not pay for these drugs for people with MAC. One month's supply can cost hundreds of dollars.

The most commonly reported side effects from the antibiotics used to treat MAC are nausea and vomiting, diarrhea, abdominal (belly) pain, and rashes. Because you usually take two or more of these drugs at the same time, it's hard to tell which drug is causing which side effect. It can take a month or more before you will know if the drugs are clearing up the infection.

Tuberculosis (TB)

Tuberculosis is caused by the bacterium (see Page 18) *Mycobacterium tuberculosis*. Anyone can become infected with TB; you don't have to have a weakened immune system. TB bacteria can spread from person to person through coughs, sneezes, and breathing, but usually only after lengthy exposure or close contact with a person with active TB in their lungs or throat. TB is usually treatable, even if you have HIV/AIDS. It's a common illness in people with HIV around the world. TB is spread through the air, so it has long been associated with overcrowded living or working conditions, poor ventilation, and lack of medical care.

TB infection

TB germs enter your body by being inhaled (breathed in). They settle in your lungs and cause a minor infection, usually with no obvious symptoms. Your body develops "walls" around the TB germs and they are forced to stop growing (they become dormant). But the germs remain in your body. If you have dormant TB germs in your lungs, you're said to have TB infection. If the germs remain dormant, you have no symptoms, and you can't spread the disease to anybody else.

108

OPPORTUNISTIC INFECTIONS AND RELATED CONDITIONS
Bacterial infections
- *Mycobacterium avium complex (MAC) / Mycobacterium avium intracellulare (MAI)*
- *Tuberculosis*

Active TB

If you have a dormant TB infection and your immune system gets weaker, the TB germs can start to grow again and multiply. This is called active TB. If you have active TB, you will probably have symptoms, and you can pass the infection on to other people.

Symptoms

Active TB in your lungs can cause a wet cough (you cough up mucus or fluid), chest pain, and difficulty breathing. It can also cause lack of appetite, weight loss, night sweats (see Page 157), tiredness, and fever. Other symptoms will depend on where the TB is in your body.

Diagnosis

The most common method for diagnosing TB infection is a skin reaction test called the PPD (purified protein derivative), or Mantoux. A tiny drop containing proteins of the tuberculosis bacteria is injected under your skin, usually on your forearm. If the spot where the needle went in raises a small bump within a couple of days, that's called a positive reaction.

A positive skin test doesn't necessarily mean that you have active TB, or that you will ever get it. It may just mean that your body has been exposed to TB before and could possibly develop active TB at some point in the future. Many doctors recommend that you have a PPD done once a year to make sure you haven't been infected with TB. However, because your immune system may be weakened if you have HIV, this test isn't always reliable. Your doctor may also do an anergy panel (a kind of skin test) to see if your immune system is strong enough to respond to the PPD test. Doctors often do chest X-rays to make sure you don't have active TB. They may also do tests on your sputum (stuff you cough up), blood, urine (pee), or stool (shit), as well as tissues from your bone marrow (see Page 64), lymph nodes (see Page 19), or brain, to check for active TB in other parts of your body.

Prevention

TB infection can become active TB soon after you get infected with HIV, even if you have as many as 500 T4 cells (see Page 27). Some people who have had a history of positive reactions to the PPD skin test, and have fewer than 500 T4 cells, take preventive medication to stop TB from becoming active. The most common preventive drug is isoniazid taken with Vitamin B6. Preventive drugs may have to be taken for as long as twelve months.

If you have active TB, it's important to make sure you don't infect anyone else. For the first two weeks after beginning medication, you should sleep in a separate and well-ventilated room and take care to cover your mouth every time you sneeze or cough. TB is considered a contagious disease, and is routinely reported to the public health department. A public health nurse may contact you to tell you how to avoid passing on the infection, and may talk to other people you spend a lot of time with, like family, friends, and co-workers.

If you're HIV positive, you should take special care around anyone who has active TB. You may want to wear a face mask to avoid getting infected.

Treatment

All TB drugs are provided free in Canada through regional public health departments. TB is usually treated by a combination of drugs such as isoniazid, pyrazinamide, rifampin, ethambutol, ethionimide, streptomycin, and cycloserine. Several of these drugs may cause side effects, including liver and kidney problems, skin rash, vomiting, and diarrhea. Isoniazid and rifampin can interact (react badly) with keto-conazole (Nizoral – see Page 114). Rifampin can interact with dapsone (see Page 119), a treatment for PCP (see Page 118), with birth control pills, with methadone, and with protease inhibitors, especially ritonavir. Treatment usually continues for at least six to twelve months. It's important to complete the entire course of treatment, even after your TB symptoms go away (usually after three weeks). Stopping too soon or not taking the drugs as prescribed can create new kinds of TB (called drug-resistant TB) that can't be treated with the usual drugs. This creates new problems in prevention and treatment. If you refuse to take medication to treat TB, you can be isolated in a hospital by medical or legal authorities.

OPPORTUNISTIC INFECTIONS AND RELATED CONDITIONS
Bacterial infections
• *Tuberculosis*

Pelvic inflammatory disease (PID)

PID is an infection of the organs of a woman's pelvis. The infection can start in your vagina, and travel through your cervix, into your uterus (womb) and to your fallopian tubes and ovaries. PID is caused by bacteria – usually the same bacteria that cause gonorrhea and chlamydia (see Pages 149 and 149). Women with healthy immune systems can get it. However, in women with HIV, it's more common, can be harder to treat, and takes longer to cure. PID can often develop over a long period of time and get worse before it's properly diagnosed.

Symptoms

Symptoms of itching, burning, soreness when your belly is touched, pain during intercourse (fucking), unusual vaginal discharge, or changes in your menstrual period should be reported to your doctor. These may be symptoms of chlamydia or gonorrhea. If those infections are not treated, they can develop into PID. Severe belly pain accompanied by fever may be symptoms of PID.

Diagnosis

If you report symptoms that sound typical of PID, your doctor will examine you and take samples for testing. PID is diagnosed by using a cotton swab to take a small sample of fluid and cells from your cervix (the entrance of your uterus [womb]). The sample is then sent to the lab to be tested for bacteria. If belly pain is severe, your doctor may do a laparoscopy. A small incision (cut) is made in your belly button and an instrument called a laparoscope is inserted into your belly. This allows your internal organs to be examined, because PID can sometimes cause abscesses on your ovaries or uterus. Any abscesses found may be treated during the laparoscopy.

Prevention

Using condoms can help prevent transmission of some of the bacteria that cause PID. Women who use intrauterine contraceptive devices (IUDs) to prevent pregnancy are at higher risk of developing PID.

Treatment

PID can usually be successfully treated with antibiotics. The antibiotics used often include one or two of the following: cefoxitin, cefotetan, doxycycline, clindamycin, gentamicin, probenecid, amoxicillin, clavulanate, ofloxacin, and metronidazole. If your pain is severe, your doctor may want to keep you in the hospital for the first days of treatment. If you have internal abscesses (see above), you may need to have surgery to remove them.

Bacterial pneumonia

Pneumonia is a swelling of the tissue of your lungs, and can have many different causes. Pneumonia caused by bacteria can occur at any stage in HIV infection. Bacterial pneumonias are more common in HIV-positive women than in HIV-positive men. These pneumonias are caused most often by two bacteria: *Streptococcus pneumoniae* and *Haemophilus influenzae*.

Symptoms

The most common symptoms of bacterial pneumonia are a sudden fever and a cough that produces sputum (stuff that comes up from your lungs).

Diagnosis

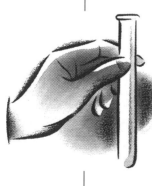

If you report symptoms that sound typical of bacterial pneumonia, your doctor will examine you by listening to your lungs through a stethoscope and taking your temperature. A sample of sputum is sent to the lab to be tested for bacteria. A sample of blood may also be taken and sent to the lab for a culture (see Page 31).

112

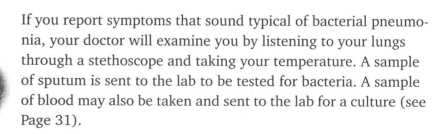

Prevention

Pneumovax (pneumococcal vaccine) and *H. influenzae* Type B vaccine (Hib vaccine) are sometimes offered as protection against bacterial pneumonia. Vaccinations of any kind often cause a short-term increase in HIV viral load (see Page 28).

Treatment

Bacterial pneumonia is treated with antibiotics. The type of antibiotic used depends on the type of bacteria that caused the pneumonia. Some of the drugs used are penicillin, erythromycin, ampicillin, and amoxicillin.

Penicillin and penicillin-like drugs can cause allergic reactions in some people. Let your doctor know if you've had a reaction to penicillin in the past. The most common side effects of these antibiotics are nausea, vomiting, diarrhea, and skin rash.

Other bacterial infections

There are many other kinds of bacteria that can cause illness. These include bacteria that cause food poisoning (see Page 99). Most bacterial infections can be successfully treated with standard antibiotics such as ampicillin, ciprofloxacin, tetracycline, and TMP/SMX (see Page 119).

Fungal infections

Candidiasis (thrush or yeast infections)

Candidiasis is the most common fungal infection in people who have HIV. Candida is a yeast found in most people and is normally kept under control by "friendly" bacteria in your body. The most common fungus (see Page 18) that causes candidiasis is called *Candida albicans*.

OPPORTUNISTIC INFECTIONS AND RELATED CONDITIONS
Bacterial infections
- *Bacterial pneumonia*
- *Other bacterial infections*

Fungal infections
- *Candidiasis (thrush or yeast infections)*

Symptoms and diagnosis

Doctors usually diagnose oral candidiasis, or thrush, just by examining your mouth. Candidiasis can appear as white patches on your gums and the sides of your tongue, where it can cause a burning feeling, swelling, redness, and changes in the way things taste. Candidiasis can also appear in your esophagus (the tube that connects your mouth and stomach), where it can cause sore throat and difficulty swallowing. Esophageal candidiasis may be diagnosed with a barium swallow and X-ray. Sometimes an endoscopy and biopsy (see Page 31) are done. In women, symptoms of candidiasis include itching and burning around the outside of the vagina, and a thick, white or yellow vaginal discharge. This is called a yeast infection.

Prevention

The risk of developing candidiasis increases if your T4 cell count (see Page 27) falls below 400, although many people with much higher T4 counts show signs of candidiasis. Sugars can encourage the growth of candida. Some people go on sugar-free diets to decrease the risk of getting candidiasis. Others take a drug like fluconazole (Diflucan – see Page 114) or ketoconazole (Nizoral – see Page 114) to help prevent the infection. Rinsing your mouth with water and a few drops of hydrogen peroxide (see Page 77), tea tree oil (see Page 87), or grapefruit seed extract (see Page 86) may be effective in preventing thrush.

Treatment

Mild thrush (candidiasis in your mouth) can sometimes be treated by rinsing your mouth several times a day with water and the substances described above. The bacteria called acidophilus, which is found in some brands of yogurt and also comes in pill form, may help reduce thrush. Sugar can make candidiasis worse, so you may want to eat less of it. An Aboriginal remedy called pitch uses the sap from certain trees as a mouthwash to treat thrush. Some people use a mouthwash made with apple cider vinegar (see Page 84) and warm water.

There are several drugs used to treat fungal infections like candidiasis. These include fluconazole (Diflucan), nystatin (Mycostatin), clotrimazole (Mycelex), ketoconazole (Nizoral), itraconazole (Sporanox), and amphotericin B (see Page 116). Most come in pill

114

OPPORTUNISTIC
INFECTIONS
AND RELATED
CONDITIONS
Fungal infections
- *Candidiasis (thrush or yeast infections)*

form, but some are available as lozenges, mouth rinses, or vaginal suppositories. Amphotericin B can be taken intravenously (IV, or injected directly into a vein), as a lozenge, or as a specially prepared oral (taken by mouth) solution. Fluconazole and ketoconazole may cause nausea and headaches and, in rare cases, liver toxicity (poisoning). The sinus medications Seldane and Hismanal should be avoided if you're taking ketoconazole or erythromycin. Nystatin in high doses can cause upset stomach or diarrhea. Since IV amphotericin B has many serious side effects, it's often used only as a last resort.

Some women who get yeast infections use over-the-counter medications such as Monistat or Canesten.

Cryptococcosis

Cryptococcosis is caused by a fungus (see Page 18) called *Cryptococcus neoformans*, which is found all over the world, especially in soil contaminated by bird droppings (shit). Most people have probably already been exposed to this fungus, usually by breathing it in. There is no evidence that infection is spread from one person to another. This fungus can infect your central nervous system (causing meningitis – see below), your lungs (causing pneumonia), or other organs and tissues (causing disease elsewhere in your body).

Symptoms

Meningitis – a swelling of the lining around your brain or spinal cord – is a life-threatening infection and should be treated as quickly as possible. Symptoms of meningitis may include fever, headache, tiredness, stiff neck, blurred vision, confusion, and nausea. Symptoms of cryptococcal pneumonia include low-grade fever, coughing (with some spitting up), and difficulty breathing. Symptoms of cryptococcosis that has spread throughout your body include painless skin lesions (sores).

115

OPPORTUNISTIC INFECTIONS AND RELATED CONDITIONS
Fungal infections
- *Candidiasis (thrush or yeast infections)*
- *Cryptococcosis*

Diagnosis

Doctors may diagnose cryptococcal meningitis using a lumbar puncture (or spinal tap, in which fluid is removed from your spine and examined) or a CT scan (see Page 31). Samples of spinal fluid are treated with India ink, which stains the fungus and makes it visible. Chest X-rays are used to diagnose cryptococcal pneumonia.

Prevention

The risk of developing cryptococcosis increases if your T4 cell count (see Page 27) is below 100. There is no proven medication to prevent cryptococcal infections. However, it's been shown that people taking fluconazole or ketoconazole (see Page 114) seem to have a much lower chance of getting cryptococcosis.

Treatment

The two main treatments for cryptococcosis are intravenous (IV – injected directly into a vein) amphotericin B and fluconazole.

Amphotericin B can cause serious side effects such as fever, chills, kidney problems, and anemia (see Page 26). A new form of amphotericin B, called liposomal amphotericin B (AmBisome), sandwiches the drug in microscopic layers of fat. This seems to be as effective as regular amphotericin B in treating cryptococcal meningitis, and has fewer side effects. Unfortunately, it's very expensive and may be hard for your doctor to get. Since amphotericin B must be given intravenously for this infection, and must be taken for at least six weeks, you may have to stay in the hospital while you're taking it. Doctors sometimes give you another medication, such as ibuprofen (e.g., Advil), acetaminophen (Tylenol), or Demerol, to reduce the side effects.

Fluconazole (Diflucan – see Page 114) may not be quite as effective as amphotericin B, but it has far fewer side effects. Also, fluconazole can be taken orally (by mouth).

Treatment for cryptococcal infection is lifelong; you have to keep taking it in order to keep the fungus from making you sick again. You may have to take oral fluconazole daily.

116

OPPORTUNISTIC
INFECTIONS
AND RELATED
CONDITIONS
Fungal infections

• *Cryptococcosis*

Histoplasmosis

Histoplasmosis is a rare infection caused by a fungus (see Page 18) called *Histoplasma capsulatum*. In North America, this fungus is found in the soil of the mid-western USA (particularly the Mississippi River valley) and in the lower St. Lawrence River valley in Canada. The fungus can be inhaled (breathed in) and infect your lungs.

Symptoms

Symptoms of histoplasmosis may include high fever, weight loss, difficulty breathing, skin lesions (patches), anemia (see Page 26), enlargement of the liver and spleen, and swollen lymph nodes (see Page 19).

Diagnosis

Histoplasmosis can be hard to diagnose. Doctors may take a biopsy (small sample of tissue) from your bone marrow (see Page 20), lymph nodes, or lungs to look at under a microscope. Blood and urine (pee) tests may also be used.

117

OPPORTUNISTIC
INFECTIONS
AND RELATED
CONDITIONS
Fungal infections
• *Histoplasmosis*

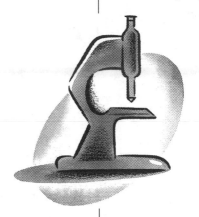

Prevention

The risk of developing histoplasmosis increases if your T4 cell count (see Page 27) is below 100 and if you live in an area where the fungus is found. Currently, there is no medication for prevention.

Treatment

If left untreated, histoplasmosis is a life-threatening illness. It is usually treated with intravenous (IV) amphotericin B, which can cause serious side effects (see Page 116). Itraconazole pills (Sporanox) are being studied as a treatment for histoplasmosis. Once the infection has been brought under control, you need lifelong treatment to keep the fungus from making you sick again.

Pneumocystis carinii pneumonia (PCP)

Pneumonia is a swelling of the tissue of your lungs, and there can be many different causes. PCP is caused by a fungus (see Page 18) called *Pneumocystis carinii*. For many years, *Pneumocystis carinii* was thought to be a type of protozoan (see Page 18), but it is now known to be a fungus based on its genetic structure. PCP is the most easily prevented infection in AIDS.

Symptoms

PCP may cause a dry cough (one that doesn't produce any fluid or mucus). It can also cause fever, shortness of breath, sweating, and tiredness.

Diagnosis

If you report symptoms that sound typical of PCP, and especially if your T4 cell count (see Page 27) is below 200, your doctor will examine you and order some tests. PCP can often be diagnosed with a chest X-ray. Another diagnosis method is to examine mucus from your lungs through an "induced sputum" test. You breathe in a mixture of salt and water, which has been turned into a mist. This causes you to cough up mucus, which is then tested. Or you may be given a gallium scan, in which a small amount of radioactive solution is injected into your body two to three days before the test. Then you lie on a table while a special camera creates images of the radioactive fluid inside your body.

If none of these tests is able to reveal the cause of your symptoms, your doctor may do a bronchoscopy. A thin, flexible tube (called a bronchoscope) is inserted through your nose, down your windpipe, and into your lungs. Then small amounts of saline solution (water with salt) are flushed down the tube. This is called a broncho-alveolar lavage (BAL). The saline solution washes the *Pneumocystis carinii* fungus off the surface of the inside of your lungs (bronchi and alveoli). The saline solution is then sucked back up the tube and sent to the lab for testing. Your doctor will give you medications to help you relax and avoid discomfort during this procedure.

OPPORTUNISTIC
INFECTIONS
AND RELATED
CONDITIONS
Fungal infections

• *Pneumocystis carinii pneumonia (PCP)*

Prevention

The risk of developing PCP increases if your T4 cell count (see Page 27) is below 200. The most commonly used preventive treatments are TMP/SMX, aerosolized pentamidine, and dapsone (see below).

The antibacterial drug TMP/SMX (trimethoprim and sulfamethoxazole) may be the most effective treatment for preventing PCP. It is often sold under the name Bactrim or Septra. Side effects include diarrhea, dizziness, headache, nausea, and vomiting. Some people are hypersensitive to the sulfamethoxazole, and may react with symptoms of itching, skin rash, aching joints, sore throat, difficulty swallowing, fever, and liver problems.

Since TMP/SMX works so well in preventing PCP, a "desensitization protocol" has been developed for it. This involves using increasing amounts so your body can slowly adjust to the drug. Between 60 and 70 per cent of people who start out being allergic to TMP/SMX are able to take it after desensitization. However, desensitization is not readily available.

Pentamidine is an antiparasitic drug (it works against parasites – see Page 159). You breathe it in through a machine called a nebulizer, which changes it into a mist that coats your lungs. Sometimes it helps to use a spray called Ventolin before the treatment, to relax your lungs. The most common dose of aerosolized pentamidine (that means the kind that you breathe in) is 300 mg every four weeks. Aerosolized pentamidine can leave a bad (metallic) taste in your mouth. You may want to suck on candy or chew gum afterwards to get rid of the taste. Other common side effects are tiredness, shortness of breath, decreased appetite, dizziness, rash, and nausea. Because pentamidine can cause pancreatitis (see Page 65), your doctor will monitor your amylase levels (see Page 28) regularly. If you decide to use pentamidine, your doctor will recommend that you don't use any other drugs that also cause pancreatitis (for example, ddI – see Page 65). Pentamidine can also be used intravenously (IV, or injected directly into a vein).

Dapsone (sold in Canada as Avlosulfon) is an antibacterial pill used, but not approved, for preventing PCP. It may have such side effects as skin rash, loss of appetite, headache, and anemia (see Page 26). A few people may have hypersensitive reactions to dapsone. These reactions usually occur within the first six weeks of use.

**OPPORTUNISTIC
INFECTIONS
AND RELATED
CONDITIONS**
Fungal infections
- *Pneumocystis carinii
  pneumonia (PCP)*
Protozoal infections
- *Toxoplasmosis*

Treatment

The treatments for PCP depend on how severe your infection is, and how you react to a given drug. The most common drug treatment is TMP/SMX (see above), which is also used for prevention. For severe cases, TMP/SMX can be given intravenously (IV, or directly into a vein) for two to three weeks.

One of the alternatives to TMP/SMX is IV pentamidine, which can have serious side effects. These include nausea, vomiting, low blood pressure, low blood sugar, diabetes, anemia (see Page 26), neutropenia (see Page 64), and kidney or liver problems. Because pentamidine can also cause pancreatitis (see Page 65), doctors prefer to use TMP/SMX when possible.

Another alternative is atovaquone (Mepron), which can cause headache, nausea, diarrhea, rash, and fever. Some people are given dapsone and trimethoprim. (Trimethoprim is one of the two drugs in TMP/SMX – see Page 119). A combination of the antibiotics primaquine and clindamycin is also effective. Mild cases of PCP can be treated with aerosolized pentamidine (see Page 119). Once PCP has been successfully treated, prophylaxis (preventive treatment) should continue in order to avoid a new infection.

In some people, the swelling in their lungs may get worse even though the fungus is being killed. Doctors may prescribe corticosteroids (usually prednisone) along with TMP/SMX or IV pentamidine. Corticosteroids have an anti-inflammatory effect; they help reduce the swelling of air passages and make it easier to breathe. They don't kill the fungus, but do help get rid of the symptoms and reduce the risk of lung failure.

Protozoal infections

Toxoplasmosis

Toxoplasmosis (toxo for short) is caused by a protozoan (see Page 18) called *Toxoplasma gondii*. People can get toxo by eating raw or undercooked meat (especially pork or lamb) which has been contaminated with the germ. Toxo has been found in the feces (shit) of about one per cent of pet cats. Toxo gets into your body through your mouth and digestive system. It can spread through your blood to many different organs. When people with healthy immune systems are infected with toxo they usually have no symptoms and their immune systems are able to contain the infection. But if your immune system is weakened, toxo can flare up and cause disease. Toxo most often infects your nervous system and causes encephalitis, which is an inflammation or swelling of the brain.

Symptoms

The symptoms of toxoplasmosis can be vague and are often easily ignored. A dull and constant headache is the most common symptom. Sometimes there may be fever. As toxo progresses, there may be symptoms like mood changes, confusion, difficulty thinking, and seizures.

Diagnosis

If you report symptoms that sound typical of toxo, and especially if your T4 cell count (see Page 27) is below 50, your doctor will examine you and order some tests. Toxo is usually diagnosed by a CT scan (see Page 31) of your brain. A sample of your blood may be examined for antibodies to toxo.

Prevention

The risk of developing toxoplasmosis increases if you test positive for toxo antibodies, meaning you have been exposed to toxo and your immune system has been able to respond to it, and if your T4 cell count (see Page 27) drops below 200.

You can reduce the risk of toxo infection by making sure any meat you eat is well cooked (to an internal temperature of 66° Celsius [150° Fahrenheit] for ten minutes). If you have a cat, wear latex gloves when you clean the litter box. The toxo "eggs" in cat feces only become infectious 24 to 48 hours after they are shed from the body, so the litter should be cleaned daily.

If you are taking TMP/SMX (see Page 119) to prevent PCP (see Page 118), it may also help protect you from toxo infection.

Treatment

Toxoplasmosis is most often treated with a combination of pyrimethamine and either sulfadoxine (this combination is called Fansidar), or clindamycin. Pyrimethamine can interfere with your body's ability to absorb the B-vitamin, folic acid. Your doctor may recommend taking leucovorin (an artificial form of folic acid) daily to make up for this. Other side effects of these drugs can include nausea, vomiting, diarrhea, skin rash, kidney problems, and a drop in the level of white blood cells (see Page 20). Other drugs being studied as treatments for toxoplasmosis include azithromycin and Mepron (see Page 120).

Once toxo infection has been brought under control, you need lifelong treatment to keep the bacteria from making you sick again.

Microsporidiosis

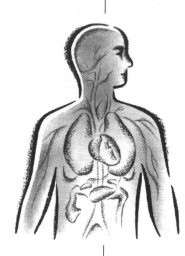

Microsporidiosis is caused by two types of protozoa (see Page 18). *Enterocytozoon bieneusi* usually infects your intestines (guts). *Septata intestinalis* can cause disseminated (throughout your body) disease by infecting macrophages (see Page 20), which can then carry these protozoa to your lungs, liver, kidney, intestines (guts), and even your eyes. It's not clear how people get microsporidiosis. Prior to AIDS, only a few microsporidiosis infections were reported. The protozoa that cause microsporidiosis are likely to be found in contaminated water or food, and the disease may be transmitted by feces (shit) and oral-anal sex (licking someone's asshole, also known as rimming).

Symptoms and diagnosis

Microsporidiosis causes diarrhea in people with HIV. Other symptoms include nausea, abdominal cramps, gas, and malabsorption (being unable to properly use the food you eat). Weight loss is usually substantial, but tends to be slow. Microsporidosis is hard to diagnose because it's caused by a very small protozoan. A special kind of microscope, called an electron microscope, is needed to see it in a sample, which is usually taken from stool (shit) or from a biopsy (tissue sample) of an infected organ.

Prevention and treatment

The risk of developing microsporidiosis increases if your T4 cell count (see Page 27) falls below 50. Paying attention to water and food safety (see Pages 97 and 97) can help protect you against this infection. So can practising safer sex (see Page 151).

People with microsporidial diarrhea can get relief with antidiarrhea treatments (see Page 160).

Several drugs have been studied. The most promising is albendazole, which has been shown to reduce diarrhea and stop weight loss in people infected with *Enterocytozoon bieneusi*. However, it does not get rid of this protozoan. Albendazole is effective in controlling *Septata intestinalis*. It's not yet known whether maintenance (continual) therapy is needed to prevent this infection from coming back. Other drugs have also helped relieve the symptoms, but the protozoa remain present. These drugs include metronidazole (Flagyl), Mepron (see Page 120), paromomycin (Humatin), and TMP/SMX (see Page 119).

OPPORTUNISTIC INFECTIONS AND RELATED CONDITIONS
Protozoal infections
- *Microsporidiosis*
- *Cryptosporidiosis and isosporiasis*

Cryptosporidiosis and isosporiasis

Cryptosporidiosis ("crypto" for short) is caused by a protozoan (see Page 18) called *Cryptosporidium parvum*. You can get it from eating undercooked meat or from drinking water contaminated with crypto. It may also be spread through oral-anal sex (rimming, or licking someone's asshole).

Isosporiasis is caused by the protozoan *Isospora belli*. This germ is most commonly found in tropical or subtropical climates.

Symptoms

The symptoms of cryptosporidiosis and isosporiasis include lots of watery diarrhea, stomach cramps, nausea, vomiting, tiredness, weight loss, and loss of appetite. Sometimes you may be infected and not have any symptoms.

Diagnosis

Both infections are diagnosed from tests of stool (shit). In very rare cases, a biopsy (tissue sample test) of your small intestine (gut) may be required.

Prevention

The risk of developing either cryptosporidiosis or isosporiasis increases if your T4 cell count (see Page 27) is below 100. People travelling to tropical or subtropical climates should be careful about food and drink (see Page 101).

Treatment

There is no standard treatment for cryptosporidiosis. Often, crypto diarrhea goes away on its own. Unfortunately, it can suddenly come back on its own, too. Doctors may try several drugs, including paromomycin (sold as Humatin), azithromycin (Zithromax), diclazuril, letrazuril, and octreotide, but these drugs don't always work. Diet and antidiarrhea medications like loperamide (Imodium) or diphenoxylate (Lomotil) may help manage the symptoms.

Nitazoxanide (NTZ) is an anti-parasite drug which is being studied as a treatment. Early information looks promising. NTZ is available through a compassionate access program. Your doctor can contact the Emergency Drug Release Program (EDRP – see Page 170) for details.

It's important to replace all the fluids lost because of diarrhea. You may have to spend some time in the hospital, where you'll get intravenous (IV, or injected directly into a vein) fluids to prevent dehydration.

Isosporiasis is usually treated with TMP/SMX (see Page 119) or Fansidar (see Page 122). You may have to keep taking medication permanently to keep this infection from coming back.

Viral infections

Cytomegalovirus (CMV)

Cytomegalovirus (CMV) is a member of the herpes family of viruses. In Canada, approximately half the adult population has been infected with CMV. When people with healthy immune systems are infected with CMV, they may have no symptoms at all, or they may have a short, flu-like illness. People with weakened immune systems, including people who have received organ transplants or people with AIDS, can develop serious problems from CMV.

Symptoms

CMV can infect cells in different parts of your body, including your eyes, digestive system, lungs, and brain. The symptoms depend on where it appears.

CMV retinitis: The most common place that CMV causes disease is in a part of your eye called the retina. The retina is a layer of cells in the back of your eye that is sensitive to light. When you look at something, the lens of your eye makes an image on your retina and your retina sends the picture to your brain. CMV retinitis can cause blindness. It usually affects only one eye at a time, but can also spread to the other eye. The most common symptoms are blurred vision, floaters (spots floating across your vision), and blind spots (dark spots in your vision). CMV retinitis is usually painless.

Gastrointestinal CMV: The second most common place that CMV causes trouble is in your digestive system. This includes your esophagus (the tube that connects your mouth and stomach), small intestine (gut), and colon. Your colon (or large intestine) carries waste to your rectum (the inside of your ass). CMV infection is most common in the colon, and it can cause fever, watery diarrhea, weight loss, and loss of appetite. CMV in your esophagus can cause difficulty swallowing or pain when you swallow.

Pulmonary CMV infection: CMV infection in your lungs is called CMV pneumonitis. This is very rare with HIV. The symptoms are the same as those of PCP (see Page 118).

126

**OPPORTUNISTIC
INFECTIONS
AND RELATED
CONDITIONS**
Viral infections

- *Cytomegalovirus
  (CMV)*

Diagnosis

If you report any vision problems, your doctor will examine your eyes, and refer you to an ophthalmologist (eye specialist). The ophthalmologist will give your eyes a detailed examination, which may include taking photographs of your retina.

If you report symptoms typical of CMV colitis (CMV infection of the colon [bowel]), you may be examined by colonoscopy (using a tube to look inside your colon through your anus [asshole]).

If you report symptoms typical of CMV esophagitis (CMV infection of the esophagus), you may be examined by endoscopy (using a tube to look down your esophagus). A bronchoscopy (see Page 118) may be used for symptoms typical of CMV pneumonitis. With each of these "scope" tests, a biopsy (tissue sample) will probably be done. The piece of tissue removed will be cultured to see if CMV will grow. Since culture tests can take several weeks to show results, doctors sometimes begin treatment right away if they think you may have a CMV infection.

Be aware of any changes in your vision. The Amsler grid (see Page 129) can help you figure out whether you have any vision problems.

Call your doctor right away if you notice a lot of floaters (little specks) in front of your eyes. They're easiest to see if you look at the sky or at a plain, light-coloured background. You should also call your doctor if an area of your vision is missing or seems blocked by a curtain or veil. It's important to diagnose and treat CMV retinitis as soon as possible. If not treated, it can cause blindness in as little as two months.

Prevention

The risk of developing CMV disease increases if your T4 cell count (see Page 27) falls below 100. CMV infections in people with HIV are usually a re-activation of the CMV that they got earlier in life. CMV is usually passed on through sexual contact or sharing needles. Practising safer sex (see Page 151), and using clean needles if you're shooting up (see Page 155), may help prevent a new infection, or re-infection.

Treatment

Ganciclovir (sold as Cytovene) and foscarnet (Foscavir) are antiviral drugs (drugs used to fight viruses). They are the most commonly used treatments for CMV infection. If you are diagnosed with CMV retinitis, you may have to be admitted to hospital for a couple of weeks of intravenous (IV, or injected directly into a vein) treatment with either ganciclovir or foscarnet (it depends on where you live). In larger cities you will not have to stay at the hospital. Once the retinitis has been stabilized, lifelong maintenance treatment is given to keep CMV from making you sick again. You can learn to take your daily intravenous treatments by yourself, in your own home. Because the treatment is taken so often, in-dwelling catheters (see Page 128) are put into your body to protect your veins.

Ganciclovir is available in pill form for maintenance therapy; it is taken daily after the retinitis has been stabilized. It is poorly absorbed and not much active drug gets used by your body. But oral (pill form) ganciclovir has far fewer side effects than IV ganciclovir. Also, many people find being hooked up to an IV limits what they can do.

Ganciclovir can also be given as a injection directly into your eye (intravitreal injection) every two weeks or so.

An experimental form of ganciclovir is the intravitreal implant ("intra" means "in" and "vitreal" refers to the jelly-like material in your eye). This is a small plastic film that's filled with ganciclovir and put into your eye, where it slowly and constantly gives off the ganciclovir. Because the implant is in your eye, very little of the drug gets into your blood. This means that the intravitreal implant can't be used to treat CMV anywhere except in your eye. This product is available through the Emergency Drug Release Program (see Page 170) but it's very expensive (at the time of writing, about $5,000 per implant), and has to be replaced every six months. If you had CMV retinitis in both eyes, you'd need intravitreal implants in both eyes.

Ganciclovir, particularly the intravenous form, can have serious side effects. The most frequent side effects are thrombocytopenia (see Page 27) and neutropenia (see Page 64). Ganciclovir can also cause kidney damage, headache, nausea, vomiting, diarrhea, rash, confusion. If you're taking AZT (see Page 64), your doctor will want to watch your blood tests closely and may take you off the AZT if neutropenia occurs. Sometimes doctors will also give you one of two drugs – G-CSF and GM-CSF – to help your body make more white blood cells. This is common in the USA, but not in Canada. Side effects from the ganciclovir implant itself include bleeding, infection, and the risk of

OPPORTUNISTIC
INFECTIONS
AND RELATED
CONDITIONS
Viral infections
• *Cytomegalovirus
(CMV)*

**OPPORTUNISTIC
INFECTIONS
AND RELATED
CONDITIONS**
Viral infections

• *Cytomegalovirus
(CMV)*

retinal detachment (your retina coming loose from your eye) where the implant was inserted.

Foscarnet (Foscavir) is an antiviral drug given intravenously (IV, or injected directly into a vein) and sometimes injected directly into the eye. You can learn to take your daily intravenous treatments by yourself, in your own home. Because the treatment is taken so often, in-dwelling catheters (see below) are put into your body to protect your veins. Foscarnet can cause serious kidney damage. Drink lots of fluids if you're taking it. Other side effects include anemia (see Page 26), tiredness, fever, muscle weakness, headache, nausea, and vomiting.

People whose white blood cell count (see Page 26) is low to begin with may be given foscarnet instead of ganciclovir. Sometimes people may switch back and forth between foscarnet and ganciclovir, and some doctors may use ganciclovir and foscarnet together in lower doses, in the hope that the side effects of each can be reduced.

A new drug, cidofovir (Vistide) is currently being studied. Cidofovir is taken intravenously once every two weeks. Not all the side effects of cidofovir are known, but it can cause serious kidney damage. A drug called probenecid is given at the same time to help prevent kidney problems. Cidofovir is currently available in Canada through the Emergency Drug Release Program (see Page 170).

Treatment with intravenous ganciclovir or foscarnet, the most common drugs for CMV retinitis, is taken every day. In-dwelling catheters are used for easy access to the vein. A central venous catheter (CVC) is a flexible tube that is placed in your upper chest wall area to allow medication to be delivered directly into your bloodstream through the veins in your chest. CVCs are put in by a surgeon. The two most commonly used types are: percutaneous CVC lines and implanted venous ports. The percutaneous line is often referred to as a "Hickman" catheter. It is a one-piece catheter. Usually six to eight inches of it remain on the outside of your chest. An implanted venous port (usually called a Port-a-Cath) is a catheter that is implanted under the skin on your chest wall, so that nothing remains on the outside of your chest. A specially designed needle with a short piece of tubing attached to it must be inserted into the port itself.

The Amsler grid

Use the following Amsler grid to check your eyes regularly. If you notice any vision problems (with or without the grid), see your doctor.

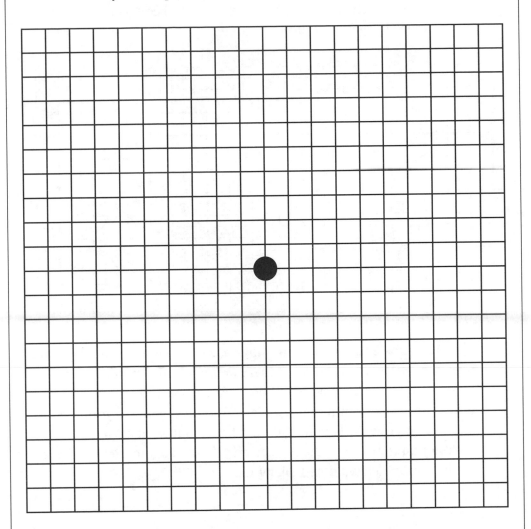

OPPORTUNISTIC INFECTIONS AND RELATED CONDITIONS
Viral infections
- *Cytomegalovirus (CMV)*
  - *The Amsler grid*

1. Test yourself in good light. If you use glasses, wear them.
2. Hold the Amsler grid at a comfortable reading distance.
3. Cover one eye and look at the black dot in the centre.
4. Keeping your eye on the black dot, note whether the lines look straight and whether the squares are all the same size (as on graph paper).
5. Repeat for the other eye.

6. If any area of the Amsler grid looks distorted, blurred, or discoloured – or is missing – contact your doctor. There is a natural blind spot in the outside of your vision (for your left eye, for example, it's to the far left). This is where the nerves of your retina (which convert light into images) all connect to send the picture images to your brain.

130

OPPORTUNISTIC
INFECTIONS
AND RELATED
CONDITIONS
Viral infections
- *Cytomegalovirus
  (CMV)*
  - *The Amsler grid*
- *Herpes simplex virus*

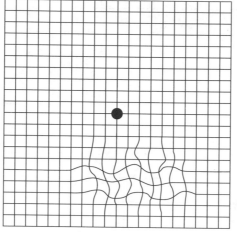

Example of distortion

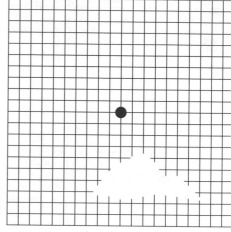

Example of area missing

The Amsler grid does not diagnose CMV retinitis or any other eye disease. It simply shows if there are any problems with your vision. These can have many different causes, including drug side effects. It's important to mention any vision problems to your doctor, so he or she can check your eyes and figure out what's wrong. Ask your doctor how to use the Amsler grid if you need more information about what you should be looking for.

Herpes simplex virus

Symptoms and diagnosis

There are two kinds of herpes simplex viruses. Herpes simplex I is the main cause of blisters or ulcers and itching on your lips. Herpes simplex II is the main cause of blisters on your genitals. But each virus can infect both your genitals and your mouth. Diagnosis is usually made by history of symptoms, physical examination, and viral culture: a cotton swab is used to take a sample from a moist sore and sent to the lab to be examined.

Prevention

Many people have been exposed to herpes. It can be passed on through sex, or from a mother to her baby during delivery (which can be very dangerous for the newborn baby.)

When you're first infected, herpes can cause an outbreak of sores. These outbreaks usually become fewer and further apart over time. Some people who have had herpes before and who have a T4 cell count (see Page 27) below 500 take acyclovir (Zovirax – see below) regularly to help prevent further outbreaks.

Treatment

Active herpes infections are usually treated successfully with acyclovir (Zovirax), which can be taken in pill form, as a cream or gel, or intravenously (IV, or injected directly into a vein). Doctors sometimes use foscarnet (Foscavir – see Page 128) for herpes infections that don't respond to acyclovir. New treatments include famciclovir (Famvir), valaciclovir (Valtrex), and trifluorothymidine (TFT or trifluridine) cream. L-lysine (see Page 94) has also been used for the prevention and treatment of herpes simplex infections.

Herpes zoster virus (shingles)

Symptoms and diagnosis

The herpes zoster virus (also called varicella-zoster virus, or VZV) is the same virus that causes chicken pox in children. Many people have been exposed to it. Inactive herpes zoster may flare up in HIV-positive people. The virus infects nerve cells and causes painful blisters called vesicles. As the vesicles heal, they form hardened layers of scabs that look like shingles on a roof. Shingles often appear on the trunk of your body (chest, belly, and back), usually only on one side. You can also get them on your arms, legs, and face. An outbreak of shingles can last weeks or months if it's not treated. Since the vesicles are on nerves, shingles are very painful. In black people, the healing vesicles can cause scars known as keloid scars. Most cases of shingles can be diagnosed just by looking at the pattern of the blisters. In other cases, diagnosis is made by testing the fluid and cells scraped from a blister.

OPPORTUNISTIC INFECTIONS AND RELATED CONDITIONS
Viral infections
- *Herpes simplex virus*
- *Herpes zoster virus (shingles)*

**OPPORTUNISTIC
INFECTIONS
AND RELATED
CONDITIONS**
Viral infections
• *Herpes zoster virus
(shingles)*
• *Progressive
multifocal
leukoencephalopathy
(PML)*

Prevention and treatment

There is no foolproof drug for preventing shingles, although acyclovir (Zovirax) pills are now often used. It's best to begin treatment as soon as possible in order to shorten the outbreak. Acyclovir works best if you start taking it within 72 hours (three days) of when the shingles appear. Early treatment can reduce the risk of nerve damage that causes post-herpetic (after herpes) neuralgia (nerve pain). It's also recommended that you take anti-inflammatory drugs (drugs that reduce swelling, such as Aspirin [ASA], ibuprofen [Advil, Motrin IB], or Naprosyn) in order to decrease the amount of damage to nerve tissue and prevent pain. Valaciclovir (Valtrex) is available in Canada. Famciclovir (Famvir) has also been approved for sale in Canada.

Progressive multifocal leukoencephalopathy (PML)

PML is caused by the JC virus. Like many of the infections that you may get, PML can be reactivated when your immune system gets weaker. It usually only happens when your T4 cell count (see Page 27) drops below 50. It hasn't been studied as much as other AIDS-related infections, probably because it's quite rare, even in people who have AIDS.

Most people have had a JC virus infection at some time in their lives. In people with healthy immune systems, this virus causes an infection of the kidneys. Most people don't know that they have the infection. After about two weeks, their bodies begin to control the virus, and the kidney infection ends. It's not known whether the infection becomes dormant (inactive) in everyone who has had the kidney infection, or whether some people get rid of the virus completely.

When your immune system becomes weaker, a dormant JC virus infection can become active again. This newly active infection can occur in your brain and causes PML. The infection is called progressive because once it happens it usually "progresses" (gets more and more severe).

Symptoms and diagnosis

Because PML affects your brain, it can cause many types of symptoms, and the symptoms can vary from one person to another. Symptoms of PML can include changes in speech or in vision (loss of vision in one area), weakness or lack of coordination in one limb or on one side of the body, and unsteadiness in walking or standing.

Other conditions that affect your brain can cause similar symptoms. These include toxoplasmosis (see Page 120), cryptococcal meningitis (see Page 115), and AIDS dementia complex (ADC – see Page 144). Your doctor may not always be able to diagnose PML from your symptoms. A CT scan or an MRI (see Page 31) of your brain may show signs of PML. A brain biopsy (removing and studying a small piece of brain tissue) is the only way to be sure of what's going on. Brain biopsies are almost never done because of the risks of damage to your brain and infection afterwards. Diagnosis of PML is usually done through a process of elimination. If symptoms and scans are not clear, treatment against toxo is started. If no improvement is seen after ten to fourteen days, then PML may be diagnosed.

Prevention and treatment

There is currently no treatment to prevent PML, nor is there any proven effective treatment. The results of one study suggest that cytosine arabinoside (ara-C, or cytarabine) injected into the fluid in your brain (a procedure called intrathecal administration) may stabilize PML. Unfortunately, other studies seem to show that this treatment doesn't make any real difference.

Occasionally, PML stops getting worse without any treatment at all. In most people, though, it keeps getting worse. Quickly progressing PML can cause death in two or three months, often due to pneumonia or suffocation (being unable to breathe).

OPPORTUNISTIC INFECTIONS AND RELATED CONDITIONS
Viral infections
- *Progressive multifocal leukoencephalopathy (PML)*

Other viral infections

Hepatitis

Hepatitis ("hep") is an inflammation (swelling) of the liver, usually caused by a viral infection. Early symptoms of hepatitis include tiredness, joint and muscle pain, and loss of appetite. Nausea, vomiting, diarrhea, and fever may follow. As the disease develops, your liver enlarges and becomes tender. Chills, weight loss, or jaundice (yellowing of your eyes and skin) may then appear. Hepatitis can affect how your liver works and can cause a liver disease called cirrhosis.

When your immune system comes into contact with one of the hepatitis viruses, it produces antibodies to help control the virus. These antibodies can then help protect your liver against future hepatitis infections. There are three main types of hepatitis virus:

◆ **Hepatitis A** is transmitted through contaminated food or water, or through contact with the stool (shit) of an infected person. The incubation time (the time between infection and the appearance of symptoms) is fourteen to 40 days. There is now a vaccine to prevent hepatitis A infection.

◆ **Hepatitis B** can be passed on through contact with contaminated blood or other body fluid, such as saliva (spit), semen (cum), or stool, or by sharing contaminated needles. The incubation time can be 40 to 180 days. There is currently a vaccine that can protect you against hepatitis B. If you are sexually active, use injectable drugs (shoot up), or are a health care worker, it's a good idea to get this vaccine (if you haven't already come into contact with hepatitis) The anti-retroviral drug 3TC (see Page 67) is sometimes used to treat hepatitis B.

◆ **Hepatitis C** used to be called non-A, non-B hepatitis. Its transmission (spread) is mainly through sharing of contaminated needles or from infected blood products, but the incubation period is closer to that of hepatitis A. There is currently no vaccine for this type of hepatitis.

◆ **Other types of hepatitis** include hepatitis D, E and G. Not much is known about these viruses.

OPPORTUNISTIC
INFECTIONS
AND RELATED
CONDITIONS
Viral infections
• *Other viral infections*
  • *Hepatitis*

There is no cure for viral hepatitis. For people with active infection, even treatment is limited. Recovery is usually up to your body's own immune system. That's why when these infections happen in people with HIV they're usually more severe and more likely to do liver damage than they would be in HIV-negative people.

Influenza

The influenza virus causes the flu. There are two basic types: Type A and Type B. Each has different strains (types), which are usually named for the place they first came from (for example, Hong Kong flu virus and Moscow flu virus). The strains can change from year to year, so that antibodies that your body has created can no longer control them. Each year, a flu vaccine is created from several virus strains that exist that year. There is a concern that these vaccines may cause HIV to reproduce faster, without protecting you from the flu. However, it's also believed that infection with the flu may stimulate HIV even more. Check with your doctor to find out the latest information on whether or not you should get a flu shot each year.

Hairy leukoplakia

Hairy leukoplakia (HL) is a condition that has been associated with the Epstein-Barr virus (EBV) and with the human papillomavirus (HPV – see Page 139). It causes white lesions (patches) that usually appear on the sides of your tongue, but it can also affect other parts of your mouth. The lesions can be mistaken for oral candidiasis (thrush – see Page 113). Under a microscope, scrapings from HL lesions have a hairy appearance. Hairy leukoplakia lesions may appear as early as the asymptomatic phase of HIV infection (see Page 21). HL usually does not cause problems, but for some people it may affect the taste of food.

Some studies have shown that high-dose acyclovir (see page 131) – more than 3,000 mg per day – taken for seven to fourteen days, followed by maintenance doses of 1,200 mg per day, can reduce or eliminate lesions.

OPPORTUNISTIC INFECTIONS AND RELATED CONDITIONS
Viral infections
- *Other viral infections*
  - *Hepatitis*
  - *Influenza*
  - *Hairy leukoplakia*

**OPPORTUNISTIC
INFECTIONS
AND RELATED
CONDITIONS**
*Other AIDS/HIV-
related conditions*
• *Kaposi's sarcoma
(KS)*

Other AIDS/HIV-related conditions

Kaposi's sarcoma (KS)

Kaposi's sarcoma is an abnormal growth of small blood vessels, usually under the skin. Sarcomas are a type of tumour (swelling).

KS was one of the first conditions identified as part of the syndrome called AIDS. Men who have had sex with men are almost the only HIV-positive people who ever get AIDS-related KS. People who use injection drugs (shoot up), people who have hemophilia, women, and people who get HIV through blood transfusions rarely get it. A few babies have been diagnosed with it.

New research suggests that KS may be caused by a herpes virus called Human Herpes Virus 8 (see Page 130). If this is true, then it's possible that the germ that causes KS was widespread in the gay community long before HIV and AIDS came along. Immune system damage created an opportunity for KS to cause harm.

Researchers believe that, if a germ does cause KS, it may be passed on through sex, and especially through oral-anal sex (rimming, or licking someone's asshole).

Symptoms and diagnosis

External KS

KS can appear anywhere on your body. It's most common in the mouth, on the face, neck, chest, and back, and on the soles of the feet. It shows up as lesions (spots) that may be purple, red, blue, or black. They're usually flat and painless, and don't itch. An early lesion can appear as a small lump under your skin and may look similar to a bruise. As the lesions progress, they can become raised and may flow together. They often appear in "showers," meaning that a lot of little lesions may show up in a short time. KS on your skin can be diagnosed with a biopsy (taking a small sample of a lesion to look at under a microscope).

Internal KS

KS can also appear inside your body on various organs, including your intestines (guts) or lungs, or in your lymph nodes (see Page 19). If your doctor suspects you may have KS inside your body, there are a number of different tests which can be done, depending on where it might be.

Prevention and treatment

Kaposi's sarcoma doesn't seem to be related to a low T4 cell count (see Page 27). It can appear in people with 400 or more T4 cells. (People diagnosed with AIDS usually have fewer than 200.) If one of the ways KS is passed on is during sex, especially oral-anal sex (rimming, or licking someone's asshole), then some people may not have been exposed yet. This is an important reason to practise safer sex (see Page 151), even with other people who are HIV positive.

Treatment of KS doesn't cure the disease, but may keep it under control. KS on your skin can be treated during the early stages and will rarely become life threatening. Visceral KS, meaning KS in internal organs (like your lungs or intestines) can be harder to treat. It's usually treated with systemic chemotherapy, that is, intravenous (IV, or injected directly into a vein) drugs, given once every week or two.

People who have only a few lesions may choose not to take treatment. A few people with KS are still alive more than ten years after diagnosis. Many people choose to have lesions treated, because of how they look. Make-up can also be used to cover up lesions.

Cosmetics for KS

Make-up can help hide KS lesions. The best way to learn about how to use cosmetics for this purpose is from other people with KS. You may have a friend who can help you learn the basics of make-up. There are professional make-up artists who can teach you effective techniques. Contact your nearest AIDS group (see Page 243) to see if they offer this service, or if they can refer you to someone who does.

Radiation therapy

Radiation therapy is a local treatment (only the affected area is treated) that may reduce the number and size of KS lesions. This treatment is normally used only if the lesions are causing you problems. It can be used on your skin, including the skin of your feet, in the area of your genitals or anus (asshole), and in your mouth. The

OPPORTUNISTIC INFECTIONS AND RELATED CONDITIONS
Other AIDS/HIV-related conditions
• *Kaposi's sarcoma (KS)*

OPPORTUNISTIC
INFECTIONS
AND RELATED
CONDITIONS
*Other AIDS/HIV-
related conditions*

• *Kaposi's sarcoma
(KS)*

doctor puts a shield around the lesion and X-rays it. Radiation therapy may be given at low doses, five days in a row over four or five weeks, or it may be given once at a high dose.

Some people who get radiation therapy get such side effects as nausea, skin irritation, low white and red blood cell counts (see Page 26), and skin discolouration (changes in skin colour). It can also sometimes cause sores when used in your mouth, and diarrhea when used on your anus.

Cryotherapy

Doctors can sometimes treat small lesions by freezing them with liquid nitrogen. This is called cryotherapy.

Chemotherapy

Chemotherapy (which literally means "treating diseases with chemicals") involves giving drugs intravenously (IV, or injected directly into a vein). This means that the treatment works throughout your body, unlike radiation therapy, which is only used on a specific area. Chemotherapy is most often used to treat KS in internal organs, where it can slow the disease down. Several drugs may be used, including vinblastine, vincristine, etoposide, doxorubicin (Adriamycin), and a combination known as ABV (short for Adriamycin, bleomycin, and vincristine).

Side effects can include nausea, vomiting, tiredness, liver and kidney problems, hair loss, peripheral neuropathy (see Page 143), and immune suppression (your immune system getting weaker). Experienced doctors can often reduce these problems by alternating drugs and by giving you blood transfusions or a drug like GM-CSF or G-CSF, which can help your body produce more white blood cells (see Page 20).

New forms of anti-cancer drugs have recently been released. These drugs have been packed into little balls of fat called liposomes, and are supposed to be less toxic (poisonous) than other forms of chemotherapy. Doxorubicin (Doxil) or daunorubicin (DaunoXome) are two of these drugs, which you may be able to get through the Emergency Drug Release Program (see Page 170).

Alpha interferon

Alpha interferon is a protein made naturally by certain white blood cells in your body. It's been approved for use in the treatment of Kaposi's sarcoma. It's usually injected under your skin every day for eight to twelve weeks. People who respond well usually keep getting maintenance (ongoing) treatment with injections three times a week. It seems to be more effective in people with more than 200 T4 cells (see Page 20).

Alpha interferon can cause side effects that include flu-like symptoms such as tiredness, chills, fever, muscle aches, nausea, vomiting, and diarrhea. These side effects can sometimes be reduced by taking a lower dose, taking pain medication just before the injection, and taking the injection just before bedtime. A few people also develop liver problems, leukopenia (see Page 26), dizziness, low blood pressure, and hair loss.

Intralesional therapy

Sometimes small amounts of a medication can be injected directly into the KS lesion with a small needle. Because the medication is injected into the lesion, higher levels of the drug go to where it may help, and less drug goes all over your body. Intralesional therapy can sometimes cause infection, pain, and scarring. Vinblastine and alpha interferon can be given as intralesional therapies. hCG (human chorionic gonadotropin) is a hormone which is sometimes given by injection to treat KS.

OPPORTUNISTIC INFECTIONS AND RELATED CONDITIONS
Other AIDS/HIV-related conditions
- *Kaposi's sarcoma (KS)*
- *Cervical dysplasia and cancer*

Cervical dysplasia and cancer

Cervical cancer is cancer of the cervix – the lower part of your uterus (womb), which joins with the back of your vagina (birth canal).

Women with healthy immune systems can develop cervical cancer, but women with weakened immune systems are more likely to. The risk is greater in HIV-positive women with low T4 cell counts (see Page 27).

Cervical cancer is associated with a virus called human papillomavirus (HPV). HPV can cause changes in the cells in your cervix which eventually cause them to become cancerous. There are many types of HPV. Most cause warts and some strains cause genital warts (see Page 150). Currently, while cervical cancer is an "AIDS-defining illness" (an illness that is officially identified as part of the syndrome called AIDS), HPV infection is not. And pre-cancerous changes caused by HPV in the skin cells of your cervix (cervical dysplasia, or CIN – cervical intraepithelial neoplasia) are not considered part of the definition of AIDS.

OPPORTUNISTIC
INFECTIONS
AND RELATED
CONDITIONS
*Other AIDS/HIV-
related conditions*
• *Cervical dysplasia
and cancer*

HPV-related cancer can appear in the lower genital tract and in the anus (asshole) in both men and women. Anal Pap smears (see Page 33) for men who have sex with men, or for women who have anal sex, are suggested. Cervical cancer in HIV-positive women can be more difficult to treat, may recur (come back) faster, and can get worse much faster than in other women.

Symptoms and diagnosis

Many women can have an HPV infection and experience changes in the skin cells of the cervix without knowing it. A pelvic examination with a Pap smear (see Page 33) and colposcopy (a visual examination of the cervix through a magnifying instrument inserted into your vagina) together with a biopsy (a tiny piece of tissue being removed from your cervix and examined) can let you know if you've been exposed to HPV, and if you have cervical dysplasia. If your test results show minor changes to the cells of your cervix, you and your doctor may decide to repeat the examination every three months.

Symptoms of cervical cancer may include bleeding from your vagina after intercourse (fucking), between periods, or after menopause. There may be unusual discharge, problems urinating (peeing), or pelvic (genital area) pain.

Prevention and treatment

There is no known way to prevent cervical dysplasia or cervical cancer. Early diagnosis can lead to more effective treatment. Women who have HIV may decide to have a pelvic exam and Pap smear (see Page 33) done every six months.

Cervical dysplasia may be treated in several ways.

◆ Cryotherapy involves freezing the affected tissue.
◆ Electrocautery involves burning away the tissue with a metal probe heated by an electric current.
◆ Laser surgery uses a very intense beam of light to remove tissue. It can be done in a doctor's office or in hospital under a local or general anesthetic.

Cervical cancer can be treated by laser surgery. If the cancer has spread through the tissue of your cervix or uterus, a hysterectomy may be done. This is a major operation done in hospital under general anesthetic. The surgeon makes a cut in your abdomen (belly) and removes your uterus (womb – including your cervix) and lymph nodes (see Page 19), and possibly your fallopian tubes and ovaries. You may spend a week or so in the hospital after the operation.

141

OPPORTUNISTIC INFECTIONS AND RELATED CONDITIONS
Other AIDS/HIV-related conditions
- *Cervical dysplasia and cancer*
- *Lymphoma*

Lymphoma

Lymphoma is cancer of the tissues or cells of your lymphatic system (see Page 19). It's a type of cancer that anybody can develop, but it is more common in people who are HIV positive. The cells that usually grow out of control in HIV-related lymphomas are called B cells (see Page 20). These are the cells that produce antibodies. There are many different types of lymphoma. The types that are seen in AIDS are Non-Hodgkin's lymphoma, primary CNS (central nervous system) lymphoma, and Hodgkin's disease. When the first two types occur in people who are HIV positive, they're considered "AIDS-defining illnesses" (see Page 139).

Usually lymphoma occurs only when your T4 cell count (see Page 27) is below 200, but it can happen even with counts higher than 600.

Untreated primary CNS lymphoma often kills very quickly. On the other hand, non-Hodgkin's lymphoma goes into remission (goes away, at least temporarily) in more than half of healthier people who get treatment. People who have T4 cell counts above 100 do better on chemotherapy than people with very low counts.

Symptoms

Lymphoma can develop anywhere in your body, but is most common in the clusters of lymph nodes (see Page 19). Usually you get it in more than one place. Your lymph nodes can grow very large (as large as a grapefruit). One of the most common symptoms of lymphoma is swollen lymph nodes in your groin (crotch) or armpits, or along your neck. Also, you may have fevers, night sweats (see Page 157), and weight loss, and may have pain in the swollen nodes.

OPPORTUNISTIC
INFECTIONS
AND RELATED
CONDITIONS
*Other AIDS/HIV-
related conditions*

• *Lymphoma*

Lymphoma may be found in your brain, stomach, gut, liver, or lungs. In your stomach, it can cause problems in eating or in keeping food down. In your lungs, it can cause breathing problems. When lymphoma appears first in your brain it is called primary CNS lymphoma. The symptoms depend on where the tumour is.

Diagnosis

Lymphoma may be diagnosed by imaging tests, such as CT scans and MRIs,or by biopsy (see Page 31).

Diagnosing lymphoma in your brain can be difficult because the pattern that shows up on CT scans look very similar to that of toxo-plasmosis (see Page 120). Brain biopsies are rare (see Page 133).

Because of this difficulty, some people end up seeing a lot of different doctors and having a lot of medical tests. You may have to wait a while to get a CT scan or MRI done.

Prevention and treatment

There is no known way to prevent lymphoma. Treatment depends on the location and type of tumour. There are two types of treatment:

◆ Radiotherapy: using radiation (see Page 137) on a tumour. This is usually done in early Hodgkin's Disease and in primary CNS lymphoma, or if you have a large tumour that's causing a problem, are too weak for chemotherapy, or have had chemotherapy that didn't work.

◆ Chemotherapy (drug) treatments (see Page 138). These are complex; four or more drugs may used at once. Most are very strong. They include: mBACOD (methotrexate, bleomycin, doxorubicin [Adriamycin], cyclophosphamide, vincristine, and dexamethasone); COMP (cyclophosphamide, vincristine, methotrexate, and prednisone); and Pro-MACE/MOPP (prednisone, methotrexate, doxorubicin, cyclophosphamide, etoposide/mechlorethamine, vincristine, and procarbozine). Sometimes, G-CSF or GM-CSF is added to protect your bone marrow (see Page 64) from being damaged by the chemotherapy. The corticosteroid drug called prednisone may be given to help relieve some of the side effects. Drugs may also be given to help relieve nausea.

Chemotherapy drugs can be put into the fluid around your brain by injecting them into your spine. This may be done to treat primary CNS lymphoma.

Chemotherapy can cause lots of side effects, including damage to bone marrow, nausea and vomiting, hair loss, rashes, headaches, mood changes, dizziness, fever, coughing, and depression. Treatments are often given in hospital (but you don't usually have to stay there overnight).

Taking any other drugs while getting chemotherapy can be dangerous. Make sure your doctor knows about everything you take. You may want to stop drinking alcohol or using street drugs while being treated.

Peripheral neuropathy

Peripheral neuropathy is a numbness or tingling or burning sensation in your hands or feet, which can become very painful. It can be caused by several different drugs and possibly by HIV itself, so it's important to figure out what the cause is. The antiviral drugs ddI, ddC, and d4T (see Pages 65 and 66) can cause peripheral neuropathy. The neuropathy may go away if you stop taking these drugs. Sometimes, though, peripheral neuropathy can be permanent.

There is no really effective treatment for peripheral neuropathy. Treatment is usually limited to pain-killing drugs. If the neuropathy is mild, sometimes the vitamins B6 and B12 (see Page 90) can help. Sometimes acupuncture (see Page 74) or acupressure massage (see Page 79) can relieve or reduce the symptoms. Doctors may prescribe amitriptyline (Elavil) to be taken at bedtime. Amitriptyline is an antidepressant, but it seems to have an effect on peripheral neuropathy. Mexilitine is also sometimes prescribed.

Sometimes the pain is so intense that people take oxycodone (Percodan, Percocet), a painkiller that acts like morphine. Others may have to take morphine itself. These medications can leave you feeling sleepy, confused, or dizzy, and may cause nausea or vomiting. Dosage of these drugs should be individually adjusted in order to control the pain as well as possible, and to cause as few side effects as possible.

Peptide T is an experimental treatment that has shown beneficial effects in treating peripheral neuropathy. There are no known side effects from Peptide T. Although it is not approved for sale, it's

143

OPPORTUNISTIC INFECTIONS AND RELATED CONDITIONS
Other AIDS/HIV-related conditions
- *Lymphoma*
- *Peripheral neuropathy*

available from buyers' clubs (see Page 171) in the USA. It comes in two forms: a liquid spray you inhale (breathe in) through your nose (like Dristan), or a subcutaneous (under the skin) injection. The spray may irritate the lining of your nose, and some people develop bruises where the injections are given.

L-carnitine, an amino acid which can be purchased at health food stores, may help prevent or reduce symptoms of peripheral neuropathy.

OPPORTUNISTIC
INFECTIONS
AND RELATED
CONDITIONS
*Other AIDS/HIV-
related conditions*
- *Peripheral neuropathy*
- *AIDS dementia
complex (ADC)*

AIDS dementia complex (ADC)

One of the conditions sometimes experienced by people with AIDS is AIDS dementia complex (ADC). ADC is called a complex because it involves a number of different problems. It's more common in people who have been living with AIDS for some time. The term "cognitive impairment" (difficulty in thinking) has been suggested as more appropriate, but most people still use the word "dementia."

Dementia is an organic problem, not a psychological problem. People often think that someone whose mind isn't working properly is just "losing it." In people with AIDS, dementia is the result of physical changes in the nervous system. It should not be confused with other problems, like depression or forgetfulness.

HIV may cause dementia when it gets into your brain by infecting macrophages (see Page 20), which can carry it from your bloodstream into your brain. It's thought that HIV then somehow indirectly damages nerve cells.

Symptoms and diagnosis

Symptoms of dementia can include poor concentration, forgetfulness, and loss of short-term memory (the ability to remember what you were doing ten minutes ago, or yesterday). If the dementia gets worse, long-term memory (the ability to remember things that happened long ago) can be lost. Dementia can make it hard to think clearly, and can make you want to avoid being with other people. It can make you get angry easily and can cause you to lose some physical coordination. Serious dementia can cause your personality to change and can leave you unable to do basic tasks.

Doctors usually diagnose ADC with a test called a mental status examination, which shows symptoms like memory loss, trouble concentrating, and mood swings (fast, frequent changes of mood). They may also do a CT scan (see Page 31) or a lumbar puncture (see Page 116). The fluid taken from your spine may show more than the usual amounts of certain white blood cell (see Page 20) proteins. This increase has been shown to be related to ADC. Tests which culture (see Page 31) fluid from your spinal cord sometimes show high levels of HIV.

Prevention and treatment

Researchers do not yet understand exactly how HIV damages brain cells. This has made it difficult to prevent and treat ADC, although there is some evidence that people who are taking the anti-HIV drug AZT (see Page 64) are less likely to develop it.

Larger-than-usual doses of AZT (around 1,000 mg each day) may help treat ADC. Other antiretroviral drugs that get into the brain may help prevent or reduce symptoms of ADC. These drugs include d4T (see Page 67) and nevirapine (see Page 68).

B vitamins (especially B6 and B12 – see Page 90) may help reduce symptoms of dementia.

Sometimes doctors use drugs like haloperidol (Haldol), methylphenidate hydrochloride (Ritalin), and diazepam (Valium) to treat the symptoms of ADC. These treatments don't stop ADC from progressing but they may help keep the symptoms under control. Some psychiatric drugs, like haloperidol, should be used with caution, as they can have very serious side effects. Other drugs that are being studied include nimodipine and Peptide T (see Page 143).

How to manage better

Here are some things that may help you cope with changes in your memory and your ability to concentrate:

◆ Use a datebook to record appointments and phone numbers. Make a list of things that need to be done each day, and check it often.

OPPORTUNISTIC INFECTIONS AND RELATED CONDITIONS
Other AIDS/HIV-related conditions
• *Peripheral neuropathy*
• *AIDS dementia complex (ADC)*

146

OPPORTUNISTIC
INFECTIONS
AND RELATED
CONDITIONS
*Other AIDS/HIV-
related conditions*
• *AIDS dementia
complex (ADC)*
• *Skin problems*
  • *Seborrheic
    dermatitis*

◆ Do one thing at a time. For example, don't try to cook dinner and talk on the phone at the same time. Try not to leave the room while you're cooking, ironing, or filling the bathtub. Keep in mind that TV and radio can distract you from what you're doing.

◆ Schedule appointments for the early part of the day. Take someone along with you to help keep track of information. Keep your evenings free for rest and relaxation. It's harder to think clearly when you're tired.

◆ Schedule time in the day to do nothing but relax. You may want to try stress reduction and relaxation techniques (see the section beginning on Page 77). Your nearest AIDS group (see Page 243) may provide free massages.

◆ Avoid stressful situations. If you don't like crowds, try doing your shopping during off-hours. Find a friend to help balance your chequebook, deal with insurance companies or the welfare office, etc.

◆ Exercise regularly, but don't overdo it. Exercise can help reduce stress. The more activities you take part in that need coordinated movements, the longer you'll be able to keep your movements coordinated.

◆ Get a pill box that beeps when it's time to take your next dose. This will give you one less thing to forget.

Skin problems

Skin problems are common in people who have HIV. Your skin is a part of your immune system, which normally keeps many germs that live on your skin under control (see Page 19). When your immune system is weakened, these germs can cause problems. Betadine scrub (an anti-germ wash) can be applied to the skin to help kill germs.

Seborrheic dermatitis

Seborrheic dermatitis is the most common skin disease in people with HIV/AIDS. It's called dandruff when it happens on your scalp. It's caused by a fungus (see Page 18) called *Pityrosporum ovale*. If you have HIV, this fungus can cause red, greasy, scaly patches on your face (especially around your eyebrows), on your chest and back, and in your groin (crotch) and armpits. Sometimes it can be itchy. When the problem is on your scalp, dandruff shampoos like Selsun or Head & Shoulders can sometimes keep it under control. Ketoconazole (see Page 114) shampoo is also available. When the dermatitis is on your face or other parts of your body, ketoconazole cream together with hydrocortisone cream may keep it under control. People with severe cases may try taking ketoconazole, fluconazole (Diflucan – see Page 114), or itraconazole (Sporanox) pills for a short time. Some people use dandruff shampoo (or antifungal soaps), instead of regular soap, all over their bodies. Vitamin E (see Page 90) levels may be low in people with seborrheic dermatitis, so taking Vitamin E may help get rid of the condition.

Psoriasis

Psoriasis may look a lot like seborrheic dermatitis, except that it tends to have thicker scales with a silvery tinge. It can appear in your armpits or on your groin (crotch), elbows, knees, or lower back. Creams that contain corticosteroids, anthralin, or tar may help treat mild cases of psoriasis. More serious cases can be harder to treat. Some people have used phototherapy, which involves exposing the psoriasis to concentrated light rays. However, this can also stimulate HIV production. Psoriasis varies from one person to the next – see your nearest psoriasis clinic.

Folliculitis

Folliculitis appears as small, red, pus-filled bumps around the roots of hairs (follicles) on your skin. It can appear anywhere on your body, but most often appears on your chest or back. Bacterial folliculitis is caused by a kind of bacteria called *Staphylococcus* and is usually treated with antibiotics like dicloxacillin. It usually gets better in a week or two. Another kind of folliculitis, called eosinophilic folliculitis, can cause an extremely itchy rash on your upper chest, back, or arms. It may be caused by a fungus and can be treated with itraconazole (Sporanox) or ketoconazole (Nizoral – see Page 114) pills, or with ketoconazole cream. Like psoriasis, eosinophilic folliculitis can sometimes be helped by light therapy (phototherapy – see above).

OPPORTUNISTIC INFECTIONS AND RELATED CONDITIONS
Other AIDS/HIV-related conditions
- *Skin problems*
  - *Seborrheic dermatitis*
  - *Psoriasis*
  - *Folliculitis*

Molluscum contagiosum

Molluscum is a viral infection which consists of little "papules" on your skin that look like a cross between a pimple and a wart. A papule is usually hard, round, and slightly flattened, and may have a small dimple on top. Molluscum is quite common, but doesn't usually cause papules unless your immune system is weakened. In people with HIV, the papules seem to grow bigger and cover a wider area. Usually the papules don't cause pain or itchiness, and are harmless. Small, individual papules can be cut away or treated with cryotherapy (using liquid nitrogen to freeze them), but they often come back again. Some people have found that using DNCB can reduce the size of the papules or get rid of them. You may want to use an electric razor if you have molluscum, since a regular "straight" razor could cut the papules. Cantheridin is a "vesicant," or blistering agent. It is applied directly to the molluscum and washed off four to six hours later. It should be applied only by your doctor.

Other skin problems

Other skin problems can be caused by viruses like herpes simplex (see Page 130) and herpes zoster (see Page 131). Human papillomavirus (HPV – see Page 139) can cause warts on your skin and especially your genitals (see Page 150).

Sexually transmitted diseases (STDs)

People living with HIV or AIDS may can get STDs more easily than other people, and often have more serious cases. You can reduce your chances of getting any STD by practising safer sex (see Page 151). If you're sexually active, it may be a good idea to get tested for STDs regularly.

OPPORTUNISTIC
INFECTIONS
AND RELATED
CONDITIONS
Other AIDS/HIV-
related conditions
• *Skin problems*
  • *Molluscum*
    contagiosum
  • *Other skin*
    problems
Sexually transmitted
diseases (STDs)

Chlamydia

Chlamydia trachomatis is a bacterium (see Page 18) that causes one of the most common STDs. Symptoms of chlamydia include a burning feeling when you're urinating (peeing) and a discharge from your penis or vagina. Chlamydia can also infect your throat, rectum (the inside of your ass), and eyes. Many people, especially women, won't have any symptoms at all. If left untreated in men, chlamydia can cause an inflammation of the epididymis – the thin tube that connects your testes (balls) to your urethra (the tube you pee through). In women, it can cause pelvic inflammatory disease (PID – see Page 111). Chlamydia can be treated with antibiotics. (Erythromycin is safe to use during pregnancy.) If you have chlamydia, anyone you're having sex with should be treated; otherwise, you and they can get re-infected again and again.

Gonorrhea

Gonorrhea is caused by the bacterium (see Page 18) *Neisseria gonorrhoeae*. It may cause a thick discharge (stuff that comes out) from your penis or from your vagina, and sometimes a burning feeling while you're urinating (peeing). In many people, especially women, there may be no symptoms. Gonorrhea can also occur in your rectum (the inside of your ass) or throat. It can develop into a chronic, serious infection if not treated. It can spread through your blood to other parts of your body, and can lead to sterility (inability to have children). In women, it can cause pelvic inflammatory disease (PID – see Page 111). Gonorrhea is treated with antibiotics. If you have it, anyone you're having sex with should be checked, and, if necessary, treated.

Syphilis

Syphilis is caused by the bacterium (see Page 18) *Treponema pallidum*. If left untreated, it goes through three stages, with different symptoms at each stage. In the first stage, a single chancre (a painless sore) forms on your genitals, rectum (the inside of your ass), or mouth or throat. It will disappear on its own in three to six weeks, without

149

OPPORTUNISTIC INFECTIONS AND RELATED CONDITIONS
Sexually transmitted diseases (STDs)
- *Chlamydia*
- *Gonorrhea*
- *Syphilis*

treatment. The second stage happens up to six months later. Sores and a rash may occur anywhere on your body. You may feel like you have the flu, with headache and aches and pains in your joints or bones. In addition, you may experience hair loss and flat, wart-like growths inside your anus (asshole) or vagina. Without treatment these symptoms may come and go. Symptoms of the third stage may take ten to 30 years to develop. They can be very serious and can result in blindness, heart or brain damage, and, in some cases, death. People with HIV/AIDS seem to develop third-stage syphilis much faster than others. Syphilis is diagnosed by a series of blood tests. The first test, called the VDRL, is a screening test. Usually, if this test is negative, you don't have syphilis. However, people with HIV/AIDS may have false-negative VDRL tests. If you suspect you have been exposed to syphilis, you may want to ask your doctor to run two other tests, called the FTA-ABS and the MHA-TP. The usual course of syphilis may be faster and harder to treat in people with HIV. Syphilis is treated with large doses of penicillin G, given as injections into a muscle (usually in your butt) for several weeks. Penicillin is the only proven effective treatment for syphilis. If you're allergic to it, your doctor may "desensitize" you to its effects. This is done by giving you tiny doses at first, and slowly building up the dosage until you can take the full amount.

Genital herpes

Genital herpes is caused by herpes simplex virus (Type II). For more information, see Page 130.

Genital warts

Genital warts are caused by the human papillomavirus (HPV – see Page 139). They are big, rough warts that occur, often in large numbers, around the head of your penis, on your vulval (cunt) lips, in your vagina, on your cervix, on your anus (asshole), or in your rectum (the inside of your ass). The warts are ugly but generally painless. They may make sex less pleasant. HPV is associated with cervical dysplasia and cervical cancer (see Page 139) in women and with anal dysplasia and anal (ass) cancer in both men and women. Women who have had HPV should have regular Pap smears (see Page 33). Men

150

OPPORTUNISTIC INFECTIONS AND RELATED CONDITIONS
Sexually transmitted diseases (STDs)
- *Syphilis*
- *Genital herpes*
- *Genital warts*

who have had HPV should have regular rectal exams, and possibly Pap smears of the rectum. The warts can be removed by cryotherapy (freezing with liquid nitrogen) or laser surgery, or with a chemical called podophyllin (a toxic [poisonous] plant extract that is painted onto the warts).

Scabies

Scabies is caused by a small mite (a kind of parasite – see Page 159) that's hard to see without a magnifying glass. It's frequently spread through sex, but you can get it from infested clothing or pets. The scabies mite digs little burrows into your skin. One of the most common places is the skin between your fingers. Scabies is also likely to infect your elbows, wrists, waist, genitals, breasts, and buttocks (butt). In people who have HIV, scabies can occur anywhere, and the characteristic burrows may not be visible.

Scabies is extremely itchy. Treatment is usually a cream (such as NIX) or a lotion (such as Kwellada) that's put on infected areas. All clothing and bedding must be washed. If you have scabies, anybody you have close contact with (including anybody you have sex with or live with) may need treatment also.

OPPORTUNISTIC INFECTIONS AND RELATED CONDITIONS
Sexually transmitted diseases (STDs)
- *Genital warts*
- *Scabies*
Safer sex

Safer sex

Safer sex is an important way of taking care of your health. It can help protect you from most sexually transmitted diseases and from hepatitis (see Page 134). Safer sex can also protect you against parasites (see Page 159) and other organisms sometimes found in feces (shit). Some parasites can cause serious problems for people with HIV.

Finally, there are different types of HIV. Some researchers think that some types may do more damage than others. If you are infected with a type from someone else who is HIV positive and who has developed a resistance to a certain treatment, you may also become resistant to that treatment. This will limit the treatment options available to you. By practising safer sex, you may be able to avoid types of HIV that you may not yet have been exposed to. This can help you stay healthy longer.

The basic rule for having safer sex is that you don't want your partner's blood (including menstrual blood), semen (cum), pre-cum (the fluid that leaks out of your penis before you come), or vaginal fluid (juices) to get into your body, and you don't want any of your fluids to get into him or her. You can hug, neck, lick, massage, dry hump, masturbate each other (jerk each other off), share fantasies, have phone sex, dress up, and do lots of other fun things. Safer sex is a great excuse to be inventive with your partner(s).

Using condoms

If you're having intercourse (fucking – meaning putting a penis into a vagina or an anus [asshole]), make sure you use a latex condom. Polyurethane (plastic) condoms protect against HIV, STDs (see Page 148), and pregnancy, but break more easily than latex ones. Natural (lambskin) condoms do not provide protection against HIV. It doesn't matter whether your penis is going inside someone else or his penis is entering you. HIV and other STDs go both ways.

Use a water-based lubricant (lube), such as K-Y Jelly. There are many other brands available. Oil-based skin lotions, cooking oil, Vaseline, Crisco, butter – anything oily – can cause condoms to break. Medications used to treat problems in your anus or vagina (such as suppositories for fungal infections or creams for hemorrhoids) can also damage condoms.

Put a drop of lube inside the tip before you put the condom on. Place the condom on the penis with the tip sticking out. Press the tip so that there are no air bubbles in it. Unroll the condom to the base of the penis. If you're having anal sex (putting a penis in someone's anus), make sure the condom is always slicked up with lots of water-based lube, such as K-Y jelly, so that the penis can enter smoothly and the condom isn't likely to slide off. If you want to be really careful, use an extra strong condom. If one partner is allergic to latex, use a "natural" (lambskin) condom and a latex one, keeping the natural one next to the penis, vagina, or anus of the allergic person. (A polyurethane condom can be used instead of the natural condom.)

When you're finished having sex, take the condom off while the penis is still hard. Hold the open end of the condom while the penis comes out to prevent any semen from leaking out. Throw the condom out. Never use a condom more than once.

All condom packages should carry an expiry date. Throw them away if the date has passed. Never store condoms in direct sunlight or in places that are very hot or cold.

Some safer sex pamphlets suggest using condoms or lubes that contain a spermicide (something that kills sperm for birth control purposes) called nonoxynol-9. Studies have shown that, although nonoxynol-9 may give you some protection against sexually transmitted diseases, it doesn't appear to lower the risk of passing on HIV. And it can cause irritation in your vagina or anus. This could actually increase the chances of a germ getting into your body. So it's probably best to avoid it. (The best way to test whether you're going to have an allergic reaction to a spermicide or cream is to test it first on the skin of the inside of your wrist.)

Women who have sex with men can protect themselves from pregnancy with contraceptives (birth control pills, spermicides, etc.), but until recently had no way of protecting themselves against sexually transmitted diseases and HIV, except by convincing their sexual partners to wear condoms. If your partner refuses to use a condom, you can refuse to have his penis inside you.

A condom for women (made of polyurethane, and sometimes called a "female condom") has recently been developed which gives women a new option for protection. It's shaped like a large condom and has two flexible rings, one on the top and one on the bottom (where it's open). The top ring is inserted into your vagina and covers your cervix (much like a diaphragm). The bottom ring remains outside your vagina. It can be inserted minutes or hours before intercourse.

It's important to note that this is a new product. It's known that the polyurethane does not allow HIV to get through. Early studies to see if this method protects against pregnancy show that it works as well as regular condoms.

Some safer sex pamphlets suggest using a vinegar douche (squirting watered-down vinegar into your vagina or anus) if you have sex without a condom or if the condom breaks. However, a douche (of any kind) may actually spread the virus and irritate your mucous membranes (skin lining your vagina or rectum [the inside of your ass]).

Oral sex

There's been a lot of debate about oral sex (going down, or licking or sucking someone's genitals; or rimming – licking someone's anus [asshole]) and how risky it is in terms of spreading HIV. The main risk in oral sex is passing on other STDs (see Page 148), hepatitis (see Page 134), and parasites (see Page 159). Oral sex is considered low risk for transmitting HIV. If you want to play as safely as possible, you or your partner could put a condom on the penis, or cover the labia (cunt lips) or asshole with a dental dam (one of the little rubber squares that your dentist uses) or plastic wrap (use the non-microwavable kind). Or, use a condom in the following way: first cut the top off, then cut the condom lengthwise, then open it up. Safer sex guidelines suggest using a non-lubricated condom for oral sex. If you don't use a condom, dental dam, or plastic wrap for oral sex, don't brush your teeth beforehand, since this can cause tiny cuts in the lining of your mouth. If you don't use a condom when someone else is going down on you, try to urinate (pee) as soon as possible after sex.

Sex toys

Dildos and other sex toys can be part of safer sex. You just have to make sure that you keep them clean. Wash them with soap and water before and after you use them. Better yet, use warm water and a little bit of bleach, and then rinse really well. Or, if you don't want to bother with all that running to the bathroom, use condoms on your toys, or wrap them in non-microwaveable plastic wrap. Don't use your sex toy in one person's body and then put it into someone else's without changing the condom or plastic. Ideally, everyone should have his or her own set of toys that are never used inside anyone else.

For everyone living with HIV/AIDS, but people with hemophilia in particular, you should be cautious of anything going into your body that might lead to hemorrhaging (heavy bleeding).

You can get more information on safer sex (and STDs – see Page 148) from your nearest AIDS group (see Page 243) or public health office. You (or you and your partner[s]) may also want to talk about sex with a counsellor. Counsellors are available at many AIDS groups.

The Canadian AIDS Society has a book called *Safer Sex Guidelines*, which you can get from the National AIDS Clearinghouse (see Page 242) or from your nearest AIDS group.

154

OPPORTUNISTIC
INFECTIONS
AND RELATED
CONDITIONS
Safer sex
• *Oral sex*
• *Sex toys*

Using street drugs

Hepatitis (see Page 134), syphilis (see Page 149), and other types of HIV can be passed from one person to another through sharing works (needles, syringes, spoons, cotton, etc.) used for shooting up (also called intravenous [IV], or injection drug use). This means injecting drugs into yourself. Germs can be spread by infected blood on a needle, in the syringe, or on any of the things used to prepare drugs for injection. The safest way to avoid spreading germs is to use a new, disposable fit (needle and syringe) every time. Needle exchange programs can provide new fits free of charge. Unfortunately, many areas of Canada do not have needle exchange programs, and some of these programs enforce a strict one-for-one policy about the number of needles and syringes they will provide.

Try not to share needles. If you do share, always clean the needle and syringe with bleach and water. Here's how:

Some needle exchange programs can give you bottles of sterile water and bleach. If these are not available, use boiled water if possible. As a last resort, use soapy water or water right out of the tap. Any brand of household bleach will do.

Step 1.   Fill the syringe completely with water. Shake and tap the syringe. Squirt out the water (**not back into the container**). **Do not reuse this water.**

Step 2.   Fill the syringe completely with **full strength bleach.** Leave the syringe with the bleach in it for at least **30 seconds.** Shake and tap the syringe. Squirt out the bleach (**not back into the container**). **Repeat Step 2 at least twice, and use new bleach each time.**

Step 3.   In order to rinse the bleach completely out of the syringe, repeat Step 1 **at least twice with new water. Do not reuse the water from the first rinse.**

Also, remember to clean your cooker (spoon, for example) with bleach and water and use a new filter (for drawing the prepared drug into the syringe) every time.

If you would like more information about injection drug use you can call a needle exchange program, if you have one in your area.

155

OPPORTUNISTIC
INFECTIONS
AND RELATED
CONDITIONS
Using street drugs

**OPPORTUNISTIC
INFECTIONS
AND RELATED
CONDITIONS**
Using street drugs
Piercing and tattoos
Constitutional
symptoms

Street drugs can make you think less clearly. Under the influence of drugs, it may not seem so important to avoid sharing works, or to practise safer sex. Anything that makes you think less clearly can put you at risk, including alcohol, amyl nitrate (poppers), marijuana (pot), barbiturates (downers), amphetamines (speed), cocaine (coke), and crack (smokable cocaine – crack can also cause sores in your mouth that increase the risk of getting STDs through oral sex).

There are several community groups that run needle exchanges and provide counselling. Their services are free and confidential. Some needle exchanges can be found in the section beginning on Page 243. Or you can contact your nearest AIDS group (listed in the same section).

Piercing and tattoos

You can be exposed to hepatitis (see Page 134), syphilis (see Page 149), and other types of HIV through piercing and tattooing if you share needles, tattoo guns, guitar strings, staples, or threads. Make sure the person doing the piercing or tattooing has sterilized all the equipment. If you have to share it, clean it with bleach and water first. The person doing the work should wear latex gloves.

Constitutional symptoms

There are a lot of symptoms that are "constitutional," or common to many of the conditions associated with HIV and AIDS. One thing to keep in mind is that many infections have the same symptoms. Sometimes symptoms may be caused by HIV itself. If you develop diarrhea, weight loss, headaches, or fever, talk to your doctor. He or she may want to do some tests to find the cause of the problem. Some of the common symptoms, such as fever, fatigue, and pain, are discussed briefly below. Since dealing with weight loss and diarrhea is so important in managing HIV and AIDS, the information about these conditions is more detailed.

Fever

Fever is one of the most common general symptoms that people living with HIV/AIDS may experience. Fever is one of your body's ways of fighting infection. Many of the diseases discussed in this chapter can cause fever. So can HIV infection, and some drugs. Remember, though, that often a simple cold can cause fever. Also remember that, although you may feel warm or hot when you have a fever, you can also feel very cold. Using a thermometer can help you decide the most appropriate way to treat a fever. Thermometers are inexpensive: ask your pharmacist to help you choose one and teach you how to read it accurately. If you have a mild fever, taking Aspirin (acetylsalicylic acid, or ASA for short), acetomenophen (Tylenol), or ibuprofen (Advil, Motrin IB) can help reduce it. If your temperature is quite high, or if your fever has lasted for more than 48 hours, call your doctor for advice.

Night sweats

Night sweats can occur at any time in HIV infection. They can be symptoms of opportunistic infections, like PCP (see Page 118) or MAC (see Page 106). They can also happen when your T4 cell count (see Page 27) is within the "normal range," and may be associated with lymphadenopathy (see Page 22). If you develop night sweats, let your doctor know, and include details like how long the sweats have been happening, and how often. A report of night sweats may help your doctor diagnose an infection in its early stages and offer you treatment faster. To help cope with night sweats, some people wear a T-shirt or pyjamas to bed so they can just change if they have a "light" sweat. But sometimes the sheets get so wet that you have to change the bed. You can purchase several types of pads lined with plastic or rubber to protect your bed from getting wet. You can also purchase ski underwear that moves sweat away from your skin. Wear something else over it to absorb the sweat. (Obviously, using a heavy blanket when it's hot can also make you sweat more than usual at night.)

157

OPPORTUNISTIC
INFECTIONS
AND RELATED
CONDITIONS
Constitutional
  symptoms
• *Fever*
• *Night sweats*

158

OPPORTUNISTIC
INFECTIONS
AND RELATED
CONDITIONS
Constitutional
symptoms
• *Fatigue*
• *Pain*

Fatigue

Fatigue is feeling tired or lacking energy, even if you haven't done anything to tire yourself. Like fever, fatigue can be a sign that your body is fighting infection. Almost all of the opportunistic infections and cancers associated with HIV/AIDS can make you feel tired. So can not getting enough nutrients (food) to satisfy your body's needs (see Page 88), or not sleeping well. Many of the drugs used to fight HIV and opportunistic infections can cause fatigue. Depression, stress, frustration, and other emotions can drain your energy too.

It's best to find the cause of the fatigue and take care of it. Your doctor may be able to identify the cause of the fatigue with the help of your own reports of your symptoms, a physical exam, and some tests (including checking your hemoglobin – see Page 26 – and thyroid hormone levels). Getting regular, moderate amounts of exercise can increase your general energy levels, but be careful not to tire yourself out. If you find yourself feeling tired during the day, take a nap. Getting enough sleep will give your body the break it needs. It will also make stress easier to handle.

Pain

Pain is always a sign that there's something wrong. Where you get pain, and what type of pain you have, depends on what's causing it. Sometimes the pain is all over (as when you have the flu); sometimes it's only in one place. Sometimes it feels dull (like a toothache); sometimes it's very sharp (like a stab wound). It can be throbbing (as when you hit your thumb); it can happen every few minutes (like cramps); or it can be constant. A lot of conditions can be diagnosed by the type of pain you have. Think about how you're going to describe your pain so your doctor has a better idea of how and what you're feeling. As with the other general symptoms, the best way to deal with pain is to get rid of whatever is causing it. If you can't do this, there are lots of drugs that can stop pain, from over-the-counter drugs (like Aspirin or ibuprofen) to narcotics (like morphine).

People with HIV/AIDS should avoid the use of acetaminophen (Tylenol) because it may worsen liver damage caused by hepatitis (see Page 134). As well, use of Tylenol may reduce your body's already low levels of glutathione (see Page 95).

There's no reason to live with serious pain, unless you choose to. Your doctor can help provide you with a pain management plan that will control your pain. Many people with HIV use complementary therapies (see Page 74) to deal with pain. Acupuncture (see Page 74) and meditation (see Page 81) are two popular ways to do this.

Diarrhea

OPPORTUNISTIC
INFECTIONS
AND RELATED
CONDITIONS
*Constitutional
symptoms*
• *Pain*
• *Diarrhea*

Diarrhea means having bowel movements (shitting) more often than usual and/or having watery bowel movements. For most people, it's just a nuisance; it happens for a day or two, then goes away, and they're back to normal. When you have HIV, diarrhea can be much more serious. Having diarrhea for weeks or months can leave you so weak and tired that your quality of life is greatly decreased. Diarrhea can also make you feel dependent on others and very embarrassed. If you have diarrhea for a few days in a row, you should call your doctor.

Causes of diarrhea

Many of the infections and cancers that people with HIV may get can cause diarrhea. These include cryptosporidiosis (see Page 123), MAC (see Page 106), CMV (see Page 125), isosporiasis (see Page 123), giardiasis, and infections by the bacteria *Salmonella* or *Campylobacter* (see Page 99) or *Shigella*. Parasites (tiny animals or plants that live in or on other living things) can also cause diarrhea. So can some drugs. Some people who use anti-HIV drugs report diarrhea as a side effect. Antibiotics can also cause diarrhea. And some of the drugs given to treat cancers like Kaposi's sarcoma or lymphoma can cause diarrhea. So can high doses of some vitamins and minerals.

Another cause of diarrhea is lactose intolerance: many adults can't drink milk or eat dairy products (like cheese and yogurt) because a sugar in the milk, lactose, bothers their guts. They get bloating, gas, cramps, and diarrhea. People who are very sensitive to lactose will get these symptoms even if they add just a spoonful of milk to their coffee.

If you have lactose intolerance, you can use lactase enzymes (such as those found in Lactaid) to help break down lactose (milk sugar). These are available in pill form, as drops to put in milk, or in specially processed milk. Staying away from milk products is also an option.

One reason that diarrhea can be serious is that it upsets the salt and water balance in your body. It causes electrolyte imbalances (see Page 29) and dehydration.

OPPORTUNISTIC
INFECTIONS
AND RELATED
CONDITIONS
*Constitutional
symptoms*
• *Diarrhea*

Prevention

It may not always be possible to prevent diarrhea. The most important thing is to be careful when you prepare food (see Page 97). You may decide to avoid any foods or beverages that you know are likely to give you "the runs." Some people find that adding bulk fibre (such as bran or psyllium) to their diet can reduce diarrhea. Try eating some oat bran cereal or a bran muffin each day.

Treatment

The best way to deal with diarrhea is to get rid of its cause. There are standard, effective treatments for food poisoning. Treatments for infections that cause diarrhea are described earlier in this chapter.

If a drug is causing your diarrhea, your doctor may be able to change it. Many people who can tolerate milk products (see lactose intolerance, above) find that yogurt (with live cultures), or acidophilus (in capsules – see page 93), helps with drug-induced diarrhea.

What you can do

Whether you can get rid of your diarrhea or not, you should try to reduce the amount of it. Drink plenty of fluids. Follow the advice in the Prevention section (see Page 160). What you eat may affect your diarrhea. Drink fluids such as water, Gatorade (or similar products), and chicken soup (or other clear broths). Avoid anything with Vitamin C in it, such as fruit juices or fruit. Vitamin C can irritate the lining of your guts and cause more problems. Avoid drinking alcohol, coffee, or tea. Bananas, papayas, and apple sauce can help with diarrhea. If you can't eat or drink enough to correct your salt imbalance, you may have to have fluids injected intravenously (IV, or directly into a vein).

There are drugs that slow down the action of your bowel, although they don't treat the cause of the diarrhea. The most common are loperamide (Imodium) and diphenoxylate (Lomotil). If these drugs don't work and the diarrhea continues, narcotics, such as codeine and morphine, are used, because they can cause constipation. The amount of narcotic you have to take is low, so there aren't many side effects. But these drugs can affect your mood and thinking.

Weight loss

Losing weight when you don't want to is a very common problem for people living with HIV. This can happen when not enough food is getting into your body, or your body's demand for food is too high. How well and how quickly you use food is called your metabolism. If you have a high metabolism, you use up a lot of food quickly. HIV infection almost always increases metabolism. If you get sick, your metabolism will increase even more. Physical exercise can also increase your metabolism. But even if you don't do as much physical work as you used to, your metabolism can still be very high.

If you don't use all of the food you eat, your body can store it as either fat or muscle. Food stored in your muscles is called lean body mass (LBM). Several studies have shown an increased risk of death in people who fall below 66 per cent of their normal LBM weight. LBM is created by building muscles, so exercise such as weightlifting is recommended. If you can't eat enough to provide energy for everything you have to do, the energy stored as fat or muscle will be used up.

People with HIV need lots of calories. It's good to use blender drinks (e.g., regular, soy, or rice milk blended with bananas and/or apples, plus some bottled fruit nectar) or liquid food supplements (see Page 96). Studies have shown that not getting enough calories from protein is a major problem when you're HIV positive; you may require up to twice as much protein as HIV-negative people. It's important to eat kinds of fat that are easy to digest, such as those found in vegetables, fish, and dairy products. Medium chain triglycerides (MCTs) are easily digestible fats found in coconuts and butter. It seems to be easy to get enough calories from normal amounts of carbohydrates. Starchy foods are best for this.

Everybody's weight goes up and down. Sometimes you eat more or exercise less, and you gain weight. Sometimes you eat less or work more, and you lose weight. If you lose 10 per cent (one-tenth) or more of your "normal" weight in a month or two (for example, if you normally weigh 150 pounds and you lose fifteen pounds without trying to), that's considered "significant" (serious) weight loss.

161

OPPORTUNISTIC
INFECTIONS
AND RELATED
CONDITIONS
*Constitutional
    symptoms*
• *Diarrhea*
• *Weight loss*

OPPORTUNISTIC
INFECTIONS
AND RELATED
CONDITIONS
Constitutional
symptoms
• *Weight loss*

Causes of weight loss

◆ **Diarrhea** (see Page 159) can lead to weight loss. With serious diarrhea, food goes through your gut so fast that your body can't absorb it.

◆ **Lack of appetite** can happen when food doesn't taste right, when you're depressed, when you have an upset stomach, or when you just don't feel well. Try to eat three or four meals every day. If you can't seem to eat all your food, refrigerate it for later in the day (leftovers should only be kept for a day or two). Keep your favourite foods on hand. Do moderate exercise before you eat. Try to avoid stress around meal times. Eat in pleasant surroundings, perhaps with a friend. Add cheese, butter, or cream to food, if you can tolerate dairy products. Appetite stimulants are described on Page 163.

◆ **Nausea and vomiting** are symptoms commonly seen in people who have HIV/AIDS. The causes can include many of the drugs used to fight HIV or opportunistic infections; radiation or chemotherapy for cancer; and several gut infections. Try eating more slowly. Don't force foods down, and rest after you eat. If you're nauseous in the morning, try eating melba toast, dry toast, or crackers when you first get up. If you're throwing up a lot, you have to make sure you're drinking enough liquids, particularly soups and watered-down fruit juices. Try not to eat your favourite foods at this time, since the nausea could turn you off of them.

◆ **Sores in your mouth** can be caused by infections, Kaposi's sarcoma or other cancers, and dental (teeth and gum) problems. First, try to get treatment for the infection, and go to a dentist to get teeth or gum problems taken care of. Try rinsing your mouth several times a day with warm salt water, or water with a little sodium bicarbonate (baking soda). Several alternative treatments, when used as mouthwashes, may be effective in treating mouth sores. These include aloe vera, tea tree oil, grapefruit seed extract, and food-grade hydrogen peroxide (see Pages 84 to 87 and Page 77). They may ease some of the discomfort; commercial mouthwashes may be too harsh. Use a toothbrush with soft bristles. Spicy foods or things with acid (like vinegar or lemon juice) can make your mouth hurt more.

Appetite stimulation

Many things can cause loss of appetite, including nausea, vomiting, infections, and depression. There are several ways to stimulate your appetite when you don't feel like eating. Some people have a glass of wine, or a bottle of beer, before and during their meal. Marijuana (pot) can also increase appetite.

Several drug treatments are used to stimulate appetite:

◆ **Megace** (megestrol acetate) has been approved for stimulating appetite in people with HIV. It's a female hormone that causes feelings of hunger. Studies have shown that it increases appetite and weight. However, the weight gained is mostly fat and not lean body mass (see Page 161), unless a male hormone (such as testosterone) is also used. Megace can actually reduce levels of testosterone, which is required to build lean body mass (such as muscle tissues).

◆ **Dronabinol** (Marinol, nabilone) is a drug that contains THC, which is the active ingredient in marijuana that causes "the munchies." It's also used as an anti-nausea treatment. Besides its effect on your appetite, this drug may also cause other effects usually noted with marijuana use (such as feeling high).

◆ **Thalidomide** is currently used as a treatment for oral (mouth) and anal (asshole) ulcers in AIDS. It also appears to stimulate appetite and increase weight. It is available through the Emergency Drug Release Program (see Page 170).

163

OPPORTUNISTIC
INFECTIONS
AND RELATED
CONDITIONS
*Constitutional
symptoms*
• *Weight loss*

You may also feel more like eating if you make your meals special. Invite friends over or eat peacefully alone. If you don't feel like cooking, and if you can afford it, order food in.

If your weight starts to go down steadily, keep in regular contact with your doctor and any other health professionals who work with you. It's especially important that your doctor keep track of your blood tests, paying attention to sedimentation rate (ESR), liver enzymes, and levels of potassium (see Pages 28 to 30) and albumin (a form of protein). A nutritionist who is well informed about HIV can help. Contact your nearest AIDS group (see Page 243) or the Community AIDS Treatment Information Exchange's HIV/AIDS Treatment Information Network (see Page 242) for more information.

If you feel bloated when you eat, you may want to try taking a tablet that contains a mixture of enzymes to help you digest your food (see Page 94). Also, a tablet of either betaine hydrochloride or glutamic acid hydrochloride with your meal may help.

Wasting

Wasting is very serious weight loss. You don't get enough energy from food you're eating, or from stored food, to meet the needs of your metabolism. So your body starts using up your muscle tissue. Wasting is often most visible in the face or upper chest.

Some people are naturally very thin. Just because somebody is thin does not mean he or she is wasting.

If your body can't get all the food it needs, there may be some things it won't do. It may become less able to fight HIV or other infections. It may stop letting you do the things you want to do.

Controlling wasting

Once wasting has started, it can be hard to stop. There are drug treatments that you can try: steroids and human growth hormone.

Anabolic steroids are based on the male sex hormone testosterone. They help your body build muscle tissue. The most common steroids used for wasting are Durabolin and Deca-Durabolin. They're given by injection into a muscle.

The use of steroids is very controversial. Your doctor may not want to give you a prescription for steroids, but some HIV primary care physicians (see Page 36) are willing to consider them. Steroids work best for gaining weight if you eat properly (especially lots of protein) and exercise regularly.

Human growth hormone is another drug that may help fight wasting. It does have some side effects, like headache and changes in the level of sugar in your blood, but it's generally very safe for short periods of use. Researchers don't know how well it controls wasting, but preliminary results show that it helps. Unfortunately, it's very expensive and hard to get.

Complementary treatments (see Page 74) that may help stop wasting are l-carnitine (see Page 94) and NAC (see Page 95).

Getting Treatments

Approved and unapproved treatments

Approved treatments are the ones the Canadian government says can legally be prescribed by your doctor and sold in drug stores.

This usually means that they've been tested according to government regulations. The tests are called clinical trials (see Chapter 9). Their purpose is to see how well the treatments work and whether they have any harmful effects ("side effects"). Clinical trials don't always provide accurate information about the treatments being tested. Sometimes new information is learned about a treatment after it's been tested. If a treatment meets the government's standards, it's approved. Because this process takes a long time and costs a lot, usually only large drug companies can put new treatments on the market. In Canada right now, AZT, ddI, ddC, d4T, 3TC (see Pages 64 to 67), saquinavir, ritonavir and indinavir (see Pages 69 to 70) are the only treatments that have been approved to treat HIV. The protease inhibitor nelfinavir (see Page 70), and the non-nukes delavirdine and nevirapine (see Page 68) are likely be approved in 1997.

Experimental treatments are drugs or therapies that have not yet been approved but are being tested. This includes many anti-HIV and related treatments being tested in Canada and elsewhere. It's not yet known whether these treatments are effective, whether they have any serious side effects, or what doses are best. But there is hope that one, or several, of them will help keep people with HIV healthy.

How to get approved treatments

Approved treatments (treatments listed on the Drug Formulary – see below) can be prescribed by your doctor and are available through most drug stores and hospitals. Provincial or territorial health insurance pays many of your medical costs. But it doesn't always pay for prescription treatments. Depending on what province or territory you live in, you may get a "drug card" if you receive social assistance (welfare, etc.). Some people may qualify for a drug card without collecting social assistance. If you present your drug card to your pharmacist, he or she can get the government to pay for most approved treatments. If your province or territory doesn't issue a drug card, your doctor may be able to make arrangements with a pharmacy or hospital to have treatments provided to you free of charge. If you're working and have a private insurance plan, you may be paid back for the cost of your treatments. If you're working but don't have private insurance, you'll probably have to pay for treatments yourself. Some people get treatments without having to pay, through HIV clinics (see Page 44) or treatment centres which are part of larger hospitals. A few AIDS groups have emergency funds to help people pay for medication.

The Drug Formulary and other government drug plans

People with HIV who are no longer working and who are on social assistance can get the provincial or territorial government to pay for approved treatments that are on a list called the Drug Formulary. The Formulary lists approved treatments for specific conditions. But most

166

GETTING TREATMENTS
Approved and unapproved treatments
How to get approved treatments
- *The Drug Formulary and other government drug plans*

new or experimental treatments are not on the list. And you may have to pay a deductible (a certain portion of the total cost of the treatment).

Registered status Indians (according to Bill C31 – for more information about how to qualify as a status Indian call your nearest Friendship Centre or Band Office, or regional office of Indian and Northern Affairs) may be eligible to get drugs paid for through the federal government's Non-Insured Health Benefits Program (NIHB) drug benefits list. For more information contact your regional office of Health Canada's Medical Services Branch (see Page 242 for the national number).

There is also a second list of treatments, which is called the non-formulary benefits list, or the over-the-counter (OTC) list. In order for you to get a product on this list paid for, your doctor may need to complete a non-formulary benefits or OTC form. You take this form, along with your prescription, to the pharmacy. The products on this list vary from one region to another.

Besides the Formulary and the non-formulary benefits list, in some provinces and territories there is a third category of treatments – a category that the provincial or territorial government created, which includes treatments for specific illnesses like HIV/AIDS (sometimes called a "facilitated access" list or an "exceptional drug" program). These lists vary. In order for you to get these treatments paid for, your doctor's name may need to be on a special list of doctors who are allowed to prescribe them. Most doctors dealing with people with HIV are already listed. Your doctor must put his or her College of Physicians and Surgeons registration number on the prescription. If your doctor's name isn't on the list, he or she can call the drug program of the provincial or territorial health department.

If a medication you need isn't on any of these lists, your doctor can apply to the provincial or territorial health department for it to be covered. Each province and territory has a different application procedure. Some doctors and pharmacists don't know about the facilitated access list or of the procedure for getting drugs covered if they aren't on any of the lists, so you may need to tell them to check for you. If your doctor has any questions, he or she can call the health department or your nearest AIDS group (see Page 243). Getting this kind of information can take a long time, but if you need the drug urgently the health department should respond within a few days.

GETTING TREATMENTS
How to get approved treatments
- *The Drug Formulary and other government drug plans*

GETTING
TREATMENTS
*How to get approved
treatments*
• *The Drug Formulary
and other government
drug plans*
• *Private insurance
coverage*

In addition to the specific treatments covered by the programs already mentioned, most provinces and territories have programs that cover the cost of all prescription treatments on the basis of HIV status and/or income. These programs vary and you should check with your nearest AIDS group to find out how to use them.

Very few complementary treatments (see Page 74) are covered by provincial or territorial health insurance. Many are expensive; ask the therapist if he or she has a sliding scale of fees. (This means that how much you pay depends on how much money you make or how much money you have.)

Some AIDS groups provide vitamins and supplements (see Page 92) free of charge.

If you're moving to another province or territory, you should find out in advance whether or not prescription drugs will be covered by your old provincial or territorial health insurance while you're waiting for your new health insurance. It usually takes three months for you to get health insurance from the province or territory you're moving to, so you may want to get a three-month supply of the drugs you need before you move. Also, not all provinces and territories provide the same degree of financial aid for prescription drugs, so you may want to get additional drugs before you leave.

Private insurance coverage

If you have a job, or are on long-term disability benefits from work, you may have a health coverage plan that includes drug and other treatment benefits. The insurance company will pay for all or part of the cost of treatments prescribed for you by a doctor. Usually the list of treatments that private insurance companies cover is very similar to the provincial or territorial government Drug Formulary (see Page 166). Some insurance companies will not pay for some treatments, such as Vitamin B12 (considered a treatment therapy for preventing malnutrition – see Page 88) for people with HIV, because they don't see them as drug treatments. Most complementary therapies (see Page 74) are either not covered or only partly covered by private insurance.

If you're new to a job, you may not be able to get private medical insurance because of your HIV status. If you do have private insurance through work, this may be a factor in deciding whether or not to leave your job. For more information, see Page 205.

Off-label use of drugs

The term "off-label use of drugs" refers to any use of a drug for which the drug hasn't formally been tested or approved. Often a private insurance company will not cover the costs of off-label drug use. You should speak to your doctor about this; he or she may be able to find a way to get the insurance company or the provincial or territorial government to cover the cost.

Paying for treatments yourself

If you're not on social assistance and aren't a status Indian (see Page 167), and you have no private insurance – or if the treatment you want isn't on the government Formulary or the OTC list (see Pages 166 and 167) – you may have to pay for treatments yourself. If your job doesn't provide any insurance, you must either pay for your medication (which can come to several hundred dollars a month or more), or do without. If you can't afford to buy the medication you need, call your nearest AIDS group (see Page 243) to find out about other options that may be available. The group may provide vitamins, supplements (see Page 92), and/or emergency funds, or may be able to find other ways of getting your medications covered.

HIV clinics

Certain treatments which have been approved for use by people who have HIV or AIDS, but which are still being tested, are distributed province- or territory-wide through HIV clinics (see Page 44) or centres to other hospitals and clinics. You must have a prescription for these treatments and pick them up at a hospital pharmacy or special clinic, since they aren't available at regular drug stores.

If you live in a rural area and travel to a city hospital in order to get a treatment, you may be able to arrange for a hospital closer to you to give it to you. You or your doctor can call an HIV clinic and tell them who you are and what hospital you want the treatment sent to.

GETTING
TREATMENTS
*How to get approved
treatments*
- *Off-label use of drugs*
- *Paying for treatments yourself*
- *HIV clinics*

How to get unapproved or experimental treatments

You can't get a regular prescription for unapproved or experimental treatments. But there are several ways to get these treatments, including the Emergency Drug Release Program, friends, buyers' clubs, and compassionate arms of clinical trials.

The Emergency Drug Release Program (EDRP)

This program allows your doctor to try to get experimental treatments that haven't yet been approved in Canada. According to government regulations, you can get these treatments when there's a medical emergency or when standard therapy isn't working.

Currently, your doctor applies, on your behalf, to Health Canada's Health Protection Branch (HPB) to get a particular treatment. Staff at the EDRP negotiate with the drug company directly. They authorize the drug company to release, on an emergency basis, new treatments that are not yet approved, including treatments that are being tested. Apparently, the HPB is prepared to release most treatments for HIV as long as:

◆ there is information available on what dose is safe
◆ your doctor has tried all the standard treatments and they're not working
◆ the people at the EDRP feel that your doctor knows what he or she is doing

The EDRP is making some changes. It's possible that in the future your doctor may be able to negotiate on your behalf directly with the drug company, with the government playing a monitoring role.

The EDRP gives a drug company permission to provide you with a specific amount of a treatment. But the drug company doesn't have to agree. And there's no rule about who's supposed to pay for the treatment if it is released, so it may be up to you to pay for it. This means that you may not be able to afford some treatments.

**GETTING
TREATMENTS**
*How to get
unapproved or
experimental
treatments*
• *The Emergency Drug
Release Program
(EDRP)*

Your doctor can contact the EDRP through the Bureau of Human Prescription Drugs at (613) 941-2108 or the Bureau of Biologics at (613) 975-0362 – or at (613) 941-3061, after hours – for requests for any treatment.

If you have trouble getting a treatment through the EDRP, contact the Community AIDS Treatment Information Exchange (see Page 242).

GETTING TREATMENTS
How to get unapproved or experimental treatments
- *The Emergency Drug Release Program (EDRP)*
- *Friends and buyers' clubs*
- *Compassionate access*

Friends and buyers' clubs

Many people who have HIV or AIDS feel they don't have time to wait for officials to figure out what's best for them. Some have found their own ways to get experimental treatments, such as sharing with friends. AIDS activists have worked hard to make it easier to get treatments. Many groups have networks to get certain treatments to people who have HIV or AIDS as cheaply as possible. In the USA, some private companies have been formed which sell treatments; these are called buyers' clubs. There are no buyers' clubs in Canada at this time.

Buyers' clubs don't all have the same source for treatments, so if you're looking for a specific treatment, you may have to search for the right one. You have to pay for these treatments. Sometimes, in addition to getting drug treatments, you can buy vitamins and supplements (see Page 92) at very good prices. You can contact the Community AIDS Treatment Information Exchange (see Page 242) for information about buyers' clubs.

It is legal for anyone in Canada to bring in prescription treatments (a maximum three-month supply) from another country for his or her own use. You need to get a prescription and arrange everything yourself (or with help from friends).

Compassionate access

In order to find out how well a new treatment works and what bad effects it may have, researchers study the treatment in a clinical trial (see Chapter 9). Each clinical trial has rules that say who can join it and who can't. Sometimes, a trial will have an extra section or "arm," called a compassionate (or open) arm, to allow people who can't take

**GETTING
TREATMENTS**
*How to get
unapproved or
experimental
treatments*

• *Compassionate access*

part in the study to get the treatment being tested. Usually the treatment is provided free until it's approved. Generally, a compassionate arm is conducted at the same time as the Phase 3 trial (see Page 175), which means most of the side effects are known, and the treatment seems to have some benefit. Some compassionate arms use a lottery or slot system to determine who can join as well as having restrictions on who is eligible. Even if you qualify to be part of the trial, you may still not be able to join the compassionate arm. This may be because your name was not drawn in a lottery. Or it may be that the maximum number of people from the slot you were placed in (according to a set of qualifications) has already been reached.

You can find out which clinical trials have compassionate arms by contacting the Canadian HIV Trials Network or the Community AIDS Treatment Information Exchange (see Page 242).

Clinical Trials

What is a clinical trial?

A clinical trial is a scientific experiment, sponsored by the maker of the treatment under study or an institution like a hospital or university, in which people take a certain treatment to find out whether it's safe and whether it works. If treatments were made available without testing, there would be no information about them. Because not everything is known about a treatment when it's being tested in a clinical trial, there is some risk involved if you choose to participate in one. It's important to keep in mind that many clinical trials discover that a treatment doesn't work.

Clinical trials don't always provide completely accurate information about the treatments being tested. Sometimes the information learned from a trial proves to be inaccurate over time, or as more people use the treatment. Some clinical trials are poorly designed. So you should be cautious about how you use the information that comes from a trial.

Every treatment sold in Canada must be approved by Health Canada's Health Protection Branch (HPB). The HPB looks at the information from clinical trials to see how safe a treatment is and how well it works. If a treatment is approved by the HPB, then the company that makes it can sell it. Except in special cases (see Chapter 8), it's against the law to sell a treatment that hasn't been approved by the HPB.

When the HPB approves a treatment, that doesn't mean the treatment will work all the time for everyone. It means that it works often enough, in enough people, to make it worth trying. It doesn't mean that the treatment is totally safe, either – only that most of the dangers are known and that the benefits outweigh the risks for most people.

CLINICAL TRIALS
What is a clinical trial?
Complementary therapies and clinical trials
The phases of a clinical trial
• *Phase 1: Is the treatment safe?*

Complementary therapies and clinical trials

Clinical trials are usually not done for such complementary treatments (see Page 74) as herbs or homeopathic remedies (see Page 76), or for therapies like acupuncture (see Page 74) or massage. This is slowly starting to change, and there are a few trials involving complementary therapies. These studies tend to be smaller and have been run by hospitals, universities, or AIDS groups. In evaluating complementary therapies, you may find it useful to talk to friends who have already tried them, or to other people living with HIV or AIDS. Another possibility is to refer to alternative medical and health publications. Some AIDS groups receive such publications and/or keep files on complementary therapies.

The phases of a clinical trial

After a treatment has been tested in the lab and on animals, it's tested on people. There are four steps, or phases, of trials done with people.

Phase 1: Is the treatment safe?

A Phase 1 trial is the first time the treatment is given to people. It's meant to find out how safe the treatment is. In particular, the researchers are concerned with bad effects which might be caused by the treatment. These range from bad breath, headaches, nausea, and vomiting to more dangerous, and even life-threatening, reactions. It's important to find out how much of the treatment can be taken without causing serious side effects, as well as what side effects might appear. Everyone in a Phase 1 trial gets some of the treatment, but since these trials sometimes try to find out the best dose (amount) of the treatment, different people are sometimes given different doses.

A treatment in Phase 1 has not been tested on people at all, so very little is known about it. This makes Phase 1 trials riskier than Phase 2 trials. Phase 1 trials are usually three months long or less, and usually involve about a dozen people. As well as studying how safe a treatment is, they may also collect early information on how well it works.

Phase 2: Does it work?

If a Phase 1 trial finds that the treatment is safe enough, a Phase 2 trial is done. In this phase, more people are given the treatment to see whether it works at the dose figured out from Phase 1, and to study the effects more carefully. Researchers try to find out whether the treatment is effective; for example, does it raise your T4 cell count (see Page 27) or clear up an infection? Phase 2 trials can last from a few weeks to a few months and may involve fewer than 100 people.

Phase 3: How well does it work?

If the Phase 2 trial shows that the treatment seems to work, a Phase 3 trial is started. By this time, the researchers have information about the most common side effects and the best dose to take. In a Phase 3 trial, usually hundreds or thousands of people are given the treatment to see whether it works for most people and whether it causes problems over a longer period of time. Researchers look for rare side effects that only show up in a few people or after a few years. So Phase 3 trials may go on for several years.

175

CLINICAL TRIALS
The phases of a clinical trial
- *Phase 1: Is the treatment safe?*
- *Phase 2: Does it work?*
- *Phase 3: How well does it work?*

Combined phases

Treatments usually have to go through all three phases before they're approved by the Health Protection Branch. But phases are sometimes combined in order to answer more than one question at a time or to speed up the approval and availability of the treatment. For example, Phases 1 and 2, or Phases 2 and 3, can be combined into one trial.

Phase 4: Post-marketing trials

Researchers don't always do post-marketing trials – trials done after the medicine is available at drug stores – but these are becoming more important now that some treatments are approved earlier than in the past. They allow for more testing over a longer period of time, to see whether any problems develop over the long term.

Controlled trials

In a Phase 1 trial, you will know what treatment you're taking and how much. But in a Phase 2 or 3 trial, you probably won't. The people in these trials are divided randomly into different groups:

◆ One group, called the study group, takes the new treatment (sometimes this group will take the new treatment in combination with the approved treatment taken by the second group). There may also be a number of study groups taking the new treatment at different doses, to show which dose works best and has the fewest side effects.

◆ Another group, the control group, takes an approved treatment (such as AZT, ddI, or ddC – see Pages 64 to 66) to see how it works in comparison with the new one.

◆ Sometimes the control group takes a substance that does nothing (known as a placebo – see Page 177).

Usually no one – not even the doctors – knows who's taking what until the trial is over. This is called a double blind study.

Controlled trials are done to make sure that the treatment really works. If everyone in the trial gets the new treatment, there's no way to tell if it's the treatment making them better or if something else is doing it. They may be getting better because they're seeing a doctor regularly, or because they're eating better or taking better care of themselves. So a new treatment is compared to something else to see which is more effective.

Also, if people in the trial believe they're taking a treatment that works, they may feel better, even if the treatment doesn't work or they are receiving a placebo. (Feeling better from taking an inactive substance, or placebo, is known as the "placebo effect.") For example, in a trial to test a treatment to fight diarrhea, half the people who took the new treatment got better. But half the people who took the placebo got better, too. This means the treatment didn't work any better than the placebo.

Placebos

Placebos (see above) are still used in some Phase 2 and 3 trials. When the first AIDS-related clinical trials were done, some people received placebos and nothing else. But now that there are a number of anti-retroviral drugs which have been approved to fight HIV, this is no longer done in tests of anti-HIV treatments. If you join a trial using a new treatment to fight HIV, you should get either approved treatments or the new treatment plus approved treatments. But the trial may still use a placebo in this way:

◆ One group would get the new treatment plus approved treatments.
◆ One group would get a placebo plus approved treatments.

For some of the illnesses that people with AIDS can get, there are no approved treatments. In trials for treatments for these illnesses, a placebo may be used alone. However, the use of placebos is becoming rare.

A placebo used in a trial has to look – and be given – exactly like the treatment being tested. So if the treatment is injected into your vein for two hours, the placebo will be injected into your vein for two hours.

Many AIDS activists have questioned the use of placebos in clinical trials. They believe that it is wrong for a person to have to give up other treatments in order to participate in a trial and possibly receive no treatment for an existing infection, or to be exposed to infections that might otherwise have been prevented. This is one reason why AIDS activists fight to have treatments in clinical trials available through compassionate access (see Page 171).

Why join a trial?

CLINICAL TRIALS
Placebos
Why join a trial?
Who can join a
clinical trial

In ideal circumstances, the reason to join a clinical trial would be to help yourself and other people with HIV/AIDS find out whether a new treatment works. However, for some people, joining a clinical trial may be the only way to get free access to a treatment or diagnostic test. Although clinical trials provide access to new treatments and provide medication free of charge, you should be careful not to treat the trial as a form of care. Trials are scientific experiments and, cannot replace the care you receive from your doctor.

If you join a clinical trial to get a new treatment, you should check with trial organizers to make sure you're in the group receiving that treatment. If they can't guarantee that you will receive the treatment, you can ask to join the compassionate arm of the trial (see Page 171), if there is one. Or you can try applying to the Emergency Drug Release Program (see Page 170) instead.

Who can join a clinical trial

Every trial has strict rules about who can join, called inclusion and exclusion criteria. Inclusion criteria are what you need to have or be in order to join the trial. For example, you may need to have a T4 cell count (see Page 27) within a certain range, or be above or below a certain age. Exclusion criteria are things that will keep you out of the trial – for instance, you can't have certain illnesses or take certain treatments while in the trial.

If a particular condition is to be treated or prevented, the inclusion criteria are meant to bring in people who have or are likely to get that condition. The exclusion criteria are intended to keep out people who are at greatest risk of harm from the experimental treatment. In practice, the inclusion and exclusion criteria have sometimes been used unfairly to prevent people from participating in a clinical trial.

Pregnant women and drug users are often kept out of trials. Women may have to use birth control because the effects of an experimental treatment on a fetus are unknown, or are suspected to be harmful. Drug companies are unwilling to take the risk of being sued and therefore try to keep out women who don't use birth control. It's important that women be included in clinical trials, because women's bodies are different from men's and may require different doses and types of treatment. More research is needed on treatments for diseases like cervical dysplasia and cancer (see Page 139), which are more common and harder to treat in HIV-positive women. The relationships between HIV and cervical cancer, and HIV and PID (see Page 111), also need further research. In general, not enough is known about how AIDS develops in women and in children.

Drug users are often kept out of trials because it's hard for researchers to know what they're taking (since most street drugs are not pure). They may also be seen as unreliable and in poor health. However, more information is needed on drug use and HIV.

If you are kept out of a trial because of the inclusion or exclusion criteria, or because the trial is full, and you want access to the experimental treatment, you may consider joining the trial's compassionate arm (see Page 171) – if there is one – or getting the treatment through the Emergency Drug Release Program (see Page 170). If you're being kept out of a trial because of your age, pregnancy, drug use, or hemophilia – or for other reasons – you can talk to the organizers of the trial or to someone at the Canadian HIV Trials Network (see Page 242). You may be able to file a discrimination complaint with your provincial or territorial Human Rights Commission (see Page 243). Your nearest AIDS group (see Page 243) may also be able to help.

How to join a trial

Your doctor can refer you to a trial. But you may have to find out on your own about what trials are taking place (see Page 186). If you find a trial that interests you, the first step is to call a trial site (one of the places doing the trial), which is usually at a hospital. The staff at the site will ask questions over the phone to find out whether you would be eligible for the trial. If you're still interested, you can arrange to

CLINICAL TRIALS
*Who can join a
    clinical trial*
How to join a trial

visit the site for an interview. You may want to talk to someone who's in the trial to get more information before you go.

During the interview, you'll be asked detailed questions about your health, medical history, and any medication you're currently using. (You may want to bring notes or your medical diary.) A medical exam and some lab tests will be done. Sometimes you may be asked to come back for a second interview.

Informed consent

After the interview(s), the people running the trial will tell you if you can join it. If you can, you'll be asked to give your informed consent. You must be informed of all the risks and rules of the trial before you consent (agree) to join. The people running the trial will talk to you about what the treatment is like, what's expected of you, what the risks are, and how the trial will affect the treatment you're getting

now. They'll give you an information package which you can take home and study. You may want to discuss the trial with your friends, partner, or family. Once you and the people running the trial feel that you understand everything you need to, you'll be asked to sign an informed consent form, if you still want to join. This document should explain all the basic elements of the trial, including its risks, in clear language. If you can't understand the form very well because it's not in your language, the trial site may provide a translator to explain it to you.

Be sure that you understand and agree with everything about the trial before you sign the form, and keep a copy for yourself. Remember, you can leave the trial whenever you want. If a child is joining a trial, the child's parent or guardian will be asked to sign the form, stating that he or she understands all risks to the child.

In order for the trial to get reliable results, you must agree to follow its rules. If you can't do everything the trial asks for (like being able to make all the appointments), talk to the people running it. They may be flexible, or they may decide that it's better for you not to join the trial but to consider joining its compassionate arm (see Page 171) – if there is one – or getting the treatment through the Emergency Drug Release Program (see Page 170).

The people running the trial have the right to take you out of the trial if you break any of the rules (for example, by not keeping appointments, not taking the treatment properly, or taking part in other trials).

New information about the trial treatment may become available while you are taking part in the trial. If that happens, the people running the trial have the responsibility to let you know. If it's important information the trial may be changed or stopped.

Cost

CLINICAL TRIALS
Informed consent
Cost
The clinical trial
- *How the treatment is taken*
- *How much of the treatment to take*

Provincial or territorial health insurance and the drug manufacturer usually pay for treatments and lab tests. Remember to ask whether other costs – like time off work, transportation, or babysitting and daycare costs – are covered. Some pharmacies charge a dispensing fee for the trial medication.

The clinical trial

Every trial is different, so it's important to learn exactly what you'll have to do before you join one. Everything you have to do while you're in the trial should be carefully explained to you, including:

How the treatment is taken

- intravenous (injected into your vein)
- intramuscular (injected into your muscle)
- subcutaneous (injected under your skin)
- a pill or liquid that you swallow
- a spray you breathe in
- a cream you rub on

How much of the treatment to take

You will be told exactly how much of the treatment to take. It's important to follow the instructions.

When to take each dose

In most trials you'll take the treatment home, and you'll be told exactly when and how to take it. In other trials, you may have to have it administered at a hospital or clinic.

CLINICAL TRIALS
The clinical trial
- *When to take each dose*
- *How often you have to come to the site*
- *Trial schedules*
- *Trial rules*

How often you have to come to the site

You may have to visit the site as rarely as once a month or as often as five times a week. At first, there may be many medical check-ups to see what the treatment is doing to you. Later in the trial, there are usually fewer check-ups.

Trial schedules

You may have to wait a few days or weeks before starting to take the trial medication. This time period allows the investigators (see Page 184) to observe your health before you start. Or, you may be asked to stop taking a certain medication and wait for a certain period of time before beginning. This allows the medication you were taking to leave your body.

You may be asked to come back after the trial is over. This allows you to let the investigators know if your symptoms return or if you are having any bad effects. They can also let you know if there's any new information about the treatment.

Trial rules

Every trial has different rules. For example, you may be asked to write down information at home about your daily activities, or you may be told not to take certain treatments. And you should find out what would cause you to be asked to leave the trial.

Taking other medication

While participating in the trial, you may not be allowed to take certain medication. The trial treatment could interfere with another treatment (either or both could be made less effective, or the combination could cause a reaction in your body). Keep a list of the medication you're taking – even over-the-counter treatments like cold tablets or cough syrup – as a reference. Check with the trial organizers if you can take any medication besides the one being tested.

Seeing your own doctor

Joining a trial is not the same as getting a new doctor. Although your health will be watched at the trial site (where the trial is carried out), clinical trials are not meant to give you comprehensive (complete) health care. It's important that you have your own doctor, who knows your complete medical history, in case of an emergency. You'll need a complete examination before you join the trial, as well as your usual check-ups and lab tests while you're in it. You may have to have some of the same tests done for the trial; your doctor and the people at the site can work out a way to share results so you only have to do a test once. And your doctor or the clinic you go to can help you decide whether or not to join the trial.

What happens if you get sick

If your health gets worse while you're in the trial, the people running it will try to find out whether it's the treatment or something else that's making you sick. Treatments can have mild side effects, like headaches or stomach aches, or dangerous ones that lead to serious illness or death. If you get sick, tell the people running the trial immediately. You may be taken off the treatment and/or be given a different treatment. If the trial is comparing two treatments, you may be offered the other one. Or you may be asked to leave the trial. You can choose to leave the trial at any time.

CLINICAL TRIALS
The clinical trial
- *Taking other medication*

Seeing your own doctor

What happens if you get sick

It's important to get the phone number of a doctor or nurse who's working with the trial who you can call at any time of the night or day, in case of emergency. If you get sick in the middle of the night, doctors in an emergency room may not know what to do, because the treatments in trials are experimental.

The principal investigator

The person in charge of the clinical trial is usually a doctor, and is called the principal investigator. He or she usually has a team of doctors (called co-investigators) and nurses at each site who do the medical exams and blood tests, etc.

The plan for the trial is called a protocol; it explains exactly how the trial will be run. If you don't qualify for a trial or if you're asked to leave because of another condition, you, or your doctor, can ask the principal investigator for an exception. This means that you may be allowed to be in the trial even if you don't exactly fit the requirements.

How your rights are protected

In the past, people in trials were not always treated properly, and some were even allowed to get sick when they should have been given treatment. To keep this sort of thing from happening, every institution that does medical research on people should have an Ethics Review Board (ERB – sometimes called a Research Ethics Board, or REB). ERBs work under guidelines put out by the Medical Research Council. The ERB is made up of scientists, doctors, and members of the public from different backgrounds, who are supposed to protect the rights and interests of the people in a trial. They must approve any trial being done by an institution, and review it every few months. They can stop a trial that doesn't do what it promised or one that might harm people. You can complain to the ERB if you think there's a problem with a clinical trial. The people running the trial will tell you how to contact the ERB. The Canadian HIV Trials Network (see Page 242) has a National Ethics Review Committee (NERC) which provides an ethics review for HIV primary care physicians (see Page 36) who enter

CLINICAL TRIALS
What happens if you get sick
The principal investigator
How your rights are protected

patients into a trial. It's important for people living with HIV/AIDS to be included on ERBs. Some trials also have data and safety management committees which keep an eye on how the trial is going.

Some trials in Canada are carried out under the Guidelines on Good Clinical Practices put out by the U.S. Food and Drug Administration (FDA).

If you have problems with a trial, you can complain to the people in charge of the trial, to the Patient Representative of the hospital where the trial is being done, or to your nearest AIDS group (see Page 243).

Leaving the trial

You can choose to leave a trial at any time, and this should not affect the care you get at the hospital or clinic in the future. If you get sick because of the treatment and are taken out of the trial, the people running the trial must make sure your medical needs are taken care of.

When a trial ends, you may have an "exit interview." If you didn't know which treatment you were taking, you may (if the study is "unblinded" at this point – see Page 176) be told during this interview. If the trial ends early because the treatment didn't work or was too dangerous, you should be told.

In some trials, people are told they can keep taking the treatment, or are offered the real treatment if on a placebo (see Page 177), after the trial is over. In the past, people who have been promised treatments sometimes didn't get them. And there is no guarantee that the treatment tested in the trial will remain available.

People enter a trial at different times, so that when one person has finished a trial lasting two years, another may still have months to go. Since the trial isn't over until everyone has finished, you may not find out what treatment you were getting until some time after you've finished it.

CLINICAL TRIALS
*How your rights are
protected*
Leaving the trial

Problems you could run into

◆ The treatment could be unsafe or have bad side effects. It could cause permanent damage to your body.
◆ If you're a clinic patient, you may have to go to another hospital or clinic, or find your own doctor, in order to participate in the trial.
◆ You may be asked to stop taking other treatments that are helping you.
◆ You may have to stay in the hospital.

How to decide

The decision of whether to join a trial is a personal one. No one should push you to enter a trial.

All trials are risky. It's important to consider the possible risks to yourself and compare them with the possible benefits, both to you and the community.

The best way to decide is to ask as many questions as you can. You can talk to your doctor. You can ask another doctor for an opinion. But remember: it's up to you whether you apply to join a trial. It's up to the researchers whether they take you.

Talk to your friends, to the people running the trial, and to people at AIDS organizations. If you know people who are in the trial or in another trial, talk to them. The more information you have, the better able you'll be to make a good decision.

How to find a clinical trial

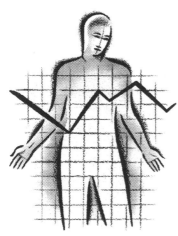

Clinical trials are carried out all over Canada. The Canadian HIV Trials Network has been set up to help people get information about trials across the country; it produces a directory of trials. For information, you or your doctor can call 1-800-661-4664, toll free.

Not all trials take place under the Canadian HIV Trials Network, so it's worth your while to talk to your doctor or to someone at the HIV/AIDS Treatment Information Network of

186

CLINICAL TRIALS
Problems you could run into
How to decide
How to find a clinical trial

the Community AIDS Treatment Information Exchange (CATIE – see Page 242) to make sure you know about all the trials that are available. Voices of Positive Women (see Page 254) publishes a pamphlet about women and clinical trials called *HIV/AIDS Research and Women*.

The information in this chapter comes from AIDS Action Now!'s booklet about clinical trials, *AIDS and HIV Drug Trials in Canada: What You Need to Know*. Its checklist of questions is very helpful if you want to join a clinical trial. You can get a copy by calling CATIE or AIDS Action Now!. Your nearest AIDS group may also have a copy or be able to get you one. The Canadian AIDS Society and the Canadian HIV Trials Network are producing an updated version of this publication, called *Clinical Trials: What You Need to Know*. All of these organizations arc listed at the back of this book (the list begins on Page 241).

CLINICAL TRIALS
How to find a clinical trial

Practical Matters

WHETHER YOU'RE WORKING, how much money you have, the kind of housing available to you, and other aspects of your social situation can affect your health.

Work

If you're working, there are many factors to take into account in deciding whether or not to stay in your job. You'll have to think about your financial situation and your emotional and physical health. You will probably find yourself seriously considering how much you really like your job, how fulfilling it is, whether you like the people you spend most of your time with at work, and whether there's something else you'd rather be doing.

Living with HIV/AIDS will have an effect on your work, especially if you're sick. You may miss work due to illness and fatigue. It may get harder to do your job. You may feel stress because you don't want your co-workers to know you're HIV positive. You may have the added responsibility of caring for a partner or family member who is also sick.

If you receive extended medical and dental benefits through work, you may wish to stay in your job for as long as possible. If you can get a disability pension through your job, and particularly if medical and dental benefits are included, leaving work will be easier. If you don't get medical benefits or your coverage isn't enough to pay for medication, you may need to leave so you can get social assistance that provides drug coverage.

Depending on what kind of work you do, you may have little security and few health care benefits. If you're self-employed or work on a contract basis, you can't collect unemployment insurance, and you probably don't have long-term disability benefits.

It may be helpful to work out exactly what your expenses are and draw up a budget. You can decide what's most important, instead of trying to deal with everything at once. Some AIDS groups provide financial counselling, or you can get help from a social worker through your nearest hospital. Friends may also be able to help.

You might want to approach your employer about flex-time (you work the same number of hours a week as before, but it doesn't necessarily have to be from nine to five). Your employer may be flexible about your duties; for example, he or she might give you a job that's less stressful or involves less physical work. You might also be able to share jobs with other employees, or work fewer hours. If you've been working full time, you may be able to change to part time. Some employers offer job retraining so you can have a different job in the same place, or learn better ways of doing your old job. But remember that approaching your employer can be risky; it might raise concerns about your ability to do your job, or about the nature of your illness.

Reducing your work hours will mean that you earn less. Your long-term disability benefit may be based on this new reduced income. Your contributions to Unemployment Insurance (UI) benefits (see Page 193) and the Canada Pension Plan (CPP) or the Québec Pension Plan (QPP) (see Page 199) will also decrease. If you're thinking about leaving work, talk with your doctor. He or she will be required to complete various medical forms stating that you can't return to work, either temporarily or permanently. And he or she will need to have enough medical details to support you in your choice.

Money

It can be hard to make enough money when you're sick. And it's hard to stay well and feel good if you don't have enough money. Many people living with HIV/AIDS use federal, provincial/territorial, or municipal government programs, such as:

◆ Unemployment insurance benefits (federal)
◆ Social assistance/welfare (municipal and provincial)
◆ Canada pension plan (federal)
◆ Income tax credits and exemptions (federal)

Your nearest AIDS group (see Page 243) can provide information about these benefits and can advocate on your behalf. Other people living with HIV/AIDS can also help you figure out what to do.

People may try to make you feel bad about using these services. But remember, you're entitled to them. People who work in social assistance offices may not treat you very well. You have the right to be treated with dignity.

Getting assistance is complicated. There are many people to talk to and forms to fill out. Often the language used in the forms or by government workers is complicated. You may need to negotiate with more than one level of government, and there are different programs at each level. (Cutbacks make getting benefits even harder.) And you're expected to know which program is right for you. If you can, get other people to help you: friends, partners, family; staff or volunteers who work with AIDS groups; or government workers. If you're uncomfortable, take someone who is familiar with the system along with you.

Many of these programs change frequently. The information in this chapter is true at the time of the writing of this book. To get more up-to-date information, contact your nearest AIDS group.

How to get financial help

You have to apply for a particular benefit or support plan. Usually, you have to go to the office which offers the benefits you need and talk with a case worker about your financial needs. Case workers are sometimes called "counsellors" or "intake workers." They'll tell you about the benefits you can apply for, and will let you know if you can get

192

**PRACTICAL
MATTERS**
Money
* *How to get
  financial help*
  * *Appealing a
    decision*

them. Sometimes you have to really work to get information out of these workers. This is due to government cutbacks and the pressure that these workers are under to save the government money. If you can't go out, a case worker might come to your home.

You'll need to fill out forms in order to apply for benefits. Do this carefully, and get help from a friend, worker, or someone at your nearest AIDS group (see Page 243) if you need it. If you make a mistake or leave something out, it can delay the process. Usually there are also forms for medical reports. If possible, see a doctor who is knowledgeable about HIV/AIDS. He or she will know how to fill out the medical report and can give you advice.

After you fill out the forms, you may have to wait to find out what will be decided. If you need money sooner, some benefits can be made available within a week. If you need emergency assistance, such as somewhere to sleep, or a meal, you can usually get help right away.

Appealing a decision

If your application is rejected, you can appeal that decision. This means you don't agree with the decision, so you ask for your case to be looked at again. You will have to fill out an appeal form. The appeal process is complicated and is different for each program, so get help. In addition to your case worker, you can contact your nearest AIDS group (see Page 243), or a group such as legal aid or a legal services society, to find someone who will work with you through your appeal. Often you have a limited amount of time to make an appeal. It's important to appeal, because many people who are turned down at first have appealed the decision and won. You may also be eligible for interim assistance during this period. You may need to ask or apply specifically for this.

Generally, to appeal the decision you must:

◆ tell your worker you want to appeal and get an appeal form; the worker should put down why your application was turned down

◆ complete your part of the appeal form (an advocate can help you); you'll need to state why you're appealing the decision

◆ include any updated medical information from your doctor if this will help your appeal

◆ take the completed appeal form back to the appropriate office within the time limit specified

If the decision isn't changed, you can often ask for a tribunal hearing. Your case will be heard by a panel and they'll decide whether or not the correct decision was made. Many appeals have been won at this level.

Unemployment Insurance (UI) benefits

There are two kinds of benefits you can get from the Unemployment Insurance Commission (UIC):

- ◆ Regular UI benefits are paid to people who are unemployed because they were laid off or their job ended. You can collect them for up to one year, depending on how long you worked, when you last claimed UI, and the rate of unemployment in your region.
- ◆ UI illness benefits are paid to people who leave work because they get sick.

The rest of this section deals with UI illness benefits, which are the kind people with HIV/AIDS usually get. The amount you get is usually about half of what you used to make at your job.

Eligibility

To be considered eligible for UI illness benefits you must:

- ◆ have worked in insurable employment (where you were paying UI premiums)
- ◆ have worked for a minimum amount of time
- ◆ have a medical certificate signed by your doctor

The most you can get on any one illness claim is fifteen weeks per year. The number of weeks you'll get depends on the type of illness you have. Presently, UI provides fifteen weeks of illness benefits for claimants with symptomatic HIV or AIDS (see Page 22) whose doctor clearly states in the medical certificate that they can't go back to work for the full fifteen weeks. Otherwise you may have to return for medical certificates whenever asked by a UI agent.

PRACTICAL MATTERS
Money
- *Appealing a decision*
- *Unemployment Insurance (UI) benefits*
- *Eligibility*

PRACTICAL MATTERS
Money

- *Unemployment Insurance (UI) benefits*
  - *Eligibility*
  - *How to apply*

If you're collecting regular UI benefits and you become unable to work due to your health, you must report that; then you can be switched to illness benefits. If you're already collecting benefits, you've already served the two-week waiting period, so illness benefits are payable right away. And there's no waiting period if you returned to work and became ill again and did not use up the full fifteen weeks from your first claim. If you're considered eligible for group wage-loss payments, you can serve your waiting period during the last two weeks covered by your wage-loss payments. If you get paid sick leave from your employer, you may be able to skip the normal two-week waiting period.

Usually any money you make while collecting benefits reduces the amount of money you get from UI. All money you make working will be taken off your benefits. Money you get from CPP/QPP disability (see Page 199) won't be taken off, because it's not considered employment earnings. Therefore, you can collect UI benefits and CPP/QPP at the same time. Money paid by a group wage-loss insurance scheme is treated as earnings; money from individual sickness insurance is not. If you get paid sick leave from your job or money from a group wage-loss insurance plan which is less than your weekly UI benefit, you can claim the difference from UI. Any amount of benefit you get will affect the number of weeks for which you can collect UI. In some cases, you might be better off not to apply for UI illness benefits until all the sick pay from your employer or insurance runs out. That way, you get temporary financial help now, and money from UI later on. An agent at your employment centre can give you advice about when to start your claim.

How to apply

The first step in applying for UI is to pick up an application form from the closest Canada Employment and Immigration Centre, as well as a blank medical certificate, which must be filled out by your doctor. If you're too sick to visit the centre, call, write, or send someone to pick up and return your application. You'll also need a record of employment from your employer. If you can't get all the documents you need immediately, don't wait. Send in your application right away and explain why you don't have all the information. A UI agent can help you get the needed information.

If you're eligible for UI benefits, you may be eligible for some form of social assistance until you receive UI benefit payments.

Social assistance/welfare

When your UI benefits run out (or if you don't qualify for UI and have no private insurance) you can apply for social assistance (welfare). This gives you a monthly amount for living expenses. You may get a drug card or the equivalent (see Page 166) that pays for most prescription drugs. Basic eye care needs, emergency dental services, and ambulance services may also be covered.

There are different kinds of social assistance programs; usually they are for either temporary or permanent unemployment. However, many of these programs are being changed.

If you're unemployed and have little money, you can receive benefits through the social assistance plan of your province or territory. If you're judged to have a permanent disability, you'll qualify for extra money. You may also be able to get things like a special diet allowance.

Depending on where you live, you'll get a cheque from the province or territory either once a month or every two weeks.

Eligibility

Social assistance programs are intended to help people with limited or no income and very few liquid assets (things you own that can easily be turned into cash). If you're temporarily or permanently unemployed, or disabled, or if you don't make very much money, you may be eligible. The eligibility criteria (qualifications for getting assistance) may be different for each program. And each province and territory has different programs. You can contact your nearest AIDS group (see Page 243) for more information about the programs available to you.

Social assistance isn't usually available to anyone under the age of majority (or legal adulthood – this varies, but is normally eighteen or nineteen). But if you're younger than that and can't live at home, you may get social assistance directly by seeing a social worker from the provincial or territorial ministry or department responsible for social services. You can also live with a relative who can apply for "maintenance" on your behalf and also for social assistance through the province or territory, depending upon your parents' income. Another option is for you to be taken into care by the province or territory, in which case you don't get money but are cared for in a foster home, group home, or agency.

PRACTICAL
MATTERS
Money
- *Social assistance/
  welfare*
  - *Eligibility*

How to apply

Call the welfare office for your area and say you have no income and can't work because of illness. This way, the welfare worker will know he or she should start an application for disability benefits (see Page 197).

To apply for social assistance, you must take these documents to the worker:

PRACTICAL MATTERS

Money

* *Social assistance/ welfare*
  * *How to apply*
  * *Start-up benefits*

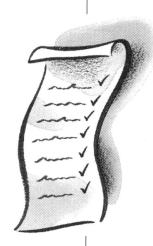

- ◆ Your birth certificate, passport, proof of Canadian citizenship, or immigrant visa
- ◆ Your health card and social insurance card
- ◆ Your lease, or the lease and a rent receipt or letter from your landlord indicating your share of the rent
- ◆ Bank statements and any other documents from financial institutions you deal with (all records for the last six months)
- ◆ Bills for municipal and school taxes, and for household insurance
- ◆ Documents concerning your belongings: car, house, etc.
- ◆ Documents that show your level of debt (credit cards, student loans, etc.)
- ◆ Pay stubs or other proofs of income over the last six months
- ◆ A medical certificate with a note from your doctor saying that you can't work because of your health
- ◆ Birth certificates and medical certificates for your partner and children, if applicable
- ◆ Any information related to a business you've owned
- ◆ Documents of all costs related to owning a home (mortgage, taxes, electricity/water/gas bills)

Start-up benefits

Start-up benefits are given to people who have been in an institution (hospital or prison) for a long time and are back in the community again. Some people have received start-up benefits after leaving an abusive partner or moving to subsidized housing for medical reasons. A doctor's letter documenting the situation will probably be needed. This money is given all at once to help you buy what you need to get started again (clothes, furniture, dishes). Provinces and territories give different amounts of money. Usually it's not very much.

Disability benefits

You can also apply for long-term benefits for people who can't work for medical reasons. Each province and territory uses a different term and looks for different things when deciding who will get disability benefits. Usually you get them for life, and qualify based on income and assets tests (how much you make and what you own). Basic medical benefits are automatically included, and bus passes (where applicable) are sometimes available at a reduced rate. Disability benefits may give you a monthly allowance. You get a drug card (see Page 166) that pays for most prescription drugs. Basic eye care needs and emergency dental services are also covered. Symptomatic HIV/AIDS (see Page 22) is considered a disability, so you may decide to apply under this category.

Eligibility

You must be between eighteen and 64 years of age, have a permanent mental or physical disability, and have little or no other income. Although symptomatic HIV/AIDS has been accepted as a disability for these benefits, getting them on these grounds is not automatic. When you apply, you'll have to show that because of the disability you need help with normal daily living, or that you have ongoing expenses for things like special diet, transportation, or other needs. You must also show that you can't be trained or retrained for regular full-time work.

You'll have to give the benefits office a report from your doctor about your health.

To qualify for these benefits, you must be considered to have both of the following:

◆ Severe disability (when you can't do ordinary things, like go grocery shopping, walk to the bus stop, keep yourself or your home clean)

◆ Prolonged disability (when your disability lasts for more than one year and will end in death).

Your doctor should write a report about things that affect your life (like your social community, education, physical and emotional problems, work history, etc.).

You will have to tell your worker about your HIV status in order to receive these benefits. The more information you can provide, the

197

PRACTICAL
MATTERS
Money
• *Disability benefits*
  • *Eligibility*

better. Bring things like updated bank books, a list of your assets (personal belongings, like a car, real estate, stereo, furniture, etc.), your rent receipts (to prove you pay rent), documents related to RRSPs or other investments, and health records or a letter from your doctor. Some provinces or territories will give you money for a couple of weeks or a month while you collect all this information.

Before you meet with your worker it may be useful to speak to a worker at your nearest AIDS group (see Page 243). Each province and territory has different rules on the kinds of assets you can have. An AIDS worker can explain these rules and give you suggestions about how to improve your chances of getting disability benefits or increase the amount you will receive.

How to apply

To apply, call the welfare office for your area. Say you have no income and can't work because of illness. A worker will come to your home and ask you about your income, living expenses, and assets. You'll be given a form to take to your doctor, who must state that you're permanently unemployable (can't ever work again). This means that you can't have any job while you're applying. If you're already on welfare, your worker may help you to apply for a disability pension. You can then collect welfare while your application is being processed. Once you start getting benefits, you stop getting welfare. You can't get both at once. If you qualify for a disability pension from the Canada Pension Plan (CPP) or the Québec Pension Plan (QPP) (see Page 199), you'll have one dollar taken off your disability benefits cheque for every dollar you get from CPP/QPP. The program expects you to call once you start getting other benefits, or if your asset level changes. If you don't, and if they find out that you're getting other money or that your assets increased, they may stop your benefits while they figure out how much you owe them, and start them up again with a monthly deduction to cover the amount owed.

It can take as long as three to five months to process an application.

198

PRACTICAL
MATTERS
Money
• *Disability benefits*
  • *Eligibility*
  • *How to apply*

Canada Pension Plan disability pension and the Québec Pension Plan (le Régime de rentes du Québec)

CPP/QPP benefits are usually paid to people who've paid into CPP/QPP and then retired. But if you've paid CPP/QPP premiums (payments you make into your pension plan) through your job for a certain amount of time and then have to stop working because of illness, you may qualify for a disability pension through CPP/QPP. There is a maximum amount available (about $850 a month), but usually you get less, depending on the premiums you were paying. The CPP/QPP also pays monthly benefits for dependent children (under the age of eighteen, or between eighteen and 25 and in full-time attendance at school, community college, or university).

Your CPP/QPP disability pension won't be affected by any other benefits you may be getting. But other benefits will go down if you get money from CPP/QPP (see Page 198).

If you've worked both inside and outside of Canada, you may be able to get at least a partial pension. You may also be able to get a partial pension from the other country.

Payments can start within six months after the date the CPP/QPP finds you to be disabled. This time period, along with the time it takes to process your application, can mean a long wait until you actually get money. So it's important to apply early. If you apply late, CPP/QPP can make up to one year of back payments.

Your payments stop:

◆ when you're no longer disabled according to CPP/QPP legislation
◆ at age 65, when your CPP/QPP retirement pension begins
◆ when you die

Any change in your condition or ability to work is re-evaluated by CPP/QPP workers to see if you can still get benefits. From time to time, they may check to see if you've become well enough to work. If CPP/QPP decides that your medical condition has improved and you haven't told them, you may have to pay back some money. As well, any attempt to work, whether full-time, part-time, or voluntary, must be reported to your CPP/QPP worker.

PRACTICAL MATTERS
Money
- *Canada Pension Plan disability pension and the Quebec Pension Plan (le Régime de rentes du Québec)*

Eligibility

To qualify for CPP/QPP disability you must:

◆ be considered disabled according to CPP/QPP legislation (according to this legislation the disability must be "severe and prolonged"; it must prevent you from doing work of any kind, and be permanent or likely to result in death)
◆ be between the ages of eighteen and 65
◆ have contributed to the CPP/QPP for a minimum number of years (at the time you become disabled, you must have paid into the CPP/QPP for two of the past three years, or five of the past ten years)
◆ be disabled within six months after the effective date of CPP/QPP retirement pension, if you're over 60

How to apply

You must apply in writing. If you can't apply on your own, someone else can do it for you. Call an Income Security Programs office for an application kit. The kit contains the information and instructions you'll need, and tells you what documents you need.

You'll need documents proving your age and your status in Canada (whether you're a citizen or landed immigrant). You'll be asked about your reason for quitting work, medications you take, future treatment you expect to need, the dates of hospital stays and the names of hospitals, and your doctor's name. You'll need to fill out a medical release form, allowing the CPP/QPP office to get information on your condition from your doctor; and a form detailing information about your former employment and education background. (See the CPP/QPP guide book.) Your doctor will have to complete a medical report. It is important to work closely with your doctor when filling out forms for CPP/QPP.

200

PRACTICAL MATTERS
Money

• *Canada Pension Plan disability pension and the Quebec Pension Plan (le Régime de rentes du Québec)*
  • *Eligibility*
  • *How to apply*

Income tax credits and exemptions

Income tax credits and exemptions are provided by the federal government to reduce the amount of taxes people with disabilities and high medical costs have to pay. They can be claimed annually when you fill out your tax return.

You may be able to claim a disability credit for the following reasons:

◆ You were severely mentally or physically impaired
◆ The impairment strongly affected your activities of daily living
◆ The impairment has lasted or is expected to last for a continuous period of at least twelve months

A disability tax credit can be claimed by:

◆ obtaining and completing a Disability Credit Certificate (you can get one from Revenue Canada)
◆ having your doctor complete a medical certificate
◆ attaching the completed form to your income tax return for the first year the claim is made

If the disability is permanent, as stated on the form, you don't have to file this form more than once, unless your circumstances change or you are advised otherwise by Revenue Canada.

You may not need all of the disability amount to reduce your federal income tax to zero. If you're supported by another person, that person may be able to claim the unused portion of your disability amount.

Under certain circumstances, your province or territory won't charge taxes on items bought to help you deal with your disability. However, many people who receive social assistance or CPP/QPP disability benefits may not be considered disabled enough for the tax credit. The strictest definition of disability is used. You'll need to talk to your doctor to see if he or she feels you are eligible.

Medical expenses

You may claim medical expenses if:

◆ they were paid for you, your spouse, or the dependents you claim
◆ they were paid in any twelve-month period ending in the year for which you're submitting your tax return and were not claimed in the previous year
◆ your total expenses are more than a specified amount or percentage of your net income, whichever is less

Allowable medical expenses:

◆ Payments to a doctor, dentist, or nurse
◆ Payments for wheelchairs, crutches, hearing aids, prescription eye glasses, and medical devices
◆ Payments for prescription drugs
◆ Premiums paid to private (non-government) health service plans
◆ In certain cases, travelling expenses (if medical treatment is not available locally)

You may not claim medical or dental expenses for which you have been or will be reimbursed (paid back). Tax regulations change each year. For more information contact Revenue Canada.

Property tax deferment

In some provinces and territories, if you're classified as having a disability, you can have the property taxes on your home deferred. The taxes are paid through a loan from the government, which must be repaid when the property is sold, or when your estate is settled (when everything you own has been distributed to your beneficiaries – see Page 205 – after you die).

PRACTICAL MATTERS

Money

• *Income tax credits and exemptions*
  • *Medical expenses*
  • *Property tax deferment*

The Federal Extraordinary Assistance Plan (EAP) and the Multi-Provincial/Territorial Assistance Program (MPTAP)

The Federal Extraordinary Assistance Plan is a one-time, tax-free benefit of $120,000, which the federal government is paying to people with hemophilia who became infected with HIV as a result of receiving blood or blood products in Canada.

Payments are made in four equal yearly amounts of $30,000. The date of the first payment depends on when your application was received, and when your eligibility is established.

Eligibility

You may be eligible if you became infected with HIV from:

◆ blood products distributed in Canada in 1978 or later to treat a blood clotting disorder (hemophilia, Von Willebrand's disease, etc.)
◆ a blood transfusion received in Canada in 1978 or later

You must be a current resident of Canada and have been a Canadian citizen or landed immigrant at the time you received the blood or blood product and became infected with HIV. You must also agree to sign a waiver protecting the federal government against court action. To apply, you must get an application form from Health Canada; call (613) 957-8266.

Qualifying for the EAP used to mean you would also be eligible for the Multi-Provincial/Territorial Assistance Program (MPTAP). The purpose of the MPTAP is to provide you (or your survivors) with financial assistance. The deadline for the MPTAP has passed, but the Canadian Hemophilia Society is trying to extend it.

Neither the principal amount of the EAP nor the money received through MPTAP is taxed, and both are exempt from social assistance calculations.

For more information call your nearest chapter of the Canadian Hemophilia Society (see Page 243).

PRACTICAL MATTERS
Money
- *Federal Extraordinary Assistance Plan (EAP) and the Multi-Provincial/Territorial Assistance Program (MPTAP)*
- *Eligibility*

Non-Insured Health Benefits Program (NIHB)

The Medical Services Branch (MSB) of Health Canada provides or arranges for the provision of Non-Insured Health Benefits (NIHB) for registered status Indians (see Page 167) and recognized Inuit. NIHB are added to the health care benefits available through provincial and territorial health care programs. The MSB will not provide or pay for health services that are provided under provincial or territorial health plans or private programs.

NIHB can include the following:

◆ Dental services
◆ Prescription drugs
◆ Medical supplies and equipment
◆ Medical transportation
◆ Vision care goods and services
◆ Professional mental health treatment

To be eligible to receive NIHB, you must be either a recognized Inuit or a registered Indian (on the official Registrar's list of Indian and Northern Affairs Canada). You must also be covered by a provincial or territorial health insurance plan. If you're registered, and have a baby, you must register him or her by the time he or she is one year old. Your baby will be covered under your registration until then. If you're in the process of registering to become a status Indian, NIHB will be paid retroactively (back dated) from the date you apply. You'll need original receipts for all eligible benefits.

Credit/debt counselling

Credit/debt counselling services are available, but differ across the country and often within provinces and territories. Contact your nearest community counselling office or AIDS group (see Page 243) to find out how to get in touch with such services.

Private insurance

Having insurance means that you have a plan, or policy (contract), for when you get sick or die. The insurance company pays for lost income or extra health care costs (such as medication, private hospital rooms, etc.) if you become sick or disabled. If you have life insurance, the insurance company will pay out money to your beneficiaries (the people who inherit from you) when you die. You pay premiums (payments you make into your insurance plan) every month or every year.

If you don't already have a private health or life insurance plan, most companies won't sell you one, because of your HIV status. Insurance companies are businesses, and don't want to lose money if you get sick and have high medical expenses which might be greater than the amount of money you'd pay into the insurance plan. Some companies may provide you with a private health insurance plan which will only cover the cost of health care not related to HIV/AIDS.

If you do approach an insurance company about health insurance, the company will ask questions about your health. If you don't tell the truth, and the insurance company later finds out, they can cancel your policy immediately. You may also lose all the money you paid in premiums.

Insurance companies can be hard to deal with. They don't always pay money when you need it. Or they may not give your beneficiaries all the money you meant to leave.

Group insurance

Some people have insurance plans through their jobs. Employers make arrangements with private insurance companies to provide drug, dental, vision, and life insurance, as well as short- and/or long-term disability plans, for their employees. Usually the employer pays all the premiums (payments made into the insurance plan) or shares the cost with the employee. You must apply in order to join a group plan, and you may be asked for information about your health, including whether you're HIV positive. You can be disqualified from some or all parts of a group insurance plan for many health conditions. People who don't know their HIV status when they join and later test positive are usually covered by these plans. People who know and admit they're positive when they apply may not be covered.

205

PRACTICAL MATTERS
Money
- *Private insurance*
- *Group insurance*

If the company you work for has lots of employees, the insurance company doesn't normally check your health before you join a group plan. They probably won't ask if you have HIV. This is because there are many people in the company who are paying in. They all contribute to the costs of payouts. If premiums go up, the amount is smaller in a large group, because the cost is spread over many people's premiums.

If the insurance company asks for information about HIV status and requires HIV testing, ask to speak with someone who works in the company's health office. They'll be familiar with all the requirements of the policy, and will know if alternatives exist. There may be circumstances under which employees aren't expected to belong to the group insurance plan. Group plan options vary from company to company; you may want to find out the specifics of the plan before becoming involved.

These plans usually cover 80 to 100 per cent of the cost of approved drugs. Dental and eye care benefits also give you coverage for all or part of your costs. Usually you have to pay for your drugs, dental work, or glasses yourself, and then put in a claim to the insurance company, asking for money back. Often there's a maximum amount you can get paid back. Certain kinds of dental work may not be covered. It is your employer who decides on the insurance plan coverage.

Talk to your personnel department, manager, or employer if you have questions about what your policy will cover, or ask if there is a booklet outlining the policy. This may be important if you need to apply for disability benefits.

If you decide to go to another job or quit working, it might be possible for you to keep the insurance plan you have by changing your group insurance to private insurance. You will not have to take any medical tests to prove eligibility. However, the company will probably charge you a higher premium.

If you're considered disabled, you may apply for a "waiver of premium." This means that, if you're approved, the insurance company can continue to insure you at no cost.

Disability insurance

There are two types of disability: short-term and long-term. Short-term disability benefits can last for up to 26 weeks, but usually only go for about seventeen weeks. You may get an amount equal to your salary, but more often you only get part of your salary; usually about 67 per cent (two-thirds). If your company doesn't provide short-term disability benefits, you may have to apply for illness benefits from UI (see Page 193). When short-term disability benefits come to an end, if you're still unable to return to work, you can apply for long-term disability benefits. However, if you know while collecting short-term benefits that you're not returning to work, you may want to start applying for long term disability, so you can avoid any gaps in income. Insurance companies usually want long-term disability claim forms at least four to six weeks before the start date of the benefit.

Long-term disability benefits can range from less than 50 per cent to more than 67 per cent of your salary. Some insurance plans provide these benefits for a limited amount of time. For example, if you worked for two years, you may be able to get two years' worth of benefits. Other insurance plans provide for long-term disability benefits until recovery, death, or age 65. To qualify, you must be considered to have a long-term, severe disability and be unable to work. The conditions and terms of private insurance plans are all different, and so is the definition of disability they use. Depending on the insurance policy, your long-term disability benefits may be reduced by the amount of any money you get from CPP/QPP (see Page 199).

You don't have to tell your employer anything about your condition in order to get this information. Even if you apply for disability benefits, your employer has no right to ask what kind of disability you have. You just need to provide a note from your doctor saying you can't work. But you'll need to provide more detailed information, including a full medical report from your doctor, to the insurance company. You will have to inform the company that you're HIV positive. It's your responsibility to provide proof of your disability.

Life insurance

The reasons for having life insurance are to leave your beneficiaries (see Page 205) money when you die and/or to get money by taking a loan from the insurance company (living benefits – see below) or selling your policy. If you have HIV or AIDS and you don't already have a regular life insurance plan, you don't have much chance of being accepted for one. Everyone has the right to apply for insurance. But most companies will ask whether you're HIV positive, or whether you've been advised to take a test but refused. You will most likely be turned down for answering yes to either of these questions.

You may have a few choices if you don't already have life insurance. Some companies offer life insurance without a medical exam. The rates are usually higher than what you pay for regular policies and they may only pay out a small amount of money if you die before a certain amount of time passes. If you're covered under a group plan at work and leave because of illness, you may be able to keep paying the premiums yourself, or apply for a waiver of premiums. A waiver means that the insurance company continues to insure you at no cost. If you start a new job that has a group plan, you probably won't have to have a medical exam.

Usually there is only one payment out from the life insurance plan, when you die. But you may be able to get money from your life insurance policy while you're still alive.

Living benefits

Some insurance companies may "lend" you money from your insurance policy. The loan is paid back with interest from the money that will go to your beneficiaries (see Page 205) when you die. This is called "living benefits," and is usually only available if your doctor has told you that you have less than one or two years to live. The insurance company will need a full medical report from your doctor confirming your condition.

If you're having problems with your insurance company because they won't pay you a "living benefit" or other benefits you feel you should get, speak to a lawyer. He or she may be able to help get them to pay you money if you need it. But this isn't always easy to do, and lawyers can be expensive. You can also contact your nearest AIDS group (see Page 243).

208

PRACTICAL MATTERS
Money
- *Life insurance*
- *Living benefits*

The Canadian Life and Health Insurance Association (see Page 242) can give you the names of companies that provide living benefits.

Viatical companies

Viatical companies or settlement firms are private businesses that will offer you money in exchange for your life insurance policy. By paying an up-front percentage (this varies from company to company and with the length of time your doctor says you have to live, but is usually around 60 per cent) of your policy's face value, these companies become the only beneficiaries (see Page 205) of your life insurance policy. And you have to pay income tax on the payment. In addition, the money you receive may affect your eligibility for social assistance. Currently, viatical settlement firms are only legal in Québec. However, if you live elsewhere in Canada, it is possible to make a viatical firm in Québec or the USA a beneficiary of your life insurance policy.

Viatical settlement firms are not insurance companies, although many standard insurance companies do provide what are called "accelerated" or "living" benefits to policy holders (see Page 208). The living benefits offered by insurance companies are usually significantly higher than those provided by viatical settlement firms.

209

PRACTICAL MATTERS
Money
- *Living benefits*
  - *Viatical companies*

Housing

Housing

One of things you may have to rethink at some point is your housing situation. Having a comfortable space to live in is important for your well-being. You might want to consider where you live, who you live with, how much you pay monthly, etc. You may need to find affordable or adequate housing because your financial situation or health changes. You may also decide to move because of concerns about such things as safety or noise, or accessibility – for example, do you have to climb a lot of stairs? Would the bathroom need to be changed to accommodate your health?

You may be able to live independently – either by yourself or with someone else – but require financial assistance. You may need help with household tasks and/or personal care (see the section on home care, Page 52). You may be unable to live on your own but not need the types of services provided by hospitals. Needs change over time.

If you live with your partner, family, or friends, you may want to discuss with them how your changing health will affect your living arrangements. You may need to find ways of balancing the support you receive from others with the desire to have quiet time for yourself.

If you need to move for financial reasons, there are several options available to you. But applying for housing can be complicated, so you may want to get someone to help you. If you have a psychiatric history or use street drugs, you may be discriminated against and denied access to housing. To read about fighting discrimination, see Page 217.

Some of the options listed below are offered in case of an emergency or as a last resort. Depending on where you live, the availability and quality of these accommodations will vary.

These are all things to think about before you actually need to move. Making arrangements in advance, while you're healthy, will decrease the stress and physical burden of moving when you're sick.

Shared housing

Shared housing usually means you have your own bedroom, but you share a kitchen, bathroom, and other living space with the other people you live with. This option is often cheaper than living on your own, but you'll have less privacy, and may not get along with your housemates.

Sometimes shared housing opportunities (or other accommodations) are posted on bulletin boards in the offices of AIDS groups (see Page 243). Talking to other people living with HIV/AIDS may also give you good hints on where to find what you want.

Housing co-operatives

Housing co-operatives provide not-for-profit housing in which members own and control the housing they live in. Rents are based on actual operating costs (what it costs to run the place) and are used to repay the mortgage and ongoing expenses of the property. Each member has a vote in the general meetings. Members volunteer to serve on committees or on the board of directors to manage the operations of the co-op. Decisions about spending money, setting out co-op goals, and creating community rules are made by the members. Membership is usually limited to residents of the co-op.

Co-op units can't be bought or sold for profit, and there's no landlord. You can stay in your unit as long as you meet the conditions set out in your occupancy agreement. In order to join a co-op, you must file an application and meet certain criteria (qualifications), which vary from one co-op to another.

Co-ops usually have a waiting list of people wishing to join, so it's important to fill in an application as soon as possible. It's best to do this before your income decreases.

Some co-ops reserve units for people with disabilities. A few are set up specifically for people with HIV/AIDS.

PRACTICAL
MATTERS
Housing
- *Housing co-operatives*
- *Subsidized housing*

Subsidized housing

If you have to live on a small amount of money, you may find it hard to find affordable housing. If you don't earn very much money and your rent is high, you'll have less to spend on other things you need. If you're in this situation, you may want to apply for subsidized housing. There are subsidized housing programs all over Canada. Housing authorities provide rent-geared-to-income housing (meaning how much you pay depends on your monthly income) for people with low incomes. More people apply for housing than they have homes for, so there are long waiting lists. Some people have to wait for a period ranging from six months to several years before they get an apartment. To decide who gets housing first, most housing authorities use a point system. They give points for health problems, disabilities, low income, and where you're living now. If you have no place to stay, or live in a place that's unhealthy for you (too crowded, bad air circulation), you get extra points. People with more points are put higher up on the waiting list.

Your doctor will be asked to complete a medical form that describes your health. People who are sicker are placed sooner. People who have been diagnosed with HIV/AIDS are higher on the list than other people. Contact your nearest AIDS group (see Page 243) for information on subsidized housing in your area.

Supportive housing

Some big cities have supportive housing for people living with HIV/ AIDS, with staff you can talk to, who can help you find services you need, and who sometimes provide medical help. In most supportive housing you have to be able to care for yourself when you move in. You have to be able to walk or get around on your own, get dressed, shop, and cook meals for yourself. If you become unable to take care of yourself, staff will help you find other housing that meets your needs. Rent is generally geared to income (see Page 211).

You must be willing to share a kitchen, a living room, and sometimes a bathroom with other people in the house. You'll be expected to help keep these rooms clean and respect the other people who live there. Living with strangers can be stressful, especially if your own health or that of the people around you is getting worse.

Recently, some apartments have been set up as supportive housing units. They are in apartment buildings that have support staff available to assist you. You'll need to discuss your needs with the staff.

To find out about housing for people living with HIV or AIDS, contact your nearest AIDS group (see Page 243).

Finding adequate housing for families where one or both partners are HIV positive can be particularly challenging. And if your partner is HIV negative he or she may not qualify to live with you. You, your partner, and/or your family may feel uncomfortable living in a home for people living with HIV/AIDS due to social stigma (see Page 3).

Hospices and nursing homes

Hospices and nursing homes are places where people who are very sick can receive 24-hour care and palliative care (see Page 46), which is given by nurses and volunteers. Space is limited and there are often waiting lists. And there are no hospices in rural areas. If you have a subsidized apartment (see Page 211), you may have to give it up if you go into a hospice. You can stay in a hospice for free.

212

PRACTICAL
MATTERS
Housing
• *Supportive housing*
• *Hospices and
  nursing homes*

Hostels and community shelters

Hostels and community shelters only provide temporary shelter. They're often full, unsafe, and dirty. You usually have to be out during working hours. Many hostels have strict rules about how long you can stay and how you behave while you're there (for example, they may not let you stay if they suspect you've been drinking or using drugs). They are a last resort if you need emergency shelter.

The YMCA/YWCA housing registry

The YMCA/YWCA housing registry is a free service which provides information and referrals to tenants, and free listings for landlords. It also provides information about social assistance programs.

In some cities the YMCA/YWCA offers cheap accommodation in residences.

Moving in with family

You may decide to move in with relatives for emotional support, or because of a decline in your health or income. If you're thinking of moving back to a rural area from a large city, you should consider the fact that you might not be able to get treatments, tests, and other forms of medical support as easily. Also, you wouldn't have the benefit of contact with many other people living with HIV/AIDS. And you might experience AIDSphobia or homophobia (fear and hatred of people with HIV/AIDS or of lesbians and gay men).

Moving in with family could be a way of stabilizing your life. Having loved ones close to you can be helpful and comforting. For some people, moving in with family may not be a matter of choice. Because of financial pressure and cutbacks to health care services, this is the only way they can get the care that they need. This may not necessarily be what either you or your family want. Be clear with them about what your needs are and when you want your privacy. Many AIDS groups provide support and counselling for families and care givers. For more information on issues related to being cared for at home, see the sections on home care and care teams (Pages 52 and 54).

213

PRACTICAL MATTERS
Housing
- *Hostels and community shelters*
- *The YMCA/YWCA housing registry*
- *Moving in with family*

Aboriginal communities

Moving to an Aboriginal community can provide social support, as well as emotional and spiritual strength. However, conditions can be difficult for people living with HIV/AIDS. Often there is no supportive housing and general housing conditions can be poor. Medical services may also be limited, depending on where the nearest hospital is. You may have to weigh the benefits of living in an Aboriginal community against the limited medical supports available.

214

PRACTICAL MATTERS
Housing
- *Aboriginal communities*

Food
- *Meal programs*
- *Food banks*

Food

Meal programs

Some agencies prepare meals and deliver them to people who can't make their own food. Usually you can either refer yourself or be referred by social service agencies, doctors, family, or friends, regardless of your income. There is a small fee for each meal, which varies from region to region. Check your telephone directory, under "Meals on Wheels." If you're on a provincial or territorial health or disability program, you may be eligible for extra money for food. Private insurance may also cover meal services. Volunteers from AIDS groups are often willing to help make and deliver meals.

Food banks

Many community agencies, including some AIDS groups, provide groceries free to people who can't afford them. Usually you're given enough groceries for a couple of days. Depending on the agency and the demand for food in your area, you can generally use these services once or twice a month. You'll need identification, and you may be asked questions about your income. If you're getting food for your family, you'll need a piece of identification for each member of your family. Most food banks can't provide food for people on special diets.

Clothing

You can often get free clothing from a local community centre or church. AIDS groups sometimes provide free clothing or money to buy clothes. In some cases, social assistance may provide a clothing allowance.

You can buy clothing cheap at second-hand clothing stores such as Goodwill and the Salvation Army.

Transportation

Some AIDS and disability groups offer transportation services. If you live in a big city and have difficulty getting around, you may be able to use public transportation for disabled people. If you're receiving disability payments, you may be able to use public transportation free, or at a discount. You may also be able to get gas tax rebates if you own or lease a car.

Legal Issues

Your rights

As a person living with HIV/AIDS you may experience discrimination, which is when someone treats you differently than they would treat someone who is HIV negative in the same situation, because of prejudice. Discrimination related to AIDS may happen because you have a visible disability, because of fear or ignorance about how HIV/AIDS is transmitted, because you're gay or assumed to be gay, or because you are or are thought to be a drug user. Discrimination is unjust, and laws have been put in place to protect people from being treated unfairly. It's important to know your rights.

Human rights legislation

The Canadian Human Rights Act and the provincial and territorial human rights codes – and the fair practices legislation in the Northwest Territories (see Page 219) – protect people living with HIV/AIDS against discrimination. They also provide protection from discrimination on a number of other grounds, including race, ethnic origin, gender, and mental and physical disability. All of Canada, except Alberta, Newfoundland, Prince Edward Island, and the Northwest Territories, forbids discrimination on the grounds of sexual orientation. Alberta and Newfoundland's codes are being interpreted as including sexual orientation, but Alberta's code is currently being challenged by the government.

The Canadian Human Rights Act is interpreted as prohibiting anti-gay discrimination. Still, in the provinces and territory that don't include sexual orientation in their codes, you can legally be discriminated against because you're gay, bisexual, or lesbian, whether or not you're HIV positive. This means you could have to prove that you were discriminated against because of your HIV status and not because of your sexual orientation.

Discrimination can take many forms. It may be direct; for example, your boss might say to you "I'm firing you from your job because I don't want to work with someone with HIV." Or it may be hidden; for example, your boss may tell you that he or she must let you go because the company is losing money and can't afford to pay all the current employees' salaries. What you may not be told is that he or she knows about your HIV status and doesn't want someone who is HIV positive working there. If you feel that you have been discriminated against (because you are HIV positive or for other reasons), you can fight back by making a formal complaint to the human rights commission in your province or territory (the Northwest Territories have no human rights code, but have fair practices legislation under which complaints can be made).

Human rights commissions have been set up under the provincial human rights codes and the Canadian Human Rights Act to help protect your legal rights. Complaints of discrimination are investigated by the commissions. The government will pay for investigating and hearing complaints.

The Canadian Human Rights Commission deals with:

◆ Services offered by the federal government or a federally controlled industry (UI, CPP [see Pages 193 and 199], banks, airlines, railways, military, federal civil services)
◆ Employment by the federal government or a federally controlled industry
◆ Housing provided by the federal government

If your complaint is not related to federal services, you can take it to the provincial or territorial human rights commission or to the fair practices office in the Northwest Territories. The human rights code of your province or territory (or the fair practices legislation) forbids certain forms of discrimination by private businesses or by provincial and municipal governments. Most cases of discrimination fall under such laws. Aboriginal people who live on-reserve come under the federal act. Those living off-reserve come under the provincial or territorial code.

If you have been discriminated against, you can get advice on whether a law has been broken, and pick up a complaint form, from the human rights commission office (or the fair practices office), or they'll send you one if you phone them. You don't have to have a lawyer or pay a fee in order to file a complaint. All inquiries are confidential.

If you file a complaint, a human rights or fair practices officer will investigate it thoroughly and submit a report. If the officer finds that you've been discriminated against, he or she will try to work things out with both parties. If this fails, an arbitration board may be appointed to hold a public hearing. If the board finds that the law has been broken, it can order the guilty person to stop discriminating and to make amends (for example, by paying you money or rehiring you).

It's illegal for anyone to try to get even with someone who's filed a complaint, given evidence, or otherwise helped with processing a complaint.

Human rights cases can take a long time. A hearing can take place within six months, but they've been known to take up to two years.

Protection from discrimination on the basis of HIV/AIDS is also provided by the Canadian Charter of Rights and Freedoms. Section 15 of the Charter provides that every individual has the right to "equal protection and equal benefit of the law" without discrimination. Like human rights legislation, the Charter protects people from discrimination on such grounds as race, ethnic origin, gender, sexual orientation, and disability.

The Charter applies to governments, so it is designed to protect you against discrimination from them. The Royal Commission on Aboriginal Peoples supports the position that the Charter protects Aboriginal people from discrimination by First Nations governments.

Human rights legislation and the Charter therefore provide protection against discrimination to all Aboriginal people in Canada, whether status or non-status (see Page 167).

Other ways to fight discrimination

There are other ways of fighting discrimination at work. The federal government has a written policy on AIDS in the workplace, which covers all federal employees. Many provinces, municipalities, unions, professional associations, and private companies have similar policies. If your company has a policy on AIDS in the workplace and you are discriminated against at work, you can complain to the personnel department or to your employer. Or you can contact your nearest Canada Employment and Immigration office or your provincial or territorial department of labour.

You can also launch a lawsuit in court, instead of filing a complaint with the provincial or territorial employment standards branch. But a lawsuit probably won't get you your job back and is usually a long and expensive process that requires you to hire a lawyer.

Your nearest community legal clinic, legal services society, or legal aid office may be able to provide you with legal assistance, even if you don't qualify for legal aid (see Page 221). Some AIDS groups also provide free legal advice or can make referrals to lawyers that specialize in HIV/AIDS-related concerns. You can also contact the Canadian HIV/AIDS Legal Network at (514) 526-1796.

If a landlord tries to evict you without legitimate cause and without giving notice as required by your lease, you may be able to delay the eviction by calling the police or taking the landlord to court.

It's hard to decide whether to fight discrimination. It may help you decide to respond if you know how you can do so. Your nearest AIDS group (see Page 243) can help.

Getting involved in AIDS activism is another way to fight discrimination. Demonstrations and lobbying can bring attention to discrimination and can help push for change.

Lawyers

Lawyers advise you of your legal rights and tell you how the law works. Also, if you need it, they will "represent" you and your case in court or in front of other decision-making groups. Generally, a lawyer acts as your advisor and advocate; he or she tells you about your legal choices and speaks for you. You hire the lawyer, and he or she takes instructions from you.

There are many reasons why you might want to see a lawyer. Maybe you've been discriminated against, or are having problems with your insurance company, or with your workplace or landlord. You can also see your lawyer to get help in completing a will, a power of attorney, or a living will (see Pages 223 to 230).

You should be able to ask your lawyer anything about your case and the law. He or she is supposed to give you good information or advise you on where to get it. Don't be afraid to ask lots of questions about your case.

If you don't have a lawyer, you may be able to find one through:

◆ word of mouth
◆ a community legal clinic
◆ a lawyer referral service or the provincial or territorial law society
◆ an AIDS group

Legal costs

Lawyers' services can be very expensive. Some lawyers charge a lower fee for people who don't have a lot of money, based on how much money you make or how much money you have. This is called sliding scale. Or a lawyer might take your case "*pro bono*" (for free), but this doesn't happen often.

Legal aid

Each province and territory offers a program of free legal services to people who can't afford lawyers. Usually this free legal service is called legal aid. Legal aid lawyers work in different areas of the law

LEGAL ISSUES
Lawyers
• *Legal costs*
  • *Legal aid*

(for example, health law or criminal law). Depending on the province or territory, legal aid may be limited to criminal matters.

Clinics

Another way you can get free legal help is through a legal clinic. Community legal clinics hire lawyers to work for people who don't have much money. Lawyers who work at a community legal clinic are paid by the clinic. See Page 243 for a list that includes legal aid head offices; you can call and ask for the telephone number of your nearest legal aid office.

Things to ask your lawyer:

◆ How much money does he or she charge per hour?
◆ Does he or she offer a "sliding scale" (see Page 221)?
◆ Can he or she give you an estimate of how much time your case will need?
◆ Will he or she take legal aid certificates?
◆ Does he or she work with student lawyers or junior lawyers (they can work on your case at a cheaper rate to keep your total costs down)?
◆ Are there any expenses you'll have to pay (faxes, court filing fees, etc.)?
◆ Does he or she have experience in the areas you need help in?
◆ What are the strong and weak points in your case?
◆ What are the chances that your case will be successful?

Planning ahead

Having HIV/AIDS doesn't mean that you will die immediately. However, planning in advance for illness and death can help you take control over your health care, your money, and your life.

There are two documents you can prepare now that will give you control over the kind of medical care you receive: a power of attorney for medical care, and a living will.

222

LEGAL ISSUES
Lawyers
• *Legal costs*
  • *Legal aid*
  • *Clinics*
Planning ahead

Medical power of attorney and living wills

Legally, you have the right to refuse treatment if you're mentally competent (able to think clearly), even if the treatment may prolong your life or cure you. However, doctors and hospitals don't all agree on what kinds of treatment you can refuse. Talk to your doctor ahead of time to make your wishes known.

If a doctor determines that you're not mentally competent to refuse or consent to a treatment, he or she must turn to a "substitute decision maker" (sometimes referred to as a proxy) to decide for you or carry out your wishes from when you were competent. If you have not named a proxy in a medical power of attorney or a living will, the doctor will usually seek consent from your next of kin – that is, your closest relative; usually your parent(s), legal (straight) spouse, grown child, or brother or sister.

A medical power of attorney (sometimes called a power of attorney for medical/personal care) or a living will (also known as an advanced directive or medical directive) is a document containing your wishes about your future health care or personal care. For example, you may not want to get certain drug treatments because they have bad side effects. You may not want to have a blood transfusion or certain medical tests done. You may want complementary therapies (see Page 74) to be explored. You may want to have treatments stopped after a period of time. You may or may not want to have medical machines hooked up to you to keep you alive (see "euthanasia," Page 226). Your instructions can be specific (for example, "no treatment for lymphoma" [see Page 141]) or general (for example, "no further treatment for any conditions after dementia [see Page 144] is diagnosed").

Because treatments are always being developed, improved, and replaced, you should keep updating your instructions. Instructions should be based on a knowledge of the medical procedures commonly used with patients who are fatally ill, and of which treatments are available at the hospitals in your area. The treatment possibilities involved are often complex. You may want to discuss these issues with your doctor or someone else who is knowledgeable and can help you tailor the document to your own health situation. A branch of the organization Dying With Dignity can also help you decide, if you're not sure. So can your nearest AIDS group (see Page 243).

223

LEGAL ISSUES
Planning ahead
• *Medical power of attorney and living wills*

To date, British Columbia, Manitoba, Newfoundland, Nova Scotia, Ontario, and Québec have passed laws recognizing living wills (Alberta and Prince Edward Island recently introduced legislation on living wills). In other provinces and territories there is no legal requirement for a doctor, or anyone else, to carry out the terms of a living will. A doctor, family member, or hospital could challenge a living will in court. Still, having a living will does indicate your wishes to the people looking after you. The more people you tell about the treatment and care decisions you've outlined in your living will, the better your chances of controlling your health care.

Your proxy should be someone you trust and who you believe would make decisions based on your instructions. Explain the kinds of decisions you want him or her to make and how you feel about different options. Make sure your wishes will be respected and that the people closest to you understand what you want. If you're concerned that your family might exclude a friend or same-sex partner from visiting you in the hospital and taking part in your care, you can name that person as your proxy. A proxy should not be a doctor or other employee of a medical facility where treatment is likely to take place. (This is against the law in many provinces.)

Other people must know that you have a medical power of attorney document or a living will, and where you keep the original. You should give copies of it to your proxy, doctor(s), lawyer, partner, trusted friends, and family members. (Have the hospital put a copy in your file.) If you discuss your instructions with these people, they'll be more likely to understand and be able to follow your wishes. Your doctor in particular is an important person to discuss the content of your living will with. He or she will let you know if it's likely to be respected. If he or she won't respect your wishes, try to find a doctor who will.

Ideally, your medical power of attorney or living will should contain both your wishes about medical care (instruction directive) and the name of the person who you want to ensure that these wishes are followed (proxy directive). However, if you don't have someone you trust to make decisions on your behalf, then you may only want to specify instructions for medical care. If you find that making decisions for a possible future illness is too difficult, then you may only want to name your proxy.

You can change your mind about your health care or other personal care decisions, or about your proxy, at any time while you are still mentally competent. If you do, you should change your medical power of attorney or living will. Re-signing these documents every so often reassures your health care providers and family and friends that what you've said is still what you want, even if there have been changes in what treatments are available. If you do change your documents, replace all copies of the old ones with copies of the new ones. You should destroy the old copies so they don't get mixed up with the new ones.

You must be of the age of majority (legal adulthood – this varies depending on which province or territory you live in) and be mentally competent in order to make a medical power of attorney or living will. You don't need a lawyer and you don't need the document notarized (certified). All you need to make these documents legal is two witnesses to your signature. The witnesses can't be related to you, can't include the people providing you with medical care, and can't be entitled to any part of your estate.

If you think your ability to make a medical power of attorney or a living will is likely to be challenged, or if it's likely that there will be disagreement about treatment between your family and your proxy, then it may be wise to have a lawyer certify your document. A lawyer can also give you specific and current information about the laws regarding medical power of attorney and living wills in your province or territory.

LEGAL ISSUES
Planning ahead
- *Medical power of attorney and living wills*
  - *A registry for living wills*

A registry for living wills

In Canada there is a "Living Wills Registry," which has a 24-hour telephone line for answering any questions you may have. For a fee, they'll send you forms to write your living will on and will register it once you send them in. They keep your living will on file and give you a card to put in your wallet, which says that you have one, in case you're in an accident or can't speak for yourself. Medical staff can call the number on the card and find out what your wishes are. Anyone in Canada can register. You can call the Living Wills Registry at (519) 273-7245. But keep in mind that registering your living will doesn't make it legally binding.

LEGAL ISSUES
Planning ahead
- *Suicide, assisted suicide, and euthanasia*
- *Enduring power of attorney*

Suicide, assisted suicide, and euthanasia

Suicide means purposely ending your life. Assisted suicide means having someone help you die, because you are physically unable to do it yourself. Euthanasia is the act of ending the life of a person who is no longer capable of functioning without life-support equipment and is incapable of deciding whether to live or to die. Some people who are very sick choose to end their lives because their physical and mental abilities have gone downhill so much. Some feel that the one thing they can control near the end is when and how they die.

It is currently illegal in Canada for anyone, including a doctor, to assist you with suicide or perform euthanasia. However, it's not illegal for you to do it yourself, and your friends can be with you. Arrange for a doctor to be nearby to officially pronounce death.

Suicide can affect your life insurance policy. Depending on the policy and how long you've had it, the benefit may be decreased or may not be given at all. If you want to read more about assisted suicide, and euthanasia, *A Gentle Death,* by Marilynne Seguin, is an excellent book on the subject. It's available at book stores and libraries. For general information on suicide, assisted suicide, and euthanasia, contact your nearest AIDS group (see Page 243) or a local chapter of Dying with Dignity. You can also talk to a doctor and/or to other people living with HIV/AIDS.

Enduring power of attorney

An enduring power of attorney (POA) is a document you sign that gives whoever you choose (your "attorney") the power to look after financial matters for you. Your attorney does not have to be a lawyer. Power of attorney allows your attorney to pay bills, operate bank accounts, pay or collect rent, and buy or sell property on your behalf if you are unable to do so.

For people living with HIV/AIDS, an enduring power of attorney can be useful. The nature of HIV/AIDS may mean that at different times you will spend periods in hospital. Also, some conditions, such as AIDS dementia (see Page 144), can prevent you from making rational decisions. At that point, it's too late to make a power of attorney. Appointing an attorney doesn't mean that you lose control of your affairs. It just means that there is someone who can look after your affairs if you can't. A doctor must first determine whether or not you are capable of making your own decisions.

You should choose someone you trust and who you know will follow your instructions. If you want to limit the attorney's powers to certain acts or certain periods, then these limitations may be written into the power of attorney document. For example, you might say that your attorney can pay your rent from your chequing account, but can't pay for anything else from that account.

In order for your POA document to be legal, it has to be written in a specific way. A lawyer can help you fill out the necessary legal papers. Lawyers and notaries charge a fee for preparing this document. If you wish, you can buy a form called a "General Power of Attorney, Short Form" from a stationery store and write up your POA yourself. You should keep a copy of your instructions and legal papers. Give the original document to your lawyer, and a copy to your attorney. This way, your attorney must go to your lawyer before he or she can start taking power over your money matters.

The kind of control your attorney has over your affairs will depend on how much power you give him or her. A general POA can be made for limited purposes, such as banking and bill paying, or you can add other responsibilities.

As long as you're mentally competent, you can cancel the power of attorney at any time. If it's never been used, you can simply destroy it. Otherwise, an enduring POA will only be ended if you cancel it, or through bankruptcy, death, or the appointment of a committee (see below).

LEGAL ISSUES
Planning ahead
- *Enduring power of attorney*
- *Committeeship*

Committeeship

If you can't manage your affairs and have not previously granted an enduring power of attorney, the court will appoint a committee (pronounced commi-TEE) to manage them for you. A committee may be one or more persons, a trust company, or the Public Trustee. It's usually appointed by a provincial or territorial supreme court judge after two doctors certify that you can't look after your affairs and/or yourself. You may fight the application either in person or by having a lawyer appear on your behalf.

As long as you're mentally competent, you may nominate whoever you want to be your committee. You can do this by completing a document called a Nomination of Committee, which must be signed in the presence of two witnesses. If you haven't nominated anyone, the court will appoint either a relative or the Public Trustee as your committee.

228

LEGAL ISSUES
Planning ahead
- *Committeeship*
- *Wills*
  - *How to write a will*

Wills

A will is a document that says what you want done with your assets (personal property) and debts (money you owe) when you die. It states your wishes about what happens to your belongings, and names whoever you want as your executor (the person who will carry out all the directions in it).

Your will should include directions for your funeral or burial if you have specific things you'd like done (see Page 233). If you are a single parent, you may want to name a legal guardian for your children under sixteen years of age and decide whether or not that person will have access to their inheritance. You might also consider setting up a trust fund for your children for educational and other purposes.

If you die without a will, you're said to have died "intestate." If this happens, your assets or estate (everything you own) will automatically be distributed amongst your nearest relatives, according to a system developed by the government. If no relatives are known or can be found, your estate will go to the government. Same-sex couples should have wills, as gay and lesbian relationships are not recognized by the government and could be contested (fought against) by family members.

You can talk to someone at your nearest AIDS group (see Page 243) about getting help writing up your will. You can also talk to a lawyer, or to someone you know who already has a will. Don't wait until you're sick; it's easier to prepare your will while you're healthy. Writing a will doesn't mean that you're ready to stop living; it only means that you want to put things in order.

How to write a will

You can write your own will, or you can hire a lawyer or notary to write it for you. If your estate is large and/or if you have large debts, a legal spouse, or legal dependents – or if your estate may be in dispute for any reason – you should have a lawyer write your will. This is the best way to make sure your will is valid and legally correct. You can call legal aid (see Page 221) for help. They might give you free advice about wills.

A lawyer or notary will write the will based on your explanation of what you want it to say. You sign the will in front of two witnesses, who then also sign it. This proves that these two people saw you sign your own will and that nobody else signed it for you or was forcing you to sign it. A witness can't be a beneficiary (see Page 205) of your will. You may ask that the will be read with no witness present, in order to keep it confidential. This is called a "formal" or "notarial" will.

If you decide to write your own will, you can fill in a standard will form that you buy at a stationery store. You can also make what is called a holograph will. It must be entirely in your own handwriting. (It can't have any printing or typing anywhere on it.) You'll have to state that this is your "last will and testament," and that no one is forcing you to write what you're writing. It must have the date on it, and must end with your signature. Your signature can be compared with the contents of your will to make sure that you are indeed the author. Because wills are very technical and have a lot of rules, it's easy for your holograph will to become invalid if you make a mistake. Holograph wills are not recognized as legal wills in every province or territory.

Before you begin to write a will, make a list of all your assets. Also make a list of what you still owe to other people or companies. If you owe money to someone when you die, it might come out of your estate before the rest is given to anyone else.

When you write a will, you should state exactly what you want to happen to everything you own. This should include a statement on where anything that you've specifically listed should go. Make sure you make it clear how you want your assets distributed. You should also name someone – called the executor (see Page 230) – who will be responsible for carrying out the instructions in the will and taking care of your estate. This should be someone you can trust to carry out your wishes. As a safeguard, you can appoint two executors, in case one is unable to act. If you don't name an executor, the Court will appoint someone (probably a relative) to administer your estate.

If there are any major changes in your circumstances, you should change your will. You can do this at any time if you are mentally competent. If you wrote out your own will, then you can make changes to it without writing the whole thing out again. But each change you make has to be done in your handwriting and you have to write your initials next to the changes. This is to make sure that nobody else takes your will and makes changes to it without you knowing. If you're making a lot of changes and your will starts to look messy or is hard to read, then you can write the whole thing over again with all the new changes. Make sure you've destroyed all the old copies. Remember to date it and sign it. If a lawyer helped you with your will, changes must be signed and witnessed in the same way as the original will was.

LEGAL ISSUES
Planning ahead
- *Wills*
  - *How to write a will*
  - *Your executor*

Your executor

Your executor is the person you've appointed to carry out the terms of your will. He or she will see that everything in the will is handled properly. The legal title of your estate (everything you own) will pass to your executor after your death. He or she will act as trustee for the heirs and beneficiaries of your estate. He or she will gather together all of your assets, pay your outstanding debts and taxes, and then distribute your money and property according to the instructions in your will. Be sure to let your executor know where you have deposited your will for safekeeping.

Anyone who is of the age of majority (legal adulthood) or older, and who is of sound mind, can be an executor. The executor can be a beneficiary (see Page 205). He or she should be someone you trust – ideally, someone who has some knowledge about business affairs. If possible, pick someone who lives in the same province as you do, to cut down on long distance phone calls and other expenses. Your spouse or partner, a friend, family member, or any of your heirs (beneficiaries) may be able to do a good job as executor. In fact, it's common practice to name your partner or main heir as executor. Be sure that the person has the time and ability to carry out the many duties of an executor. Overseeing an estate is a complex, time-consuming job, and sometimes it can include responsibilities that last for years.

After you die, your executor is responsible for making funeral arrangements, notifying your beneficiaries, giving out your assets, advertising in local newspapers if you have creditors (people you owe money to), settling debts, filing an income tax return for the last year of your life, and probating the will. (Probating means getting the courts to officially recognize the will as valid. This is important with larger estates, or where someone might try to challenge your will).

Bank accounts

After you die, personal assets, including bank accounts, are "frozen" (meaning that no money can come out). It is then the duty of your executor (if there is a will) or the administrator of the estate (if there is no will) to go over your assets and liabilities and fulfil the terms of the will (or decide what will happen to your property). Sorting all this out will take time, especially if there's no will.

If you and your partner have a joint account, when either of you dies that account will be frozen as if it were only in the name of the one who died. That could leave the survivor without funds until the will is sorted out. Rather than have that happen, you can rearrange your assets, and particularly the cash in your bank accounts, in advance.

LEGAL ISSUES
Planning ahead
- *Bank accounts*
- *Survivor benefits (CPP/QPP)*

Survivor benefits (CPP/QPP)

There are three types of survivor benefits offered by the Canada Pension Plan (CPP)/Québec Pension Plan (QPP):

- Surviving spouse's pensions
- Orphans' benefits
- Death benefit

A surviving spouse's pension is a monthly pension for the surviving spouse of a deceased contributor. A surviving spouse can be a legal or common-law spouse. A partner of the same gender does not qualify as a spouse under CPP/QPP legislation.

Orphans' benefits are flat-rate monthly benefits provided for your dependent children. To qualify for benefits, your child must be under the age of eighteen, or between eighteen and 25 and in full-time attendance at a school, university, or training program.

The death benefit is a lump-sum benefit payable to your beneficiaries (see Page 205). Your executor (see page 230), or a representative of your estate (see Page 228), should apply for the death benefit. If there is no estate, your surviving spouse, your next of kin, or the person responsible for the funeral expenses may apply.

Applications are available at most funeral homes, insurance companies, social agencies, and government offices. Some funeral services will do the paperwork for you, for a fee. Some will pay the death benefit immediately and wait the 90 to 120 days it takes the government to process a claim.

Applications for survivor benefits should be made as soon as possible after death. The benefits will be lost if they're not applied for within a year. For more information, contact your nearest Income Security Program office.

Memorials and funerals

Arranging a memorial and/or funeral is one of those things that most of us would rather not think about. It helps to remember that memorials and funerals are for the living. They give those who survive a way to celebrate your life, and a way to share grief, comfort each other, and begin to get used to their loss. You don't have to pay for your funeral right away; it can be paid after you die. Pre-planning your funeral makes things easier for the people you leave behind. Also, once you've made the arrangements, you won't have to think about them anymore. This will prevent you from having to worry about these things when you're sick. You don't have to do this planning alone; get someone else to help.

The service and the funeral can be very simple and reasonably cheap, or it can be very fancy and expensive. A simple funeral can be a very nice one. A funeral director can help you make choices which are within your budget. Don't hesitate to check out more than one option. Once you've decided on the details, ask for a contract that spells everything out. If you're on social assistance, the cost of a basic service will be covered.

In some cities you can use direct cremation and burial services, which avoids funeral homes entirely. Such services usually include:

◆ Removal from the place of death
◆ Completion of all medical and legal requirements
◆ A simple casket
◆ Transportation to the grave site or crematorium

You may also be able to buy the services of a funeral home at a reduced rate through membership in a memorial society. This is a non-profit, volunteer organization that uses collective bargaining tactics to negotiate with funeral homes for less expensive arrangements for its members, who pay a modest fee to join.

With pre-planning, you can ask to have things the way you want them. Here are some questions you may want to think about:

◆ Do you want an obituary (a death notice in the newspaper)?

◆ Will your body be cremated (burned, with the ashes put into a container called an urn), buried, or entombed (put in a tomb above ground)?

◆ Where will your body be placed? You may have a family plot where you want to be buried. Or you may choose to be cremated and leave your ashes with a spouse or partner, or have them scattered over a favourite place.

◆ How much do cemetery plots and stones cost?

◆ Where do you want your funeral to take place? Funeral services are often held in a funeral home or crematorium chapel, or in a church, synagogue, or temple. Some people have held them outdoors or at someone's house.

◆ What type of casket or urn do you want? What kind of tomb-stone or marker would you like, and what will it say?

◆ Do you want a visitation? A memorial service? A religious service? A private service? Visitations are held before funer-als. Your close friends and family gather in the funeral home, with the casket there, to receive visitors. At a memorial service, your body is not usually present. Memorial services can be led by anyone, just about anywhere you like. Religious services are usually led by a religious leader. Private services are only for those invited.

◆ Do you want an open or closed casket? (If the casket is open, that means the people at your funeral can see you.)

◆ Who will be your pallbearers? Pallbearers are the people you choose to carry the casket from the funeral home to the service, and then to the cemetery. Between four and six pall bearers can be chosen.

◆ What will you wear? Do you want to wear your finest clothes or your favourite jeans and t-shirt?

◆ Do you want flowers, or donations to a favourite charity made in your name? Or is there some other way you want people to remember you?

◆ What kind of music do you want? Do you want an organist or other musician?

◆ Do you want to be embalmed? Embalming is a process that preserves your body. The main reason for it is to allow for cosmetic work to make your body look as lifelike as possible.

LEGAL ISSUES
Planning ahead
• *Memorials and funerals*

Usually a body doesn't have to be embalmed unless it's being moved out of the province or territory. However, some provinces and territories have a rule that all bodies must be embalmed. If your casket is going to be open for visitation or during the service, your body will have to be embalmed.

Pre-paying

You can pre-arrange a service without pre-paying. Depending on what province or territory you live in, pre-paid funerals are controlled so that the majority of the pre-payment is placed in a trust and either all or some of the interest is added to the principal amount. Different regions have different rules about how much of your money is returned if you cancel your contract, depending on how long you wait to do so. Or, you could set up your own fund for funeral purposes, keeping aware of any rise in the pre-arranged costs.

A pre-paid funeral is considered a liquid asset (an asset easily turned into cash) by social assistance (see Page 195), and the value of your funeral will be added to that of all your other liquid assets. Your liquid assets must remain below a certain amount in order for you to be eligible, and continue to qualify, for social assistance.

Checklist for Managing Your Health

NOTE: Almost everything mentioned in this chapter is discussed in detail elsewhere in the book. Use the index (Page 269) to find specific references.

Things to think about

◆ Try to connect with a doctor who is well informed about HIV and AIDS. Your doctor will give you ongoing medical support and will do most of your basic blood work and keep track of your general health. How do you get along with him or her?

◆ You may want to keep a medical diary. Record any symptoms and drug side effects. Write down questions you want to ask your doctor, what tests or prescriptions you need, and any follow-up tests or appointments scheduled.

◆ Have your T4 cell count done regularly. The risk of developing some opportunistic infections increases if your T4 cell count drops. Some common opportunistic infections can be avoided with prophylactic (preventive) treatment.

◆ Get your viral load tested regularly. Consider anti-HIV combination therapy if your viral load is above 5,000 copies/ml, especially if your T4 cell count is below 500.

◆ Talk to your doctor about vaccinations which could help you avoid some infections.

◆ Look into anti-HIV treatments. Whether to take these, and when to begin them, is your decision. Information about these treatments changes constantly.

◆ Get regular dental and eye checkups.

◆ Eat well. Food gives you energy and helps your body work. If your body is strong and healthy, you have a better chance of fighting off infections, and controlling them if they happen.

◆ Talk to a nutritionist or dietitian about vitamin and mineral supplements. Consider taking a good multivitamin every day, and possibly extra Vitamin E, Vitamin C, and Vitamin A, and zinc. Talk to your doctor about getting regular doses of Vitamin B12.

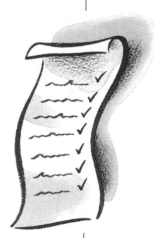

◆ Pay attention to your body's need for rest. Rest if you find yourself feeling tired during the day.

◆ Moderate exercise can help relieve depression and anxiety. It can reduce stress and help you relax, improve your digestion, and help your body take in and use more oxygen.

◆ Consider complementary therapies. Many people who have HIV have reported benefits from therapies like acupuncture, Chinese herbal medicines, and plant extracts. A naturopathic practitioner can help you make informed decisions. So can this book.

◆ Think about your living situation; your work, finances, housing, etc. If possible, make arrangements in advance while you are healthy.

Monitoring your health

There are steps you and your doctor can take to keep track of your health. This chart offers suggestions on which tests and treatments might be good for you, depending on your T4 cell count and viral load.

T4 cell count	If you are/have	Action
Any count		Find a primary care doctor and have a physical examination, including inspection of mouth and skin; blood tests, liver integrity tests, and neurological tests.
		Baseline T4 count, viral load, T8 count, T4 percentage; repeat every 6 months if over 500 T4 cells.
	Viral load greater than 5,000 copies/ml	Consider anti-HIV combination therapy.
		Baseline toxoplasmosis titre.
		HIV can interfere with the regular syphilis test (VDRL). As a precaution also have the FTA-ABS and the MHA-TP tests. If positive, treat.
		Hepatitis B antibody test. If negative, consider vaccination against hepatitis B.
		Tuberculosis PPD test. If positive, treat.
		Baseline ophthalmic eye test. Use the Amsler grid.
		Baseline dental exam; regular dental care to avoid gingivitis (inflammation of the gums) and periodontitis (weakening of the gums); if possible, have a dental exam and cleaning every 6 months.
		Consider vitamin and mineral supplements.
	If you have herpes outbreaks	Treat with acyclovir (Zovirax).

CHECKLIST FOR MANAGING YOUR HEALTH
Monitoring your health

238

**CHECKLIST FOR
MANAGING YOUR
HEALTH**
*Monitoring your
health*

T4 cell count	If you are/have	Action
	If you are a woman	Pelvic/vaginal exam every 6 months. A pelvic exam includes a Pap smear, and can detect cervical dysplasia and cancer, pelvic inflammatory disease (PID), and yeast infections, as well as sexually transmitted diseases like chlamydia and gonorrhea.
	If you have receptive anal sex (get fucked in the ass), whether you're a man or a woman	Rectal Pap smear, especially if you are at risk of getting, or have had, genital warts (HPV)
	If you're losing too much weight	Identify and treat cause; consider nutritional and supplemental therapy; try appetite stimulants.
200-500		See your doctor every 3-6 months (or as needed).
		T4/T8 percentage; Repeat every three months.
		Monitor your viral load regularly.
		Seriously consider anti-HIV combination therapy.
	If you have diagnosed mouth problems	Local treatment with mouthwash and/or complementary treatments; if severe, treat with antibiotics or antifungals.
	If you have skin problems, candidiasis, or mouth problems	See appropriate specialist.

T4 cell count	If you are/have	Action
100-200		See your doctor every 1-3 months (or as needed); treat any symptoms promptly and thoroughly.
		Monitor your viral load regularly.
		Use preventive treatment against PCP.
		Toxoplasmosis titre; test once a year.
	If you have a drop in T4 count or a rise in viral load	Switch anti-HIV combination therapy.
	If you have fevers	Identify and treat cause.
	If you have diarrhea	Identify and treat cause; treat with antidiarrheal.
Under 100		See your doctor every 1-2 months; treat any symptoms or infections promptly and thoroughly.
		Monitor your viral load regularly.
	If you have a drop in T4 count or a rise in viral load	Switch anti-HIV combination therapy.
		Continue PCP preventive treatment; consider preventive treatment for MAC, toxoplasmosis, CMV, and fungal infections.

For an updated version of the Laboratory Centre for Disease Control (LCDC) definition of AIDS call the LCDC in Ottawa at (613) 957-1777 or call the Community AIDS Treatment Information Exchange (CATIE) toll free at 1-800-263-1638.

For more information on HIV/AIDS-related treatments, contact CATIE's HIV/AIDS Treatment Information Network at the same toll-free number.

Phone Numbers of AIDS Resources

NOTE: Numbers marked with an X [×] indicate that the agency will not accept collect calls.

National agencies

Aboriginal Nurses Association of Canada	1-800-599-9066
(In Ottawa)	(613) 733-1555
Canadian AIDS Society	1-800-884-1058
(In Ottawa)	(613) 230-3580
Canadian Children With Positive Parents	(306) 652-9677
Canadian College of Naturopathic Medicine	× (416) 251-5261
Canadian Foundation for AIDS Research	
(CanFAR)	1-800-563-2873
(In Toronto)	(416) 361-6281
Canadian Hemophilia Society	1-800-668-2686
(In Montréal)	(514) 848-0503
Canadian HIV/AIDS Mentorship Program	
(CHAMP)	(416) 480-4451

Canadian HIV/AIDS Physicians Network (CHAP network)	(604) 631-5515
Canadian HIV/AIDS Legal Network	(514) 526-1796
Canadian HIV Trials Network (In Vancouver)	1-800-661-4664 (604) 631-5327
Canadian Holistic Medical Association	× (416) 485-3071
Canadian Life & Health Insurance Association	(416) 777-2221
Canadian Medical Association	× (613) 731-9321
Canadian Mental Health Association	× (905) 898-7466
Canadian National Institute for the Blind (In Toronto)	1-800-268-8818 (416) 486-2500
Canadian Naturopathic Association	× (416) 233-1043
Canadian Nurses Association	× (604) 669-1030
Canadian Palliative Care Association (In Ottawa)	1-800-668-2785 (613) 230-3343
Canadian Pediatric Society	× (613) 737-2728
Canadian Public Health Association	× (613) 725-3769
CATIE – Community AIDS Treatment Information Exchange (HIV/AIDS Treatment Information Network) (In Toronto)	1-800-263-1638 1-800-263-1638 (416) 944-1916
College of Family Physicians of Canada	× (905) 629-0900
Comité des personnes atteintes du VIH (CPAVIH)	1-800-927-2844
Emergency Drug Release Program	× (613) 941-2108
Health Canada	× (613) 957-2991
Health Canada – National Medical Services Branch	× (613) 954-7756
Health Canada – Publications Unit	× (613) 954-5995 × (613) 952-9191
HIV-T Support & Information Services	1-800-668-2686
National AIDS Clearinghouse	× (613) 725-3434
Pharmaceutical Manufacturers' Association of Canada	× (613) 727-1380

Regional agencies

British Columbia

Aboriginal issues

BC Native AIDS Awareness Project	(604) 660-2088
Healing Our Spirit – B.C. First Nations AIDS Society	× (604) 983-8774
Medical Services Branch	× (604) 666-6155
Vancouver Native Health Society (Home Outreach Project)	× (604) 254-9949

AIDS agencies

AIDS Prince George	(250) 564-1727
AIDS Prince Rupert	(250) 627-8823
AIDS Society of Kamloops	(250) 372-7585
AIDS Vancouver	(604) 687-2437
AIDS Vancouver Island	1-800-665-2437
(In Victoria)	(250) 384-4554
Asian Society for AIDS Prevention (ASAP)	(604) 681-2122
BC Coalition of People with Disabilities	1-800-663-1278
(In Vancouver)	(604) 875-0188
(TDD)	(604) 875- 8835
Black AIDS Network Society	(604) 525-3285
Grupo VIDA, Latin American AIDS Awareness Project	(604) 681-2122
Kelowna and Area AIDS Resources Education and Support	1-800-616-2437
(In Kelowna)	(250) 862-2437
Latin American AIDS Project	× (604) 255-7273
Lower Mainland Purpose Society (Youth Health & Resources Centre)	× (604) 526-0108
North Island AIDS Coalition	
Campbell River	(250) 286-9757
Comox Valley	(250) 339-6500

Pacific AIDS Resource Centre (PARC) (includes the Persons with AIDS Society of British Columbia, AIDS Vancouver, Wing House, and Positive Women's Network)	(604) 681-2122
Penticton AIDS Support Group	(250) 490-0909
Persons with AIDS Society, Victoria	1-800-434-2959
(In Victoria)	(250) 383-7494
Positive Women's Network	× (604) 681-2122
Prostitution Alternative, Counselling & Education (PACE)	(604) 872-7651
Sex Worker's Alliance of Vancouver	(604) 488-0710
Vancouver Island PWA Coalition	(250) 383-2872
West Kootenay/Boundary AIDS Network, Outreach and Support Society	1-800-421-2437
(In Castlegar)	(250) 365-2437
YouthCo AIDS Society	(604) 688-1441

Drug and alcohol issues

Alcoholics Anonymous

Vancouver	× (604) 434-3933
Victoria	× (250) 383-7744

Narcotics Anonymous

Prince George	× (250) 562-3545
Vancouver	× (604) 873-1018

Needle exchange programs

Cariboo Health Unit	× (250) 398-4600
Chilliwack: Upper Fraser Valley Health Centre	× (604) 795-3757
Courtenay: Upper Island Health Centre	× (250) 334-1141
Kamloops Society for Alcohol & Drug Services	× (604) 374-4634
Kelowna: Outreach Care Program	× (250) 868-2230
Nanaimo & Area Services for Family	× (250) 754-2773
Prince George: Native Friendship Centre	× (250) 564-1727
Quesnel: Native Friendship Centre	× (604) 992-8347
Vancouver: DEYAS Needle Exchange	× (604) 685-6561

Vernon: North Okanagan Youth & Family   × (250) 545-3572

Victoria: AIDS Vancouver Island   × (250) 384-2366

Government hotlines & other associations

British Columbia Naturopathic Association   × (604) 736-6646

Canadian Association of Nurses in AIDS Care (CANAC)   × (604) 669-1030

Canadian Hemophilia Society – BC Division   × (604) 871-4516

Canadian Mental Health Association – BC Division   × (604) 688-3236

Ministry of Health Information   1-800-665-4347

Housing & palliative care

British Columbia Hospice/Palliative Care Association   × (604) 734-4373

Langley Hospice Society   × (604) 530-1115

McLaren House Society   × (604) 669-4090

Normandy House   × (604) 261-4292

Right To Die Society of Canada   × (250) 380-1112

St. Paul's Hospital – Palliative Care Unit   × (604) 631-5060

Victoria AIDS Respite Care Society   × (250) 388-6220

Victoria Hospice Society   × (250) 370-8715

WINGS Housing Society   (604) 681-2122

Legal & financial issues

BC Council of Human Rights   × (250) 387-3710

BC Lawyer Referral Service   × (604) 687-3221

Law Society of British Columbia   × (604) 669-2553

Legal Aid/Legal Services Society of British Columbia   × (604) 660-4600

Prisoners' issues

Elizabeth Fry Society   (604) 873-5501

John Howard Society   (250) 361-1551

Spiritual issues

Living Through Loss Society   × (604) 873-5013

Treatment issues

BC Centre for Excellence (hotline for physicians treating people living with HIV/AIDS)	1-800-665-7677
(In Vancouver)	(604) 631-5515
British Columbia Children's Hospital (Oak Tree Clinic – Women and Family HIV Centre)	(604) 875-2212
Canadian HIV/AIDS Physicians Network	(604) 631-5515
Canadian HIV Trials Network National Coordination Centre	1-800-661-4644
Canadian HIV Trials Network – Regional Office	(604) 631-5036
Infectious Disease Clinic at St. Paul's Hospital	(604) 631-5060
Progressive AIDS Research and Information Society (PARIS – services complement those of AIDS Vancouver)	(604) 682-4992

PHONE NUMBERS OF AIDS RESOURCES
Regional agencies
- *British Columbia*
- *Alberta*

Alberta

Aboriginal issues

Feather of Hope Aboriginal AIDS Prevention Society	1-800-256-0459
(In Edmonton)	(403) 488-5773
Medical Services Branch	× (403) 495-5439

AIDS agencies

AIDS Calgary Awareness Association	1-800-590-8795
(In Calgary)	(403) 228-0155
AIDS Jasper: A Positive Coordinated Community Response	(403) 852-5274
AIDS Medicine Hat	(403) 527-7099
AIDS Network of Edmonton Society	(403) 488-5816
Athabasca AIDS Awareness Group	× (403) 791-0034
Banff Regional AIDS Committee	(403) 762-0690
Central Alberta AIDS Network Society	(403) 346-8858
Edmonton Persons Living with HIV Society (Living Positive)	(403) 488-5768
Lethbridge AIDS Connection Society	(403) 328-8186
South Peace AIDS Council (Grande Prairie)	× (403) 538-3388

246

Drug and alcohol issues

Alberta Alcoholism & Drug Abuse Commission
(AADAC)   × (403) 297-3071

Alcoholics Anonymous

     Calgary   × (403) 777-1212

     Edmonton   × (403) 424-5900

Narcotics Anonymous

     Calgary   × (403) 569-3427

     Edmonton   × (403) 421-4429

Needle exchange programs

     AIDS Network of Edmonton   (403) 488-5742

     Boyle Street Co-op   × (403) 424-4106

     Needleworks – Boyle McCauley Health
     Centre (Edmonton)   × (403) 422-7333

Government hotlines & other associations

Alberta AIDS/STD Information Line   1-800-772-2437

Alberta Association of
Naturopathic Practitioners   × (403) 228-1907

Alberta Government Agencies   (403) 310-0000

Canadian Hemophilia Society

     Calgary Representative   × (403) 282-0786

     Edmonton Representative   × (403) 352-4920

Canadian Mental Health Association – Alberta
Division   × (403) 482-6576

Provincial AIDS Program   × (403) 427-0836

Housing & palliative care

AGAPE Manor Hospice (palliative care)   (403) 282-6588

Kairos House (a program of Catholic Social
Services: housing for PHAs)   (403) 454-2906

Kairos II Program (a program of Catholic Social
Services: housing for HIV-positive women with
children)   (403) 473-5957

Palliative Care Association of Alberta   × (403) 352-3337

**PHONE NUMBERS
OF AIDS RESOURCES**
Regional agencies
- *Alberta*
- *Saskatchewan*

Safe House (housing for street youth
involved with prostitution)   (403) 488-3246

Society Housing AIDS Restricted Persons
(SHARP Foundation)   (403) 245-1094

Legal & financial issues

Alberta Human Rights Commission

     Calgary   × (403) 297-6571

     Edmonton   (403) 427-3116

Legal Aid Society of Alberta

     Calgary   × (403) 297-2260

     Edmonton   × (403) 427-7560

Prisoners' issues

Elizabeth Fry Society

     Calgary   (403) 294-0737

     Edmonton   (403) 421-1175

John Howard Society

     Calgary   (403) 266-4566

     Edmonton   (403) 423-4878

Spiritual issues

Interfaith Association on AIDS (Edmonton)   × (403) 448-1768

Treatment issues

Alberta Children's Provincial General Hospital   × (403) 229-7813

Canadian HIV Trials Network – Regional Office   × (403) 670-2480

Eden Valley Health Centre (Black Diamond)   × (403) 558-3656

Edmonton General Hospital   × (403) 482-8111

Pediatric Infectious Disease Clinic   × (403) 492-1680

Saskatchewan

Aboriginal issues

AIDS Regina – Aboriginal counsellors   (306) 924-8420

All Nations Hope   × (306) 924-8424

Medical Services Branch   × (306) 780-5043

AIDS agencies

AIDS Moose Jaw	(306) 693-6760
AIDS Regina Inc.	(306) 924-8420
(Facts Line)	1-800-525-0905
AIDS Saskatoon	1-800-667-6876
(In Saskatoon)	(306) 242-5005
Canadian Children with Positive Parents	(306) 652-9677
PLWA Network of Saskatchewan	1-800-266-0693
(In Saskatoon)	(306) 373-7766
Tisdale Rural Response	(306) 873-2557

Drug and alcohol issues

Alcoholics Anonymous	
Regina	✕ (306) 545-9300
Saskatoon	✕ (306) 665-6727
Narcotics Anonymous	✕ (306) 757-6600
Needle exchange programs – Health Department	
Regina	✕ (306) 777-6644
Saskatoon	✕ (306) 655-4619
	(306) 221-2442

Government hotlines & other associations

Canadian Hemophilia Society Representative	✕ (306) 933-2260
Canadian Mental Health Association – Saskatchewan Division	✕ (306) 525-9543
Saskatchewan Association of Naturopathic Physicians	✕ (306) 664-3244
Saskatchewan Provincial Government Inquiry	1-800-667-0666

Housing & palliative care

Saskatchewan Palliative Care Association	✕ (306) 359-7484

Legal & financial issues

Law Society of Saskatchewan	✕ (306) 569-8242
Legal AID Commission	✕ (306) 933-5300
Saskatchewan Human Rights Commission	✕ 1-800-667-9249
(In Regina)	(306) 933-5952

**PHONE NUMBERS
OF AIDS RESOURCES**
Regional agencies
• *Saskatchewan*

Prisoners' issues

Elizabeth Fry Society	(306) 934-4606
John Howard Society	(306) 757-6657

Treatment issues

Gay & Lesbian Health Services of Saskatoon	1-800-358-1833
(In Saskatoon)	(306) 665-1224
Prescription Drug Services Plan	1-800-667-7581
Provincial Health Council	1-800-224-7036

Manitoba

Aboriginal issues

Manitoba Aboriginal AIDS Task Force	(204) 957-1114
Medical Services Branch	✕ (204) 983-4199
West Region Tribal Council (Dauphin)	✕ (204) 638-8225

AIDS agencies

AIDS and Sexuality Peer Education Project (University of Manitoba Peer Advisor)	(204) 474-6696
AIDS Manitoba	(204) 231-2437
AIDS Shelter Coalition of Manitoba	1-800-670-6880
(In Winnipeg)	(204) 775-9173
AIDS/STD Information Line (Village Clinic)	1-800-782-2437
(In Winnipeg)	(204) 945-2437
Body Positive Coalition of Manitoba	(204) 452-7704
Brandon AIDS Support Inc.	(204) 726-4020
Facts of Life Line (Planned Parenthood)	1-800-432-1957
(In Winnipeg)	(204) 947-9222
HIV Positive Person's Support Group	
Health Sciences Centre	✕ (204) 787-3506
St. Boniface General Hospital (Pager)	✕ (204) 932-8914
Village Clinic	✕ (204) 453-0045
Manitoba Post-Secondary AIDS Project	(204) 261-8411

Drug and alcohol issues

Alcoholics Anonymous	✕ (204) 942-0126

Narcotics Anonymous × (204) 981-1730

Winnipeg Needle Exchange Program
(Street Connection) × (204) 586-1463

Government hotlines & other associations

Canadian Hemophilia Society × (204) 775-8625

Canadian Mental Health Association –
Manitoba Division × (204) 775-8888

Manitoba Association of Naturopathic
Practitioners × (204) 661-2437

Housing, home care, & palliative care

Artemis Housing Co-op Ltd.
(S.A.M. Management) × (204) 942-0991

Hospice & Palliative Care Manitoba (204) 889-8525

Kali-Shiva Society (home care, support, and
hospice) (204) 477-9506

Victorian Order of Nurses × (204) 775-0269

Legal & financial issues

Community Financial Counselling Services × (204) 989-1900

Law Society of Manitoba × (204) 942-5571

Legal Aid Manitoba × (204) 985-8500

Manitoba Human Rights Commission × (204) 945-3007

Prisoners' issues

Elizabeth Fry Society (204) 589-7335

John Howard Society (204) 775-1514

Spiritual issues

Metropolitan Community Church of Winnipeg (204) 661-2219

Pastoral care departments
  Misercordia General Hospital × (204) 788-8283
  St. Boniface General Hospital × (204) 237-2356
  Health Sciences Centre × (204) 787-3884

Rainbow Coalition (Winnipeg Presbytery,
United Church of Canada) (204) 944-8680

Sacred Journeys × (204) 284-6355

| St. Benedict's Educational Centre | × (204) 339-1705 |

Treatment issues

Fort Rouge Medical Clinic	× (204) 987-3540
Kinic	× (204) 784-4090
Misercordia General Hospital, Department of Social Work	× (204) 788-8165
Mount Carmel Clinic	× (204) 582-2311
Sandy Bay Health Centre (at Marvis)	× (204) 843-2874
Village Clinic of Winnipeg	× (204) 453-0045
Winnipeg Children's Hospital	× (204) 789-3619
Women's Health Clinic	× (204) 947-1517

Ontario

Aboriginal issues

Association of Iroquois and Allied Indians (London)	(519) 434-2761
Medical Services Branch	× (613) 952-0161
Two-Spirited People of the First Nations (Native AIDS Awareness Project)	(416) 944-9300
Union of Ontario Indians	× (705) 657-9383

AIDS agencies

Africans in Partnership Against AIDS	(416) 340-9943
African Health Services	(416) 591-7600
AIDS Action Now!	(416) 928-2206
AIDS Care Counselling Etobicoke Peel Together (ACCEPT)	(416) 394-8885
AIDS Committee of Cambridge, Kitchener/ Waterloo and Area	(519) 570-3687
AIDS Committee of Durham Region	(905) 665-0051
AIDS Committee of Guelph & Wellington County	(519) 763-2255
AIDS Committee of London	× (519) 434-1601
AIDS Committee of North Bay and Area	(705) 497-3560

AIDS Committee of Ottawa	(613) 238-5014
(The Living Room)	1-800-461-2182
(In Ottawa)	(613) 563-0851
AIDS Committee of Perth County	(519) 272-2437
AIDS Committee of Simcoe County	(705) 722-6778
AIDS Committee of Sudbury	1-800-465-2437
(In Sudbury)	(705) 688-0505
AIDS Committee of Thunder Bay	(807) 345-1516
AIDS Committee of Toronto	
(Deaf AIDS Outreach Project)	⨯ (416) 340-2437
(TTY)	(416) 340-8122
AIDS Committee of Windsor	1-800-265-4858
AIDS Memorial Committee	
(519 Community Centre)	(416) 392-6874
AIDS Niagara	1-800-773-9843
(In St. Catharines)	(905) 984-8684
Algoma AIDS Network	1-800-361-2497
(In Sault Ste. Marie)	(705) 256-2437
Alliance for South Asian AIDS Prevention	(416) 599-2727
Asian Community AIDS Services	(416) 963-4300
Black Coalition for AIDS Prevention	(416) 926-0122
Centre for Spanish Speaking People (AIDS	
Prevention Program)	(416) 925-2800
Hamilton AIDS Network	1-800-563-6919
(In Hamilton)	(905) 528-0854
HIV-T Group (provides peer support and	
information for people infected with HIV	
through blood supply)	1-800-465-4488
(In Toronto)	(416) 483-4488
Huron County HIV/AIDS Network	(519) 482-1141
Kingston AIDS Project	1-800-565-2209
(In Kingston)	(613) 545-3698
Maggie's: Prostitutes' Safe Sex Project	⨯ (416) 964-0150
Ontario AIDS Network	(416) 364-4555
Peel HIV/AIDS Network	(905) 890-8770
Perry Sound Muskoka AIDS Committee	⨯ (705) 375-1080

253

**PHONE NUMBERS
OF AIDS RESOURCES**
Regional agencies
• *Ontario*

Peterborough AIDS Resources Network (In Peterborough)	1-800-361-2895 (705) 749-9110
Positive Straight Men	(416) 923-3253
Positive Youth Outreach	× (416) 506-1400
Prisoners with AIDS Support and Action Network	(416) 920-9567
The Teresa Group (provides practical & emotional support to families with children/ parent(s) infected/affected by HIV/AIDS)	(416) 596-7703
Toronto PWA Foundation	× (416) 506-1400
Voices of Positive Women (In Toronto)	1-800-263-0961 (416) 324-8703
Youthlink-Inner City (provides information, education, referral, and counselling to people under the age of 25)	(416) 922-3335
Youth Services Bureau of Ottawa-Carleton	(613) 729-1000

Drug and alcohol issues

Addiction Research Foundation (HIV Clinic) (Intake Office)	× (416) 595-6079 × (416) 595-6128
Alcoholics Anonymous	
Hamilton	× (905) 522-8392
London	× (519) 438-9006
Ottawa	× (613) 523-9977
Sault Ste. Marie	× (705) 254-1312
Thunder Bay	× (807) 344-1712
Toronto	× (416) 487-5591
Narcotics Anonymous	
Hamilton	× (905) 522-0332
London	× (519) 661-0119
Ottawa	× (613) 236-4674
Thunder Bay	× (807) 343-9100
Toronto	× (416) 691-9519
Needle exchange programs	
Guelph	
Clean Streets Stonehenge	× (519) 837-1470

Hamilton
Hamilton AIDS Network × (905) 524-4659
Hamilton Health Unit × (905) 546-3500

Kingston
Keep Six! × (613) 545-3698

London
Counterpoint Needle Exchange × (519) 434-1601

Ottawa
SITE Clinic × (613) 232-3232

St. Catharines
AIDS Niagara × (905) 984-8684

Sudbury
The Point × (705) 673-4287

Thunder Bay
The Exchange × (807) 625-9767

Toronto
Addiction Research Foundation × (416) 595-6079
Alexandra Park × (416) 504-6131
Anishnawbe Health Centre × (416) 360-0486
Hassle Free Clinic × (416) 922-0603
Open Door Centre × (416) 366-7124
Parkdale Community Health Centre × (416) 537-2455
Shout Clinic × (416) 927-8553
Street Outreach Services × (416) 926-0744
The Works (mobile van) × (416) 392-0520
Youthlink-Inner City × (416) 922-3335

Windsor
AIDS Committee of Windsor (519) 973-0222

Government hotlines & other associations

Canadian Mental Health Association –
Ontario Division × (416) 977-5580

Hemophilia Society of Ontario (AIDS Education
& Support Program)
    London (519) 432-2365
    Sudbury (705) 674-9717
    Toronto (416) 972-0641
    Vanier (613) 744-5800

Ministry of Health AIDS and Sexual Health Hotline	(416) 392-2437
Ministry of Health AIDS Hotline (English)	1-800-668-2437
Ministry of Health AIDS Hotline (French)	1-800-267-7432
Ontario Naturopathic Association	× (416) 233-2001
Ontario Public Health Association	× (416) 367-3313

Housing, home care, & palliative care

127 Isabella Non-profit Residence	(416) 928-9458
AIDS Housing Group of Ottawa (palliative care and support housing for PHAs)	(613) 235-8815
Barrett House (Residence for PHAs)	(416) 864-1627
Brant County Home Care Program (Brantford)	(519) 759-7752
Casey House Hospice Inc. (palliative care)	(416) 962-7600
Community Hospice Association of Ontario	× (416) 510-3880
Fife House Foundation Inc. (supportive housing for PHAs)	(416) 963-8218
John Gordon Home (London – palliative home care & housing for PHAs)	(519) 433-3935
Mid-Toronto Community Services	(416) 962-9449
Ontario Palliative Care Association	(905) 436-0145
Trinity Hospice (provides palliative home care team)	× (416) 364-1666
Victorian Order of Nurses (Home Care Division)	× (416) 499-2009

Legal & financial issues

Law Society of Upper Canada (Ontario)	× (416) 947-3300
Legal Services at the 519 Church Street Community Centre	(416) 392-6874
Ontario Human Rights Commission	× (416) 965-8641
Ontario Lawyer Referral Service	× (416) 947-3330
Ontario Legal Aid Provincial Office	× (416) 979-1446

Prisoners' issues

Elizabeth Fry Society	
Hamilton	(905) 527-3097

Kingston	(613) 544-1744
Ottawa	(613) 238-1171
Toronto	(416) 924-3708

John Howard Society	(416) 604-8412
Prisoners with AIDS Support and Action Network	(416) 920-9567

Spiritual issues

Holy Blossom Temple (AIDS Committee)	×	(416) 789-3291
Metropolitan Community Church of Toronto (AIDS Care)	×	(416) 406-6228
Northern Lights Alternative Canada (Toronto Centre – "AIDS Mastery" workshop)	×	(416) 922-9276

Treatment issues

African Community Health Services	×	(416) 591-7600
Anishnawbe Health Toronto	×	(416) 360-0486
Canadian HIV/AIDS Mentorship Program		(416) 480-4451
Canadian HIV Trials Network – Regional Offices		
Ottawa General Hospital	×	(613) 737-8169
Sunnybrook Health Sciences Centre	×	(416) 480-6044
CATIE – Community AIDS Treatment Information Exchange HIV/AIDS Treatment Information Network (In Toronto)		1-800-263-1638 (416) 944-1916
Children's Hospital of Eastern Ontario	×	(613) 737-2651
Community Research Initiative of Toronto		(416) 408-1041
Hassle Free Clinic		(416) 922-3549
Hospital for Sick Children (HIV Program)	×	(416) 813-6268
Immigrant Women's Health Centre	×	(416) 323-9986
Lawrence Commanda Health Centre (Sturgeon Falls)	×	(705) 753-3312
McMaster University Medical Centre	×	(905) 521-5075
Mount Sinai Hospital, Department of Psychiatry (provides psychiatric treatment for people with HIV/AIDS)	×	(416) 586-8714

257

**PHONE NUMBERS
OF AIDS RESOURCES**
Regional agencies
• *Ontario*

St. Joseph's Health Centre of London (HIV Care Program)	(519) 646-6000 extension 4855
Sunnybrook Health Science Centre (HIV/AIDS clinic)	× (416) 480-6044
Toronto General Hospital (Immuno-deficiency Clinic)	× (416) 340-5077
Trillium Drug Program – Ministry of Health (In Toronto) (TTY)	1-800-575-5386 (416) 314-5518 1-800-387-5559
Wellesley Hospital (HIV Program)	× (416) 926-7041
West Bay Health Centre	× (705) 377-5347
West Central Community Health Centre (West Central AIDS Project)	× (416) 703-4107

Youth issues

Positive Youth Outreach	(416) 506-1400
Youthlink-Inner City	× (416) 922-3335

Québec

Aboriginal issues

Medical Services Branch (AIDS Committee Action Program/Programme d'action communautaire sida [PACS])	× (514) 283-3294
Urban Aboriginal AIDS Awareness Project (at the Native Friendship Centre)	(514) 499-1854

AIDS agencies

AIDS Community Care Montréal/SIDA bénévoles Montréal	(514) 527-0928
Association des bénévoles accompagnateurs-accompagnatrices pour personnes atteintes du SIDA (ABAAPAS)	(514) 521-3345
Bureau local d'intervention traitant du SIDA	(819) 758-2662
Bureau régional d'action SIDA	(819) 776-2727
Centre d'action SIDA Montréal (femmes) (Centre for AIDS Services of Montréal [for women only])	(514) 989-7997

Centre sida amitié (St-Antoine-des-Laurentides)	(514) 431-7432
Coalition des organismes communautaires québécois de lutte contre le SIDA (COCQ-SIDA)	(514) 844-2477
Coalition SIDA des sourds du Québec	1-800-363-6600
(In Montréal)	(514) 288-1780
Comité des personnes atteintes du VIH (CPAVIH)	1-800-927-2844
(In Montréal)	(514) 282-6673
Groupe d'action pour la prévention du sida (GAP-sida) Inc.	(514) 722-5655
Intervention régionale et information sur le SIDA (IRIS)	(819) 823-6704
Mouvement d'information, d'éducation et d'entraide dans la lutte contre le SIDA (MIEL)	(418) 649-1720
Service spécialisé SIDA Québec	(514) 699-3099
SIDAction Trois-Rivières	✕ (819) 374-5740
SIPE Lanaudiére: SIDA information, prévention, écoute	(514) 752-4004
Stella (sex workers)	(514) 282-1563

Drug and alcohol issues

Alcoholics Anonymous	
Montréal	✕ (514) 376-9230
Québec	✕ (418) 529-0015
Region sud-ouest du Québec	✕ (514) 374-3688
Multidisciplinary Outreach Team (provides housing, support, detoxification services & counselling for PHAs)	✕ (514) 281-4032
Narcotics Anonymous	
Montréal	✕ (514) 525-0333
Québec	✕ (418) 649-0715
Needle exchange programs	
Chicoutimi	✕ (418) 541-1000
Greenfield Park	✕ (514) 679-6772

Montréal

Cactus	× (514) 847-0067
Clinique communautaire Pointe St. Charles (CLIP – for youth)	× (514) 937-9251
Itinérants	× (514) 281-4010
L'anonyme	× (514) 953-2040
PIC-ATOUTS	× (514) 253-8968
Spectre de rue	× (514) 528-1700
Rouyn-Noranda	× (819) 764-3264
Victoriaville	
(exchanges at drugstores)	× (514) 528-2400
(exchanges at hospital, clinics & CLSC)	× (819) 758-2662

Government hotlines & other associations

Canadian Association of HIV Research (Québec Department of Public Health – Centre for AIDS Studies)	× (514) 932-3055
Canadian Hemophilia Society – Québec Division/Société canadienne de l'hémophilie – Section Québec	× (514) 848-0666
Canadian Mental Health Association – Québec Division/Association canadienne pour la santé mentale	× (514) 849-3291
Ministry of Health AIDS Hotline/Ministère de la Santé et des Services sociaux	1-800-463-5656

Housing, home care & palliative care

Chez ma cousine Evelyne (residence for active drug users living with HIV/AIDS)	(514) 288-7244
Maison Amaryllis (housing for PHAs, drug users, homeless people, and psychiatric patients)	(514) 526-3635
Maison Dehon (housing for PHAs)	(514) 384-9498
Maison d'Hérelle (housing for PHAs on Plateau Mont-Royal)	(514) 844-4874
Maison du Parc (housing for PHAs)	(514) 523-7420
Maison Plein Coeur (drop-in centre for counselling and food)	(514) 597-0554
Maison Ludovic (housing for PHAs)	(514) 722-8523

Palliative Care Association/Association québécoise des soins palliatifs	(514) 527-2194

Legal & financial issues

Canadian HIV/AIDS Legal Network/ Réseau juridique canadien sur le VIH/sida	(514) 526-1796
Centre des ROSÉS de l'Abitibi-Témiscamingue (Rouyn-Noranda)	(819) 764-9111
Commission des services juridiques (Québec)	(514) 873-3562
Québec Human Rights Commission/ Commission des droits de la personne et des droits de la jeunesse	(514) 873-5146
Québec Lawyer Referral Service	(514) 866-9392
	(514) 866-2490

Prisoners' issues

Elizabeth Fry Society	(514) 489-2116
John Howard Society	(514) 933-2627

Spiritual issues

Village Community Church	× (514) 679-9362

Treatment issues

Canadian HIV Trials Network – Regional Office	× (514) 843-2611
Centre hôpitalier de l'Université Laval	× (418) 654-2282
Centre Pierre Hénault Inc. (provides psycho-social support for those affected by HIV/AIDS)	× (514) 273-8603
Farha Foundation (raises funds to improve AIDS outpatient services and AIDS awareness)	× (514) 270-4900
Fonds de recherche pour étude sur la sida Québec (FRESQ) (provides support to AIDS-related cancer researchers)	× (514) 521-1572
Montréal Children's Hospital	× (514) 934-4485
St. Justine Hospital (Centre maternel et infantile sur le SIDA)	× (514) 345-4931

New Brunswick

AIDS agencies

AIDS New Brunswick	1-800-561-4009
(In Fredericton)	(506) 459-7518
(TTD)	(506) 450-2782
AIDS Saint John	(506) 652-2437
PLWHIV/AIDS Network of New Brunswick	(506) 451-4700
SIDA-AIDS Moncton	(506) 859-9616

Drug and alcohol issues

Alcoholics Anonymous

Fredericton	× (506) 450-3018
Moncton	× (506) 382-5087
Saint John	× (506) 693-9080

Narcotics Anonymous

Fredericton	× (506) 452-5558
Needle Exchange (AIDS Saint John)	(506) 652-2437

Government hotlines & other associations

Canadian Mental Health Association – New Brunswick Division	× (506) 455-5231
Hemophilia Society of New Brunswick	× (506) 857-9753

Housing & palliative care

Palliative Care Association	× (506) 452-5321

Legal & financial issues

Law Society of New Brunswick	× (506) 458-8540
Legal Aid New Brunswick	× (506) 451-1424
New Brunswick Human Rights Commission	× (506) 453-2301

Prisoners' issues

Elizabeth Fry Society

Moncton	(506) 855-7781
St. John	(506) 635-8851
John Howard Society	(506) 457-9810

Prince Edward Island

AIDS Agency

AIDS PEI   1-800-314-2437
(In Charlottetown)   (902) 566-2437

Drug and alcohol issues

Alcoholics Anonymous

    Charlottetown   × (902) 892-2103

    Souris/Montague   × (902) 838-3625

Alcohol & drug treatment centres

    Charlottetown   × (902) 368-4120

    Souris/Montague   × (902) 687-7110

    Summerside   × (902) 888-7110

Government hotlines & other associations

Canadian Mental Health Association – PEI
Division   (902) 566-3034

Housing & palliative care

Island Hospice Association   (902) 368-4498

Legal & financial issues

Law Society of PEI   × (902) 566-1666

Legal Aid   × (902) 386-6043

PEI Human Rights Commission   × (902) 368-4180

Social Assistance

    Charlottetown   × (902) 368-5330

    Montague   × (902) 838-0700

    O'Leary   × (902) 859-8811

    Souris   × (902) 687-7060

    Summerside   × (902) 888-8100

Prisoners' issues

John Howard Society   (902) 566-5425

**PHONE NUMBERS
OF AIDS RESOURCES**
Regional agencies
• *Prince Edward Island*

Newfoundland & Labrador

264

**PHONE NUMBERS
OF AIDS RESOURCES**
Regional agencies
• *Newfoundland &
Labrador*

AIDS Agency

Newfoundland and Labrador AIDS Committee	1-800-563-1575
(In St. John's)	(709) 579-8656

Drug and alcohol issues

Alcoholics anonymous

Corner Brook	✕ (709) 785-5048
Gander	✕ (709) 651-2001
Labrador	✕ (709) 944-6200
St. John's	✕ (709) 579-5215
Drug Dependency Services (Department of Health)	✕ (709) 729-0623

Government hotlines & other associations

Canadian Mental Health Association – Newfoundland Division	✕ (709) 753-8550

Housing & palliative care

Palliative Care Association Inc.	✕ (709) 368-0380

Legal & financial issues

Law Society of Newfoundland	✕ (709) 722-4740
Newfoundland Human Rights Commission	1-800-563-5808
(In St. John's)	(709) 729-2326
Newfoundland Legal Aid Commission	✕ (709) 753-7860

Prisoners' issues

John Howard Society	(709) 722-1848

Treatment issues

Janeway Child Health Centre	✕ (709) 778-4222

Nova Scotia

Aboriginal issues

Atlantic First Nations AIDS Task Force	1-800-565-4255
(In Halifax)	(902) 492-4255
Medical Services Branch	× (902) 426-6085

AIDS agencies

AIDS Coalition of Cape Breton	(902) 567-1766
AIDS Coalition of Nova Scotia	(902) 429-7922
(Toll-free)	1-800-566-2437
(Information line)	(902) 425-2437
Nova Scotia Advisory Committee on AIDS	(902) 424-5730
Nova Scotia Women and AIDS Project	(902) 429-7922
Pictou County AIDS Coalition	(902) 752-6218
Stepping Stone (sex workers)	(902) 420-0103
Valley AIDS Concern Group (Kentville)	× (902) 679-3515

Drug and alcohol issues

Alcoholics Anonymous	
Canning	× (902) 582-7734
Halifax/Dartmouth	× (902) 461-1119
Sydney	(902) 564-8851
Drug Dependency Program for Persons Living With AIDS	× (902) 634-4624
Main Line Needle Exchange	× (902) 423-9991
Narcotics Anonymous (Halifax)	× (902) 454-2913

Government hotlines & other associations

Canadian Hemophilia Society	× 1-800-668-2686
Canadian Mental Health Association – Nova Scotia Division	× (902) 466-6600
Nova Scotia Naturopathic Association	× (902) 538-8733

Housing & palliative care

Nova Scotia Hospice Palliative Care Association	× (902) 567-7846

Legal & financial issues

Dalhousie Legal Aid Services	× (902) 423-8105
Nova Scotia Barristers Society	× (902) 422-1491
Nova Scotia Human Rights Commission	× (902) 424-4111
Nova Scotia Lawyer Referral Service	× (902) 422-1491
Nova Scotia Legal Aid Commission	× (902) 420-6573

**PHONE NUMBERS
OF AIDS RESOURCES**
Regional agencies
• *Nova Scotia*
• *Yukon*

Prisoners' issues

Elizabeth Fry Society

Cape Breton	(902) 539-6165
Halifax	(902) 454-5041
John Howard Society	(902) 423-7915

Spiritual issues

CARAS (Church members Assembled to Respond to AIDS)	× (902) 428- 4055

Treatment issues

Canadian HIV Trials Network – Regional Office	× (902) 428-3742
Infectious Disease Clinic – Victoria General Hospital	× (902) 428-4140
Izaak Walton Killam Children's Hospital	× (902) 428-8498
STD Clinic, Victoria General Hospital	× (902) 428-2272

Yukon

AIDS agency

AIDS Yukon Alliance	1-800-661-0507
(In Whitehorse)	(403) 633-2437

Drug and alcohol issues

Alcoholics Anonymous (Whitehorse)	× (403) 668-5878
Needle Exchange (AIDS Yukon Alliance)	× (403) 633-2437

Government hotlines & other associations

Canadian Mental Health Association – Yukon Division	× (403) 668-8812
Communicable Disease Unit	× (403) 667-8323

Legal & financial issues

Government of Yukon (Legal Aid)	× (403) 667-5210
Law Society of Yukon	× (403) 668-4231
Yukon Human Rights Commission	× (403) 667-6226

Northwest Territories

AIDS agencies

AIDS Yellowknife	(403) 873-2626
Iqaluit HIV/AIDS Project (a program of Canadian Mental Health Association – Baffin Island Branch)	× (819) 979-3005
Kativik AIDS Prevention Program	× (819) 964-2222
Kimmirut Asapi Community Health Centre (Lake Harbour)	× (819) 939- 2217
Niviuqtit AIDS Support Group (Cape Dorset)	× (819) 897-8820
Yellowkinfe Help and AIDS Line	(403) 873-9903

Government hotlines & other associations

Canadian Mental Health Association –	
NWT Division	× (403) 873-3190
Baffin Island Branch	× (819) 979-4151
NWT AIDS Information Line (In Yellowknife)	1-800-661-0795 (403) 873-7017

Legal & financial issues

Law Society of the Northwest Territories	× (403) 873-3828
Legal Services Board of the Northwest Territories	× (403) 873-7450
Northwest Territories Canadian Human Rights Commission	× (403) 495-4040

267

PHONE NUMBERS OF AIDS RESOURCES

Regional agencies

- *Yukon*
- *Northwest Territories*

Index

A

ABV
    for Kaposi's sarcoma 138
acetaminophen 116, 158
acidophilus 93, 114
acupressure – *See* shiatsu
acupuncture 74, 79
    for pain 159
    for peripheral neuropathy 143
acyclovir 59, 237
    for hairy leukoplakia 135
    for herpes 131
    for herpes zoster virus
        (shingles) 132
ADC – *See* AIDS dementia complex
    (ADC)
Adriamycin – *See* ABV and
    doxorubicin
Advil – *See* ibuprofen
advocacy xviii
aerosolized pentamidine – *See*
    pentamidine

affirmations 82–83
AIDS
    definition 22
AIDS dementia complex (ADC) 133,
    144–146
    diagnosis 144–145
    how to manage with 145–146
    prevention 145
    symptoms 144–145
    treatments 145
albendazole
    for microsporidiosis 123
albumin 163
alcohol 30, 60, 86
    and chemotherapy 143
    and ddI 66
    and street drugs 155–156
aloe vera 84, 162
    acemannan 84
alpha interferon
    for Kaposi's sarcoma 138

alternative therapies – *See* complementary therapies

amikacin 107

amino acids 84, 85

l-carnitine 94

l-lysine 94

amitriptyline

for peripheral neuropathy 143

amoxicillin 112, 113

amphetamines 156

amphotericin B 114

and d4T 67

for cryptococcosis 116

for histoplasmosis 117

ampicillin 113

Amsler grid 126, 129–130, 237

amyl nitrate 156

amylase 65, 94, 119

anabolic steroids – *See* steroids

anal cancer

and genital warts 150

anal dysplasia

and genital warts 150

anemia 26, 64

iron 91

anergy panel 109

anthralin

for psoriasis 147

antibiotics 107–113

and diarrhea 159

antibodies 20, 21, 25

antibody immune response 20, 83

anticoagulants

and Vitamin E 90

antifungals 114–120, 238

apple cider vinegar 84

grapefruit seed extract 86

pau d'arco 86

tea tree oil 87

anti-HIV treatments 61–71, 236, 238, 239

anti-inflammatories

aloe vera 84

copper 91

licorice root 86

antioxidants 90

and copper 91

and N-acetyl cysteine (NAC) 95

bioflavonoids 93

melatonin 94

selenium 91

Vitamin C 90

Vitamin E 90

antiretrovirals – *See* antivirals

antivirals 61, 127–135

and the brain/nervous system 145

appetite stimulation 163–164, 238

apple cider vinegar 84

ara-C – *See* cytosine arabinoside

aromatherapy 76, 83

ascorbic acid – *See* Vitamin C

Aspirin 60, 157, 158

for herpes zoster virus 132

assisted suicide – *See* suicide

asymptomatic HIV infection 21

atovaquone

for microsporidiosis 123

for Pneumocystis carinii pneumonia (PCP) 120

for toxoplasmosis 122

attorneys 226

Avlosulfon – *See* dapsone

ayurvedic medicine 76, 83

azidothymidine – *See* AZT

azithromycin 107

for cryptosporidiosis 124

for toxoplasmosis 122

AZT 59, 63, 64–65, 69, 105, 165

and AIDS dementia complex (ADC) 145

and ganciclovir 127

and saquinavir 69

dose 64

drug interactions 65
side effects 64
AZT myopathy 65

B
B cells 20
B lymphocytes – *See* B cells
B vitamins 90, 92
    and AIDS dementia complex
        (ADC) 145
    and pryimethamine 122
bacteria 18
bacterial infections 61, 97, 104,
        106–113, 159
    and aloe vera 84
    and bee propolis 84
    and garlic 85
bacterial pneumonia 61, 105,
        112–113
    diagnosis 112
    prevention 113
    symptoms 112
    treatments 113
Bactrim – *See* TMP/SMX
bank accounts 231
barbiturates 156
bee propolis 84
beta endorphin 73
beta-carotene 89, 93
Betadine scrub 146
betaine hydrochloride 164
Biaxin – *See* clarithromycin
bifidus 93
bioflavonoids 93
biopsy 31
bitter melon 84
blender drinks 96, 161
bleomycin – *See* ABV
blind spots 125
blindness
    and cytomegalovirus (CMV) 125
    and syphilis 150

blood 18, 25
    tests 25–29, 237
        for Mycobacterium avium
            complex (MAC) 106–107
blood cultures – *See* culture tests
blood gases 29
blood ozonation 77
blood urea nitrogen (BUN) 30
blue-green algae 85, 93
bone marrow 20, 25, 64
Boost 96
broncho-alveolar lavage (BAL) 118
bronchoscope 31
bronchoscopy 118, 126
buyers' clubs 74, 171

C
calcium 93
calories 161
campylobacteriosis 100
    and diarrhea 159
Canada Pension Plan 190, 194,
        199–200, 207
Canadian Charter of Rights and
        Freedoms 219
Canadian Human Rights Act
        217–219
Canadian Human Rights
        Commission 218
candida – *See* candidiasis
candidiasis 77, 84, 86, 89, 96,
        113–115, 135, 238
    See also thrush
    diagnosis 114
    prevention 114
    symptoms 114
    treatments 114–115
        acidophilus 93
        bifidus 93
        pau d'arco 86
        tea tree oil 87

cantheridin
    for molluscum contagiosum 148
carbohydrates 89, 161
    and amylase 94
care teams 54
CAT scan – *See* CT scan
catheters
    CVC 128
    Hickman 128
    Port-a-Cath 128
CBC – *See* complete blood count
        (CBC)
cefotetan 112
cefoxitin 112
cell-mediated immunity 20, 72
cell-mediated response 83
central nervous system – *See* nervous
        system
central venous catheter (CVC) 128
centres locaux de services
        communautaires (CLSC) 45
cervical cancer 139–141, 238
    and genital warts 150
    diagnosis 140
    prevention 140–141
    symptoms 140
    treatments 140–141
cervical dysplasia 139–141, 238
    and genital warts 150
cervix 139
chemotherapy 162
    for Kaposi's sarcoma 137, 138
    for lymphoma 141, 142
    side effects 138, 143
children 60
    and melatonin 95
Chinese cucumber 71
Chinese medicine, traditional
        (TCM) 58, 74–75, 83
chiropractic 75, 80
chlamydia 111, 149
chromium 92, 93

cidofovir
    for cytomegalovirus (CMV) 128
    side effects 128
cimetidine – *See also* Tagamet
    and ddI 66
ciprofloxacin 107, 113
circulatory system 19
cirrhosis 134
Citricidal – *See* grapefruit seed
        extract
clarithromycin 107
clavulanate 112
clindamycin
    for pelvic inflammatory disease
        (PID) 112
    for Pneumocystis carinii
        pneumonia (PCP) 120
    for toxoplasmosis 122
clinical trials 165, 171, 173–187
    criteria 178–179
clothing 215
clotrimazole 114
clotting 60
CMV – *See* cytomegalovirus (CMV)
cocaine 156
codeine
    and ritonavir 69
    for diarrhea 161
co-enzyme Q10 94
co-factors 22
colon problems
    and aloe vera 84
colonoscope 31
colonoscopy 126
colposcope 31
colposcopy 140
combination therapy 62–63, 69,
        238, 239
    and compliance 62
    immune modulators 72
    protease (proteinase)
        inhibitors 68

committeeship 227

community health representatives (CHRs) 42

COMP (cyclophosphamide, vincristine, methotrexate, and prednisone)
  for lymphoma 142

compassionate access 171–172, 178, 179

compassionate arm – *See* compassionate access

complementary therapies 58, 74–87, 168, 174, 236
  for pain 159

complementary therapist or practitioner 42–43

complete blood count (CBC) 26
  differential 26

Compound Q 71
  side effects 71

condoms 152–153
  condom for women 153

constipation
  and aloe vera 84

constitutional symptoms 156–164

controlled trials 176–177

conventional medicine 57

copper 91, 93

corticosteroids
  for Pneumocystis carinii pneumonia (PCP) 120
  for psoriasis 147

cortisone
  and melatonin 95

counselling 14, 75
  financial 204
  legal aid 220
  peer counselling 13

counsellors 14

crack 156

creatinine 29, 30

crisis lines 13

Crixivan – *See* indinavir

cryotherapy
  for cervical dysplasia 140
  for genital warts 151
  for Kaposi's sarcoma 138
  for molluscum contagiosum 148

cryptococcal meningitis 115, 133

cryptococcal pneumonia 115

cryptococcosis 115–116
  diagnosis 116
  prevention 116
  symptoms 115
  treatment 116

cryptosporidiosis 97, 123–124
  and diarrhea 159
  diagnosis 124
  prevention 124
  symptoms 123
  treatments 124

CT scan 31, 116, 133

culture tests 31

curcumin 85

CVC – *See* catheters

cyanocobalamin – *See* Vitamin B12

cytarabine – *See* cytosine arabinoside

cytokines 20, 72
  TNF-alpha 85

cytomegalovirus (CMV) 71, 95, 104, 125–130
  and diarrhea 159
  CMV colitis 126
  CMV esophagitis 126
  CMV pneumonitis 125, 126
  CMV retinitis 125
  diagnosis 126
  gastrointestinal CMV 125
  prevention 126
  pulmonary CMV infection 125
  symptoms 125
  treatments 127–128

cytosine arabinoside
   for progressive multifocal
      leukoencephalopathy
      (PML) 133

D
dapsone 59
   and d4T 67
   and ddI 66
   and rifampin 110
   for Pneumocystis carinii
      pneumonia (PCP) 119, 120
daunorubicin
   for Kaposi's sarcoma 138
ddC 28, 62, 63, 66, 165
   and d4T 67
   and peripheral neuropathy 143
   and saquinavir 69
   drug interactions 66
   side effects 66
ddI 28, 62, 63, 65–66, 105, 165
   and d4T 67
   and molybdenum 91
   and pentamidine 119
   and peripheral neuropathy 143
   drug interactions 66
   side effects 65
Deca-Durabolin 164
deductible 167
dehydration 160
   and cryptosporidiosis 124
delavirdine 68, 165
   side effects 68
delayed type hypersensitivity
   (DTH) 73
Demerol 116
dental dams 154
dental exam 237
dental problems 162
dentists 41
depression 12, 163
   and fatigue 158

desensitization protocol 119
dexamethasone
   and melatonin 95
d4T 63, 67, 165
   and peripheral neuropathy 143
   drug interactions 67
   side effects 67
diarrhea 29, 88, 110, 159–161,
   162, 239
   causes 159–160
   prevention 160
   traditional Chinese medicine 75
   treatments 160
      acidophilus 93
      bifidus 93
diazepam – *See also* Valium
   for AIDS dementia complex
      (ADC) 145
diclazuril
   for cryptosporidiosis 124
dicloxacillin
   for folliculitis 147
didanosine – *See* ddI
dideoxycytidine – *See* ddC
dideoxyinosine – *See* ddI
diet 88–97
   anti-candida 96
   macrobiotic 96
dietitians 48, 236
Diflucan – *See* fluconazole
digestion
   and apple cider vinegar 84
   and curcumin 85
dildos 154
dinitrochlorobenzene – *See* DNCB
diphenoxylate 160
   for cryptosporidiosis 124
disability benefits 196, 197–198
disability insurance 207
disease progression 62
disulfiram
   and ddC 66

DNA 63
DNCB 73
   for molluscum contagiosum 148
double blind studies 176
doxorubicin
   for Kaposi's sarcoma 138
doxycycline 112
dronabinol 163
drug card 166
Drug Formulary 166, 166–168
drug interactions 12, 39, 40, 61, 70,
   105, 183
   and street drugs 61
   chemotherapy 143
drug use 30, 60–61, 126, 155–156
   and chemotherapy 143
   needles 6
Durabolin 164

E
EAP – *See* Federal Extraordinary
   Assistance Plan
echinacea 85
EDRP – *See* Emergency Drug Release
   Program
EFAs – *See* essential fatty acids
Elavil – *See* amitriptyline
electrocautery
   for cervical dysplasia 140
electrolytes 29, 160
Emergency Drug Release Program
   170–171
   and cidofovir 128
   and ganciclovir 127
   and naltrexone 73
   and thalidomide 163
emotions 9–16
   and fatigue 158
encephalitis 121
endocarditis 61
endorphins 80
endoscopy 31, 126

enduring power of attorney
   226–227
Ensure 96
enteral nutrition 96
Enterocytozoon bieneusi 122
enzymes 18, 19, 63, 84
   alanine aminotransferase 30
   alkaline phosphatase 30
   amylase 28
   and d4T 67
   aspartate aminotransferase 30
   creatinine phosphokinase 29
   gamma-glutomyltransferase 30
   integrase 18
   lactate dehydrogenase 30
   liver 30, 163
   protease (proteinase) 68
   reverse transcriptase 18
eosinophilic folliculitis 147
epididymis 149
Epivir – *See* 3TC
Epstein-Barr virus 135
erythrocyte sedimentation rate
   (ESR) 29, 163
erythromycin 113
   for chlamydia 149
ESR – *See* erythrocyte sedimentation
   rate (ESR)
essential fatty acids (EFAs) 94
essential oils 76
essiac tea 85
ethambutol 107
ethionamide
   and ddC 66
etoposide
   for Kaposi's sarcoma 138
euthanasia 226
exceptional drug program 167
exclusion criteria – *See* clinical trials,
   criteria
exercise 76, 80–81, 162, 164
   and fatigue 158

Extraordinary Assistance Plan – *See* Federal Extraordinary Assistance Plan (EAP)

F

facilitated access list 167
fair practices legislation (NWT) 217–219
famciclovir
  for herpes 131
  for herpes zoster virus 132
Famvir – *See* famciclovir
Fansidar – *See* pyrimethamine
fat 89
  and lipase 94
fatigue 158
  traditional Chinese medicine 75
fatty acids 94
Federal Extraordinary Assistance Plan (EAP) 203
fetus 59
fever 85, 157, 239
Flagyl – *See* metronidazole
floaters 125
fluconazole 114
  for candidiasis 114
  for cryptococcosis 116
folic acid 90, 92
  and pyrimethamine 122
folliculitis 147
food poisoning 99–100, 113
food safety 97–100, 107
food services 214
  food banks 214
  meal programs 214
foscarnet
  and d4T 67
  for cytomegalovirus (CMV) 127, 128
  for herpes 131
  side effects 128
"friendly" bacteria 93, 113

FTA-ABS test 150
funerals 228, 232–234
fungal infections 105, 113–120, 239
  treatments
    aloe vera 84
    pau d'arco 86
    tea tree oil 87
fungi 18

G

gallium scan 118
ganciclovir
  and AZT 65
  and d4T 67
  and ddC 66
  and ddI 66
  for cytomegalovirus (CMV) 127
  side effects 127
garlic 85
gastroscope 31
G-CSF
  and ganciclovir 127
  for Kaposi's sarcoma 138
  for lymphoma 142
genital herpes – *See* herpes
genital warts 33, 34, 139, 150
gentamicin 112
germs 18
giardiasis
  and diarrhea 159
gingivitis 237
GLQ233 – *See* Compound Q
glutamic acid hydrochloride 164
glutathione
  and acetaminophen 158
  and N-acetyl cysteine (NAC) 95
  and selenium 91
Glyceron – *See* glycyrrhizin
glycyrrhizin 86

GM-CSF
  and ganciclovir 127
  for Kaposi's sarcoma 138
  for lymphoma 142
gonorrhea 111, 149
gp120 18
grapefruit seed extract 86, 162
  for thrush 114
group insurance 205–206
guided imagery – *See* affirmations
gynecologists 41

H
hairy leukoplakia 135
Halcion
  and ritonavir 69
Haldol – *See* haloperidol
haloperidol
  for AIDS dementia complex
    (ADC) 145
  side effects 145
hCG (human chorionic
    gonadotropin) 139
Health Canada's Health Protection
    Branch (HPB) 58, 170,
    173–174, 176
health insurance
  private 102, 166, 168, 195,
    205–206
    complementary therapies 74
  provincial or territorial 14, 45, 52,
    63, 166, 168
  travel 102
hematocrit 26
hemoglobin (Hgb) 26
  and copper 91
  and fatigue 158
hemophilia 60, 154
  and Vitamin E 90
hemorrhaging 154

hepatitis 30, 134–135, 151, 154
  and acetaminophen 158
  and piercing 156
  and street drugs 155
  and tattoos 156
  hepatitis A 134
  hepatitis B 30, 61, 134, 237
  hepatitis C 60, 134
  hepatitis D 134
  hepatitis E 134
  hepatitis G 134
  treatments
    milk thistle 86
herbal medicine 75, 83–87
  aromatherapy 76
herbs 76
herpes 33, 34, 130–132, 237
  and bee propolis 84
  and Kaposi's sarcoma 136
  and skin problems 148
  diagnosis 130
  genital 150
  herpes simplex I 130
  herpes simplex II 130
  prevention 131
  symptoms 130
  treatments 131
    glycyrrhizin 86
    hyssop 86
    Monolaurin 95
herpes simplex 71
herpes zoster virus (shingles)
    131–132
  and skin problems 148
  diagnosis 131
  prevention 132
  symptoms 131
  treatment 132
"Hickman" catheter 128

Hismanal
  and erythromycin 115
  and ketoconazole 115
  and ritonavir 69
histoplasmosis 117
  diagnosis 117
  prevention 117
  symptoms 117
  treatments 117
HIV – *See* human immunodeficiency virus (HIV)
Hivid – *See* ddC
HL – *See* hairy leukoplakia
Hodgkin's disease 141
holistic xvi, 57, 75
home care 51, 52, 52–53
homeopathy 75, 76, 83
hormone regulation
  and melatonin 94
hormones 73
hospices 54, 212
hostels 213
housing 209–214
housing co-operatives 210–211
HPB – *See* Health Canada's Health Protection Branch
HPV – *See* human papillomavirus (HPV)
human chorionic gonadotropin – *see* hCG
human growth hormone 164
  side effects 164
human immunodeficiency virus (HIV) 103
  different types 151, 152, 153, 154, 156
  DNA 18
  infection 21–22
    asymptomatic 21
    ELISA test 25
    pregnancy 59
    primary 21
    seroconversion 21
    symptomatic 22
    tests for 25
    Western Blot test 25
  reproductive cycle 63
  resistance to treatment 62, 151
  RNA 18
human papillomavirus (HPV) 135, 139, 148, 150
human rights codes 217–219
Humatin – *See* paromomycin
humoral immunity 20, 72
hydrazaline
  and ddC 66
hydrocortisone
  for seborrheic dermatitis 147
hydrogen peroxide 77, 162
  for thrush 114
hyperbaric medicine 77
hypericin 71
  side effects 71
hyperoxygenation therapy – *See* oxygen therapy
hyssop 86
hysterectomy
  for cervical cancer 141

I

ibuprofen 116
  for fever 157
  for herpes zoster virus 132
  for pain 158
imaging tests 31–32
immune boosters – *See* immune system modulators
immune system 19–20, 103
immune system modulators 72–73
  blue-green algae 85
  licorice root 86
immunity
  cell-mediated 20
  humoral 20

Imodium – *See* loperamide
Impact 96
implanted venous port 128
in vitro 57
in vivo 57
inclusion criteria – *See* clincial trials,
    criteria
indinavir 69, 165
    side effects 70
"induced sputum" test 118
in-dwelling catheters 128
infections
    tests for 31–32
influenza 135
    treatments
        Monolaurin 95
    Type A 135
    Type B 135
informed consent 180–181
Interleukin-2 72
intestinal parasites
    treatments
        curcumin 85
intralesional therapy
    for Kaposi's sarcoma 139
intrathecal administration 133
intrauterine contraceptive devices
        (IUDs) 111
intravitreal implant 127
Invirase – *See* saquinavir
iron 91, 92, 93
Isocal 96
isoniazid 110
    and ddC 66
Isosource 96
isosporiasis 123–124
    and diarrhea 159
    diagnosis 124
    prevention 124
    symptoms 123
    treatments 124

itraconazole 114
    for folliculitis 147
    for histoplasmosis 117
    for seborrheic dermatitis 147
IUDs – *See* intrauterine
    contraceptive devices

J
JC virus 132

K
Kaposi's sarcoma 136–139, 162
    and diarrhea 159
    cosmetics for 137
    diagnosis 136–137
    external 136
    internal 137
    prevention 137–139
    symptoms 136–137
    treatments 137–139
        hyssop 86
    visceral 137
keloid scars 131
ketoconazole 114
    and ddI 66
    and isoniazid 110
    and rifampin 110
    and ritonavir 69
    for candidiasis 114
    for folliculitis 147
    for seborrheic dermatitis 147
kombucha "mushroom" 87
KS – *See* Kaposi's sarcoma
Kwellada
    for scabies 151

L
lab tests 24
lactose-intolerance 93
lamivudine – *See* 3TC
laparoscopy 111

laser surgery
 for cervical dysplasia 140
 for genital warts 151
lawyers 221–222
LBM – *See* lean body mass
l-carnitine 94
 and wasting 164
 for peripheral neuropathy 144
lean body mass 80, 161, 163
legal aid 221–222
legal clinics 222
letrazuril
 for cryptosporidiosis 124
leucovorin 122
 See also folic acid
leukemia
 and melatonin 95
leukocytes 20
leukopenia 26
licorice root 86
life insurance 205, 208, 209, 226
lipase 94
liquid food supplements 96–97, 161
 brand names 96
listeriosis 100
liver 60
liver integrity tests 29, 237
living benefits 208, 209
living wills 47, 223–225
l-lysine 94
 for herpes 131
Lomotil – *See* diphenoxylate
long-term disability benefits
 190, 205
 See also disability benefits
loperamide 160
 for cryptosporidiosis 124
loveride 68
lumbar puncture 116
lymph 18, 19
lymph nodes 19, 21, 22, 23

lymphadenopathy
 night sweats 157
lymphatic system 19, 141
lymphocytes 20, 27
lymphoma 141–143
 and diarrhea 159
 and melatonin 95
 diagnosis 142
 Non-Hodgkin's 141
 prevention 142
 primary CNS 141
 symptoms 141–142
 treatments 142–143

M

MAC – *See* Mycobacterium avium
 complex (MAC)
macronutrients 89
macrophages 20, 122
magnesium 91, 93
magnetic resonance imaging (MRI)
 scans 24, 31
MAI – *See* Mycobacterium avium
 complex (MAC)
malabsorption 88
malnutrition 88
manganese 93
Mantoux – *See* purified protein
 derivative test
marijuana 156
 and appetite 163
Marinol – *See* dronabinol
massage 75, 76, 77–79
mBACOD (methotrexate,
 bleomycin, doxorubicin
 [Adriamycin], cyclophos-
 phamide, vincristine, and
 dexamethasone)
 for lymphoma 142
MCTs – *See* medium chain
 triglycerides (MCTs)
medical benefits 190

medical expenses 202

medical power of attorney 223–225

Medical Services Branch 167, 204

meditation 76, 81–82
    for pain 159

medium chain triglycerides
    (MCTs) 161

Megace 163

megestrol acetate – *See* Megace

melatonin 94–95

memorials 232–234

meningitis 115

meridians 74

metabolic changes 88

metabolism 161

methadone 61
    and rifampin 110

methylphenidate hydrochloride
    for AIDS dementia complex
        (ADC) 145

metronidazole 112
    and ddC 66
    for microsporidiosis 123

mexilitine
    and peripheral neuropathy 143

MHA-TP test 150

microbes 18

micronutrients 89–91

microsporidiosis 122–123
    diagnosis 122
    prevention 123
    symptoms 122
    treatments 123

milk thistle 86

MiluVita Plus 96

minerals 61, 84, 85, 88, 91, 236
    See also individual mineral names
    and diarrhea 159
    multiminerals 93

molluscum
    and DNCB 73

molluscum contagiosum 148

molybdenum 91, 92, 93

Momordica charantia – *See* bitter
    melon

monocytes – *See* macrophages

Monolaurin 95

Monostat-4
    and ritonavir 69

monotherapy 62

morphine 158
    for diarrhea 161
    for peripheral neuropathy 143

Motrin IB – *See* ibuprofen

mouth problems 238

moxibustion 74

MPTAP – *See* Multi-Provincial/
    Territorial Assistance Program

MRI scans – *See* magnetic resonance
    imaging (MRI)

MSB – *See* Medical Services Branch

mugwort 74

Multi-Provincial/Territorial
    Assistance Program 203

muscle wasting – *See* wasting

Mycelex – *See* clotrimazole

mycobacteria 97

Mycobacterium avium complex
    (MAC) 30, 31, 97, 104,
    106–108, 239
    and diarrhea 159
    diagnosis 106
    night sweats 157
    prevention 107
    symptoms 106
    treatments 107
        hyssop 86
        side effects 108

Mycobacterium avium intracellulare
    (MAI) – *See* Mycobacterium
    avium complex (MAC)

Mycostatin – *See* nystatin

N

nabilone – *See* dronabinol

NAC – *See* N-acetyl cysteine (NAC)

N-acetyl cysteine (NAC) 92, 95
  and TMP/SMX 95
  and wasting 164

naltrexone 73
  dose 73

Naprosyn
  for herpes zoster virus 132

naso-gastric tube 96

naturopathic practitioners 75, 83, 236

naturopathy 75

nausea 88, 162–163

nebulizer 119

needles – *See* drug use

nelfinavir 70, 165

nervous system 23, 61, 115
  and toxoplasmosis 121

nervous system tests 32–33, 237

neuralgia
  and herpes zoster virus 132

neutropenia 64, 65
  and AZT 64
  and d4T 67
  and ganciclovir 127
  and 3TC 67

neutrophils 64

nevirapine 68, 165

niacin – *See* Vitamin B3

night sweats 157
  traditional Chinese medicine 75

NIHB – *See* Non-Insured Health
  Benefits Program

nimodipine
  for AIDS dementia complex
    (ADC) 145

nitazoxanide 124

NIX
  for scabies 151

Nizoral – *See* ketoconazole

non-formulary benefits list 167

Non-Insured Health Benefits
  Program (NIHB) 167, 204

non-nucleoside reverse transcriptase
  inhibitors (NNRTIs) 63, 68

nonoxynol-9 153

Norvir – *See* ritonavir

NTZ – *See* nitazoxanide

nucleoside analogues 63–67
  side effects 64

Nutren 96

Nutribiotic – *See* grapefruit seed
  extract

nutrition 75, 76, 88–97

nutritionists 236

nystatin 114

O

obstetricians 42

octreotide
  for cryptosporidiosis 124

off-label use of drugs 169

ofloxacin 112

open arm – *See* compassionate
  access

ophthalmic eye test 237

ophthalmologist 126

opportunistic infections 103–148

Opti Healthgain 96

oral sex 154

over-the-counter (OTC) list 167

oxycodone
  for peripheral neuropathy 143

oxygen therapy 77

ozone 77

P

pain 158–159

palliative care 46, 54, 212

pancreatitis 28
  and 3TC 67
  and d4T 67

and ddC 66

and ddI 65

and pentamidine 119

and ritonavir 69

pantothenic acid – *See* Vitamin B5

Pap smear 33, 140, 150, 238

    rectal 34, 140, 238

parasites 97, 151

    and diarrhea 159

paromomycin

    for cryptosporidiosis 124

    for microsporidiosis 123

Paxil

    and ritonavir 69

PCP – *See* Pneumocystis carinii
    pneumonia (PCP)

PEG – *See* percutaneous endoscopic
    gastrostomy

pelvic inflammatory disease (PID)
    111–112, 149, 238

    diagnosis 111

    prevention 111

    symptoms 111

    treatments 112

penicillin 113

    for syphilis 150

pentamidine 29, 59

    aerosolized

        for Pneumocystis carinii
            pneumonia (PCP) 119,
            120

    and ddI 66

Peptamen 96

Peptide T

    for AIDS dementia complex
        (ADC) 145

    for peripheral neuropathy
        143–144

    side effects 143

Percocet – *See* oxycodone

Percodan – *See* oxycodone

percutaneous endoscopic
    gastrostomy 96

periodontitis 237

peripheral neuropathy 62, 143–144

    and d4T 67

    and ddC 66

    and ddI 65

    traditional Chinese medicine 75

    treatments 143

persistent generalized
    lymphadenopathy 22

pets 100–101

phenytoin 61

    and ddC 66

photosensitivity 102

    and hypericin 71

phototherapy

    for psoriasis 147

physical examination 23, 37, 237

PID – *See* pelvic inflammatory
    disease (PID)

piercing 156

pineal gland 94

placebo effect 177

placebos 176, 177–178

plasma 25, 26

platelet count 27

platelets 26, 27

PML – *See* progressive multifocal
    leukoencephalopathy (PML)

Pneumocystis carinii pneumonia
    (PCP) 32, 59, 118–120, 239

    diagnosis 118

    night sweats 157

    prevention 119

    symptoms 118

    treatments 120

pneumonia

    and progressive multifocal
        leukoencephalopathy
        (PML) 133

Pneumovax 113

podophyllin
    for genital warts 151
poppers – *See* amyl nitrate
Port-a-Cath – *See* implanted
    venous port
potassium 93, 163
power of attorney 48
PPD – *See* purified protein
    derivative test
prednisone
    for lymphoma 142
    for Pneumocystis carinii
        pneumonia (PCP) 120
pregnancy 42, 59, 111
    and erythromycin 149
    and melatonin 95
primaquine
    for Pneumocystis carinii
        pneumonia (PCP) 120
primary care physician 36, 44
primary HIV infection 21
private insurance – *See* health
    insurance
probenecid 112
    and cidofovir 128
progressive multifocal
    leukoencephalopathy (PML)
        132–133
    diagnosis 133
    prevention 133
    symptoms 133
    treatment 133
Pro-MACE/MOPP (prednisone,
    methotrexate, doxorubicin,
    cyclophosphamide, etoposide/
    mechlorethamine, vincristine,
    and procarbozine)
    for lymphoma 142
property tax deferment 202
protease (proteinase) 94
protease (proteinase) inhibitors 63,
    68–70, 165

protein 89, 161, 164
    and protease 94
protein drinks 96
protozoa 18, 104, 120, 123
    and microsporidiosis 122
protozoal infections 105, 120–124
provincial health insurance – *See*
    health insurance
proxy 223, 224
pseudohypericin 71
psoriasis 147
psychiatrists 13, 14
psychologists 14
p24 antigen 28, 71
    test 28
pulmonary function tests 32
purified protein derivative test
    (PPD) 109, 237
pycnogenol 93
pyridoxine – *See* Vitamin B6
pyrimethamine
    and sulfadoxine 122
        for isosporiasis 124
    for toxoplasmosis 122

Q
qi 74
Québec Pension Plan 190, 194,
    199–200, 207
quercetin 93

R
radiation therapy 162
    for Kaposi's sarcoma 137
    for lymphoma 142
    side effects 138
radiotherapy – *See* radiation therapy
ranitidine
    and ddI 66
recommended daily allowance
    (RDA) 92
rectal exams 33, 34, 151

red blood cell (RBC) count 26
red blood cells 26, 29, 64
reflexology 78
reiki 79
religion 15, 51
renal (kidney) function tests 30
Rescriptor – *see* delavirdine
restaurants 99
retinal detachment 128
Retrovir – *See* AZT
retrovirus 18, 61
reverse transcriptase 63, 68
reverse transcriptase inhibitors 63,
    63–68
riboflavin – *See* Vitamin B2
rifabutin 61, 107
    side effects 107
rifampin 61
Ritalin – *See* methylphenidate
    hydrochloride
ritonavir 69, 70, 110, 165
    drug interactions 69
    side effects 69
RNA 63
rolfing 79

S
safer sex 6, 151–154, 156
    and cytomegalovirus (CMV) 126
    and Kaposi's sarcoma 137
    and microsporidiosis 123
Salmonella 97, 99
    and diarrhea 159
saquinavir 69, 165
    side effects 69
scabies 151
scope tests 31
seborrheic dermatitis 146–147
secondary infections 103
    See also opportunistic infections
sedimentation rate – *See* erythrocyte
    sedimentation rate (ESR)

Seldane
    and erythromycin 115
    and ketoconazole 115
    and ritonavir 69
selenium 91, 92, 93
sepsis 61
Septata intestinalis 122
Septra – *See* TMP/SMX
seroconversion 21
sex toys 154
sexually transmitted diseases
    148–151, 238
    and piercing 156
    and street drugs 155–156
    and tattoos 156
shark cartilage 87
shelters 213
shiatsu 79
    for peripheral neuropathy 143
Shigella
    and diarrhea 159
shingles – *See* herpes zoster virus
side effects 12, 29, 59, 105, 165,
    166, 174–175, 186
skin infections 77
    and DNCB 73
skin problems 146–148, 238
smudge 82
social assistance 166, 195–196, 209,
    234
sores
    in mouth 162
spermicide 153
spirituality 15, 51
Sporanox – *See* itraconazole
SPV-30 72, 86–87
St. John's wort 71
stain tests 31
stavudine – *See* d4T
STDs – *See* sexually transmitted
    diseases
steroids 164

stomach problems
    and aloe vera 84
street drugs – *See* drug use
stress 11, 77, 162
    and fatigue 158
subsidized housing 211
substitute decision maker – *See*
    proxy
suffocation
    and progressive multifocal
        leukoencephalopathy
        (PML) 2133
suicide 13, 226
sulfadoxine
    for isosporiasis 124
    for toxoplasmosis 122
sulfamethoxazole – *See* TMP/SMX
sulfonamides
    and ddI 66
suntanning 102
superoxygenation therapy – *See*
    oxygen therapy
supplements 75, 92–97
supportive housing 212
surrogate marker 27, 62
survival benefit 62
survivor benefits (CPP/QPP)
        231–232
    death benefit 231
    orphans' benefits 231
    surviving spouse's pensions 231
sweat lodge 82
Swedish massage 78
swollen lymph glands
    traditional Chinese medicine 75
symptomatic HIV infection 22
synergistic relationship, AZT and
        3TC 67
syphilis 149–150, 155, 156, 237
    first stage 149
    second stage 150
    third stage 150

T

T cell count 27, 60, 88
T cell function 20, 88
T cells 20
    and N-acetyl cysteine (NAC) 95
T lymphocytes – *See* T cells
T4 cell count 27, 72, 178, 235, 236,
        237, 239
    and naltrexone 73
    and SPV-30 86
    night sweats 157
T4 cells 27, 62, 71
    and zinc 91
T4 percentage 27–28, 237
T4/T8 percentage 238
T8 cell count 28, 237
    and DNCB 73
    and SPV-30 87
T8 cells 20
T8 percentage 28
Tagamet
    See also cimetidine
    and ritonavir 69
Tai Chi 81
tar
    for psoriasis 147
tattoos 156
tax credits and exemptions 201–202
TB – *See* tuberculosis
te tre oil – *See* tea tree oil
tea tree oil 87, 162
    for thrush 114
territorial health insurance – *See*
    health insurance
testosterone 163, 164
tests
    in vitro 57
    in vivo 57
    men 34
    women 33
tests of immune system cells 27–28
tetracycline 113

TFT – *See* trifluorothymidine

Th1 response 20

thalidomide 163

THC 163

therapeutic touch 78

thermometers 157

thiamine – *See* Vitamin B1

3TC 63, 67, 134, 165
    side effects 67

thrombocytopenia 27
    and ganciclovir 127

thrush 77, 89, 96, 113
    See also candidiasis
    acidophilus 114
    apple cider vinegar 84
    bee propolis 84
    grapefruit seed extract 86
    tea tree oil 87

thyroid hormone levels
    and fatigue 158

tinctures 76

TMP/SMX 59, 113
    and N-acetyl cysteine (NAC) 95
    for isosporiasis 124
    for microsporidiosis 123
    for Pneumocystis carinii
        pneumonia (PCP) 119, 120
    for toxoplasmosis 121
    side effects 119

total parenteral nutrition (TPN) 97

touch therapies – *See* massage

toxoplasmosis 120–122, 133, 142,
    237, 239
    diagnosis 121
    prevention 121
    symptoms 121
    treatments 122

TPN – *See* total parenteral nutrition
    (TPN)

Trager 79

transfusions 60

transportation 215

travel 101–102
    and cryptosporidiosis 124
    and isosporiasis 124

trifluorothymidine
    for herpes 131

trifluridine – *See* trifluorothymidine

triglyceride 65

trimethoprim
    See also TMP/SMX
    for Pneumocystis carinii
        pneumonia (PCP) 120

tuberculosis (TB) 61, 104, 106,
    108–110, 237
    diagnosis 109
    drug-resistant 110
    prevention 110
    symptoms 109
    treatments 110
        side effects 110

Tylenol – *See* acetaminophen

U

ubiquinone – *See* co-enzyme Q10

Ultra Clear 96

Ultra Maintain 96

unemployment insurance 190,
    193–194, 195, 207

V

vaccination 101, 236

valaciclovir
    for herpes 131
    for herpes zoster virus 132

Valium
    See also diazepam
    and ritonavir 69

Valtrex – *See* valaciclovir

varicella-zoster virus (VZV) – *See*
    herpes zoster virus

VDRL test 150

Ventolin 119

vesicles 131

viatical companies 209
Videx – *See* ddI
vinblastine
    for Kaposi's sarcoma 138, 139
vincristine
    See also ABV
    and ddC 66
    for Kaposi's sarcoma 138
Viracept – *See* nelfinavir
viral infections 105, 125–135
    and aloe vera 84
viral load 25, 28, 62, 237, 238, 239
    and SPV-30 87
Viramune – *See* nevirapine
viruses 18
Vistide – *See* cidofovir
visualization 82–83
Vitamin A 89, 92
Vitamin B1 90
Vitamin B2 90, 92
Vitamin B3 90
Vitamin B5 90
Vitamin B6 90, 92
    and isoniazid 110
    for peripheral neuropathy 143
Vitamin B12 90, 92
    deficiency 96
    for peripheral neuropathy 143
Vitamin C 90, 92
    and bioflavonoids 93
    and diarrhea 160
    and l-carnitine 94
Vitamin E 90, 93
    and selenium 91
    for seborrheic dermatitis 147
Vitamin K
    and Vitamin E 90
vitamins 61, 84, 88, 89–90, 236
    and diarrhea 159
    B-complex 93
    multivitamins 92
Vivonex 96

vomiting 29, 88, 162, 163
VZV – *See* herpes zoster virus

W
wasting 29, 85, 164
    and AZT 65
    and l-carnitine 94
    treatments
        N-acetyl cysteine (NAC) 95
water safety 97, 107
water-based lubricant 152
weight loss 161–164, 238
    traditional Chinese medicine 75
welfare – *See* social assistance
white blood cell (WBC) count 26
white blood cells (leukocytes) 20,
    26, 64, 127, 138
wills 228–230
    executors 229, 230, 231

X
Xanax
    and ritonavir 69

Y
yeast infections – *See* candidiasis
YMCA 213
yoga 81
YWCA 213

Z
zalcitabine – *See* ddC
Zantac – *See* ranitidine
ZDV – *See* AZT
Zerit – *See* d4T
zidovudine – *See* AZT
zinc 91, 92, 93
Zithromax – *See* azithromycin
Zovirax – *See* acyclovir